The Ecstatic Whitman

The Ecstatic Whitman

Literary Shamanism & the Crisis of the Union

George B. Hutchinson

Ohio State University Press *Columbus*

Library of Congress Cataloguing-in-Publication Data

Hutchinson, George, 1953–
  The ecstatic Whitman.

  Includes bibliographical references and index.
  1. Whitman, Walt, 1819–1892—Criticism and interpretation.
2. Shamanism in literature.   3. Prophecies
in literature.   4. Ectasy in literature.   5. United
States in literature.   I. Title.
PS3242.S52H88   1986   811'.3   86-877
ISBN 0-8142-0412-0

To Momma Anne and Poppa George

CONTENTS

Acknowledgments

I WOULD LIKE TO THANK the following people for the criticism, encouragement, and advice they provided at various stages in the preparation of this book: Robert E. Stillman, William H. Shurr, and Bethany Dumas of the University of Tennessee; Jerome Loving of Texas A & M University; and Robert G. Gunderson, Terence Martin, J. Albert Robbins, and James H. Justus of Indiana University, Bloomington. I owe special thanks to Professor Justus for directing the dissertation from which this study derives, and to my friend Keith Iams, with whom I often discussed my ideas as they first developed.

I am also grateful to Wayne State University Press for permission to use portions of my article on "The Sleepers" first published in the *Walt Whitman Review,* and to the editors at the Ohio State University Press—particularly Elizabeth A. Martin—for their patience and help.

The Graduate School of The University of Tennessee, Knoxville, and the John C. Hodges Fund of the department of English at the same institution kindly provided summer research grants which helped me to finish revisions in the summers of 1984 and 1985; and Dinah Brock helped type the final manuscript.

Neither apologies nor acknowledgments can make up for the attention scholarship has stolen from my long-suffering wife, Portia, and our little boy, Spencer, who have reason to diagnose this project as an acute and sustained episode of spirit-possession. To my parents, my best teachers, acknowledgments are equally inadequate; I can only hope they will be proud if they lurk somehow in the better pages of this book.

Finally, this study is dedicated to the memory of my grandmother, Anne Karrs Bain, and to my grandfather, George W. Bain, professor emeritus of geology at Amherst College, who has been a constant standard in my life for honesty and curiosity, for interdisciplinary probing and synthesis regarding the broadest of human concerns.

Introduction

*T*O THE STUDENT of American civilization, Whitman presents a challenge essentially three-fold, involving his aesthetic, his religious impulse, and his relation to mid-nineteenth-century American culture. In each of these realms, Whitman, as a visionary poet, is a fascinating if perplexing study. In all of them together, he is an alluring puzzle for interdisciplinary synthesis, a magnet attracting diverse methods and insights. Moreover, no figure in American literature has been more often the subject of cross-cultural investigations. Thus appeals to paradigms or correspondences in various literary and religious traditions or psychological frameworks proliferate, and bringing into coherence the different approaches now seems a hopeless task. Yet as we seek a holistic understanding of Whitman's significance we must inevitably wonder: by what method might we integrate the most important interdisciplinary and cross-cultural perspectives developed in the last thirty years? In this study I argue that interpreting Whitman's career as a form of ecstatic prophetism can accomplish such integration, and I choose shamanism as a practical model for understanding his brand of ecstaticism. The shamanistic model of prophetic role-playing reconciles various interpretations of the poet's religious orientation, his visionary ecstasies, and his psychological make-up. More importantly, while linking the rise and decline of his career as a visionary poet to historical context, it helps illuminate the ecstatic structures and techniques of Whitman's major poems as well as his view of the poet's social function.

Although scholars have frequently termed Whitman a prophet—and occasionally a shaman—we have yet to see a studied, interdisciplinary attempt to explore the implications of this terminology.[1] Knowledge of specific forms of ecstatic expression provides, of course, a necessary basis for any such investigation, and much of the following study will demonstrate how the process of the shamanistic experience sheds light on the unity and power of several of Whitman's greatest poems, as well as the *Drum-Taps* cluster as a whole. These poems are chosen not only for their reputations in the critical literature but for their importance in revealing the nature of

Whitman's inspiration. Each appears within the Whitman canon as a fountain out of the poet's psychological and spiritual reservoir, which was tapped periodically in response to crises and overflowed into new editions or clusters of verse. Most of Whitman's other poems are chiefly preliminary surges or tributaries emanating from the central inspiration that gave sustenance to *Leaves of Grass*. Yet what are we to make of the similarities between shamanism and Whitman's poetry? The answer to this question is of far greater significance than the recognition of phenomenal correspondences alone, and has to do with the basic functions of ecstaticism in human societies.

To "explain" Whitman's similarities with the shaman requires forays into anthropology and an untraditional approach to literary history—an approach that welcomes the many discoveries of influences upon the poet but subordinates these discoveries to a more fundamental notion of the relationship of ecstatic performance to cultural crisis and development. Identifiable "sources," as traditionally conceived, are secondary to the manner in which ecstatic transformation gives the visionary a method of responding to environmental change, thus "revitalizing"—in some ways reorienting, in others reinforcing—the symbolic systems of his culture. Whitman's employment of literary and popular-cultural resources is shaped by the more fundamental necessity of adaptation to a changing social order. Hence, an essential point of this book is that knowledge about the nature of ecstatic role-playing can help us explain the mystery of Whitman's transformation into a poet as well as later changes in his career. Moreover, such knowledge helps illuminate his kinship with other prophets and reformers of his age. In the attempt to define Whitman's calling and to place it culturally, one should consider the essential dynamics of the ecstatic performer's role. Such an approach is consonant with the intentions of America's greatest poet, for he sought the "origin of all poems" and of all religions in the very attempt to revitalize his culture, and his search led him to the reconstruction of an essentially shamanistic aesthetic.

It is a critical commonplace that Whitman's aesthetics were the outcome of his "mystic intuitions," though many have argued that he was not actually a mystic.[2] Henry Seidel Canby claimed that when the style of a Whitman poem failed it was because the poet had lost his inspiration, and the poet himself stated that "the great thing is to be inspired as one divinely possessed."[3] Considering the number of studies that have covered Whitman's mysticism, it would be futile to offer yet another examination of "parallels" if that examination did not help make sense of the sponge-like capacity of *Leaves of Grass* to absorb a tremendous diversity of religious traditions. As Frederik Schyberg once pointed out, Whitman's poetry exhibits "the typical characteristics of absolutely all the various mystic doctrines. Without having read them, or heard of them, they arose naturally out of his own temperament, and he has developed characteristic mystic tenets, often even more striking and paradoxical than those of his predecessors."[4] Although recent revelations of Whitman's study of world religions should eliminate any convictions of his total näiveté, a glance at the Whitman bibliography of the past thirty years bears out the main thrust of Schyberg's statement.

Whitman does not offer a full-fledged religion; instead, he presents several fundamental religious insights—concerning particularly the relation of the body to the soul, the concept of immortality, the concept of unity in diversity, and the idea of interpenetrating spiritual and physical worlds—and a form of religious experience that may be found in numerous types of mysticism probably because it provided the foundation for all of them. The essential form of the shamanic ecstasy—which many scholars date back to Paleolithic hunting communities and which Eliade places antecedent to the Vedas—is the common denominator toward which the various mystical doctrines associated with Whitman converge, for the ecstatic experience at the heart of shamanism is a universal phemomenon, its basic attributes being found in forms of mysticism the world over. Noting that the twenty-seven thousand-year-old relief at Lascaux has been interpreted as a representation of shamanic trance, Professor Eliade explains why he regards the ecstatic experience as a "primary phenomenon": "We see no reason whatever for regarding it as the result of a particular historical moment, that is, as produced by a certain form of civilization. Rather, we would consider it fundamental in the human condition, and hence known to the whole of archaic humanity; what changed and was modified with the different forms of culture and religion was the interpretation and evaluation of the ecstatic experience."[5] I should emphasize at this point that it is the phenomenon of ecstatic role-taking itself that can be considered primal, not any particular form of shamanic practice.

Ecstatic techniques have been adapted to specific environmental and social contexts, which to a certain extent differentiate them from each other. However, the forms of shamanism
documented throughout the world do share important characteristics that distinguish them particularly from the mysticisms
of systematized religions that have absorbed and subordinated
the ecstatic technique to serve their own social and theological
hierarchies.[6]

Shamanism is a relatively autonomous practice that can
function within the contexts of many different world-views, its
only ideological preconditions being the concept of a dualistic
soul and the belief in parallel spiritual and physical worlds, the
connections of which the shaman has special abilities to penetrate. The concept of the dual soul assumes that in addition to
the "fixed soul" element maintaining life (Whitman's "self")
man has a "free soul" that can exit the body under certain
conditions, including trance, sleep, and especially death.[7] The
capacities of this "free soul" are crucial to the shaman, whom
Johan Reinhard has recently defined as *"a person who at his
will can enter into a non-ordinary psychic state (in which he
either has his soul undertake a journey to the spirit world or he
becomes possessed by a spirit) in order to make contact with
the spirit world on behalf of members of his community."*[8]
Eliade emphasizes the character of shamanism as a *"technique of ecstasy,"* specifying that "the shaman specializes in a
trance during which his soul is believed to leave his body and
ascend to the sky or descend to the underworld."[9] Although
the phenomenon of soul transport is very common in
shamanism, more recent investigators have agreed with Reinhard that it is not a necessary feature; soul-possession and
soul-transport seem to be interchangeable elements of the
shamanistic seance.

The seance may be called for a wide range of reasons, but
it is always intended to reassert a state of equilibrium, whether
through a cure, a discovery of wrong-doing, a discovery of the
location of game, or a prophecy. More important than the
specific subject of the seance, however, is the fact that
the practice of shamanism reassures a community about death
and reinforces social union by providing contact with the spiritual world and with cosmic truths; for the shaman specializes
in the affairs of the soul and of spiritual realities. It is only by
virtue of the power of his soul and his spiritual knowledge that
he is able to cure or to prophesy.

The shaman is normally "called" to his vocation after enduring a period of illness or psychological affliction that is cured by trance experiences accompanied with visions and spiritual visitations. As he gradually acquires mastery over the trance, he achieves a stable relationship with one or more spirits—a relationship frequently represented as sexual union, marriage, or direct kinship.[10] These spirits give advice and information, escort the shaman to the other world, fuse with him to heighten the ecstasy, help him retrieve the soul of a patient or stand guard over it when it has been restored, and otherwise aid the shaman in his seances. Spiritual helpers or "demons" appear frequently in Whitman's poems, and a good example of their use can be found in one of his first attempts to create the verse form of *Leaves of Grass:*

I am the poet of Strength and Hope
Where is the house of any one dying?
Thither I speed and turn the knob of the door,
Let the physician and the priest timidly withdraw.
That I seize on the ghastly man and raise him with resistless will.
O despairer! I tell you you shall not go down,
Here is my arm, press your whole weight upon me.
With tremendous breath I force him to dilate.
Sleep! for I and this stand guard this night,
And when you rise in the morning you find that what I told you is
    so.
Every room of your house do I fill with armed men
Lovers of me, bafflers of hell,
Not doubt not fear not death shall lay finger [upon] you
And you are mine all to myself.[11]

It is interesting that Whitman should differentiate himself from—and replace—the physician and the priest, for the shaman is the counterpart of both, distinct from them in his mastery of spirits and spontaneous relations with the supernatural. In some cases the shaman's own soul may serve as a "helper" or a possessing agent of sorts. Ake Hultkrantz tells us that among the Naskapi Indians of Labrador the spirits may be replaced by "the shaman's power-filled free-soul, the 'Great Man' . . . [A] free-soul distanced from its owner may take on the same functions as a guardian spirit. That is, the extraordinary ecstatic powers of the shaman may be interpreted as flowing from his own semi-detached soul or an acquired spirit potency."[12] Such, I would propose, is frequently the case in

Whitman's poems. The "invitation" of the soul often sets the groundwork for the spiritual adventure.

Variations in shamanic phenomena are due to differences in socioeconomic and cultural conditions that provide the substance and content of the spiritual experience.[13] This is what lends the shamanic complex its versatility: "In being linked with the shamanic tradition complex traditional elements of different origin have become moulded in accordance with the basic ideology upholding shamanism and have gained shamanic significance."[14] Thus Whitman could fit the ideology and imagery of American democracy easily into the shamanic way. This adaptation was particularly appropriate in that shamanism forms the central religious complex in the antinomian and essentially egalitarian hunting communities of Siberia and the northwestern regions of North America. Shamanic practice is best suited to "classless" societies in which religion is not dominated by a priesthood. Thus it seems particularly appropriate for the democratic and egalitarian ethos Whitman upheld.

If one examines the literature concerning Whitman's mysticism with shamanism in mind, one finds that virtually all of the mystical characteristics convincingly used to link him to the more systematized vedantic, middle-eastern, or western religious traditions are consonant with shamanism, while the characteristics that distinguish Whitman from those traditions are typical traits of the classic shamanic complex. The most notable distinctions that should be mentioned are the important role of the senses and of sexual climax to the mystical ecstasy, and the connection of the mystical experience with symbolic activity without which the experience would be considered worthless.

Frederik Schyberg found the one thing that prevents Whitman from being "merely a mystic" to be his "strong sense of reality, a healthy enthusiasm for things in themselves."[15] The usual stumbling block in comparing traditional forms of mysticism with Whitman's has been the poet's emphasis upon the body as intimately involved in the ecstatic experience. Thus Hyatt Waggoner, comparing and contrasting Whitman with various mystic types, settles for the term "erotic mysticism," and James E. Miller, Jr., noting the seemingly paradoxical importance of the senses in the mystical transports of "Song of Myself," adopted the phrase "inverted mysticism."[16] Going further, Roger Asselineau held that "the source of his mysticism is not only a diffuse sensuality, but emotions or joys of a purely sexual nature"; "mystical joy and sexual climax are confused."[17] In a more recent book-length study of eastern religious parallels to Whitman's work—a study that attempts unconvincingly to illuminate direct sources—Professor Rajasekharaiah is unable to fit this "confusion" into his model and predictably falls back upon psychobiographical speculations to take up the slack.[18] In referring to the shamanic tradition, however, we discover that no confusion is involved, that the sexual transport can be a crucial element in breaking through the thresholds of a trance to fullest illumination. The union with a spiritual partner frequently precipitates the soul journey or possession sequence. Furthermore, the sexual roles in such trysts are interchangeable, for the shaman may adopt a sexual role opposite to the one he or she would have in "real life," just as Whitman takes the female role in his sexual episodes nearly as often as the male role.

Neurophysiologists have recently supplied fascinating material for speculations concerning the relation of sexual experience to mystical ecstasy. Eugene G. d'Aquili and Charles D. Laughlin, Jr., in a biogenetic structural analysis of ritual trance, illuminate the functional similarity of neurophysiological phenomena recorded during sexual orgasm to those recorded during "altered states of consciousness," and speculate that these similarities account for the connection of sexual experience with mystical transports.[19] Whereas the sexual nature of the experience is usually sublimated in the Eastern and Western traditions, in the shamanic complex it is fully exploited. The extent to which sensual stimuli or images of arousal are incorporated in the mystical tradition may well correspond to culture-wide attitudes toward bodily functions. And in a break with antisexual ascetic traditions we would expect the visionary to return to the more naïve form of the mystical experience, if he has the capacity to find it. Thus it will not do to consider Whitman's employment of sexual experience as anomalous; rather, we must alter our conception of the mystical substrate. Similarly, neurophysiological evidence suggests the propriety of sexual interchangeability during the ecstatic transport, for there are "no qualitative sex differences in the physiological sexual response"—that is, from a strictly neurophysiological point of view, sexual ecstasy is the same in men and women.[20] The ability to exchange sexual roles in the state of trance may be highly therapeutic as well as cathartically powerful, and certainly exemplifies the shaman's immunity from structural norms imposed upon the "profane." Such sexual interchangeability would seem threatening to the priests and ascetics of hierarchical orders, whereas the shamanic complex can exploit its affective possibilities. Diving beneath the Vedas and all established systems for his religious inspiration, Whitman found a more primal ground of mystical experience—not merely a new hybrid, but the form that was more simple because it was more whole.

Closely linked to spirituality and feelings about the body is a culture's or an individual's attitude toward death. Whitman's tendency to treat these areas together reflects a profound ontological symmetry. In "Democratic Vistas" American attitudes toward death, sex, and religion appear as the writer's greatest concerns. Whitman could not extricate these themes from each other—though he could shift their relative prominence— and at the heart of his visionary poems we see them brilliantly unified when the soul and body are in their highest powers. Hyatt Waggoner has already pointed out that Whitman was most successful when he wrote simultaneously on his three great themes—love, transcendence, and death—and that he "almost never, until very late in life, wrote on death without writing on love and transcendence at the same time."[21]

Likewise, the intimate awareness of death lies at the very center of shamanism. The ecstatic experience in nearly every instance has the lineaments of ritual death, and the power of the shaman derives precisely from his ability to plumb spiritual worlds that are normally closed to the living.[22] In fact, shamans are frequently "chosen" after apparently having died and come back to life. The experience of death in such cases functions as the initiatory vision experience that must be followed by professional training. Moreover, the sacrificial nature of the shamanic rite has been widely documented. Perhaps these observations can help us appreciate the centrality of death as well as sexuality to Whitman's poetic inspiration. Read, for example, of the ambition he expressed in a notebook dating from the months before *Leaves of Grass* appeared:

> I want the chanted Hymn whose tremendous sentiment shall uncage in my breast a thousand wide-winged strengths and unknown ardors and terrible ecstasies—putting me through the flights of all the passions—dilating me beyond time and air—startling me with the overture of some unnamable horror—calmly sailing me all day

on a bright river with lazy slapping waves—stabbing my heart with myriads of forked distractions more furious than hail or lightning—lulling me drowsily with honeyed morphine—tightening the fakes of death about my throat, and awakening me again to know by that comparison, the most positive wonder in the world, and that's what we call life.[23]

Within the compass of this passage are revealed the process of several of Whitman's finest poems and the origin of his method of dredging up the resources for *Leaves of Grass*. It is, in fact, a condensed description of a shamanic ecstasy.

One telling objection to comparing literary and mystical processes is that the mystic absorption in a state of passivity and contemplation by nature conflicts with the active process of metaphoric creation and performance. Thus Richard Chase, though conceding that the term *mysticism* may be useful "in speaking of the general tenor of Whitman's mind," has said that theories of "mystical experience" seem irrelevant to an understanding of the poems.[24] Actually, there are instances of mystical orders that are connected with performance and even poetic forms—the Persian Sufis (with whom Whitman has been compared) being a notable example. The Sufis, it turns out, have been cited as an order within an established religion that utilizes the shamanistic techniques of ecstasy to gain spiritual insight.[25] The whirling dance of the dervish has its counterpart in the frenzied, spiraling dance of the shaman as he mounts toward his trance. What distinguishes the shamanic performance from most mystical exercises, however, is its functional purpose—to cure someone, to escort the dead to a resting place, to prophesy, or to discover the source of a community affliction. The shaman gains mystical knowledge in the process of performing a practical function, and the religious experience in which all observers share is allied to the solution of a problem. Whitman's insistence upon the social functions of poetry and his impatience with those who, in his mind, overemphasized the purely aesthetic qualities of literature grew from the form of his religious impulse. He was so torn by the historical problems of his age that his poetic practice became also a means of self-cure, an act of maintaining equilibrium.[26] The symbolizing and religious functions were inherently linked in this process. Without the role that was dependent upon symbolic activity, the religious impulse alone could not help Whitman. Similarly, from the individual point of view, the shaman's artistic activity is the main factor in his life. Only after the religious calling has resulted in performance does the shaman establish his role and thus save himself, for he maintains his psychic health through artistic creation: "The result of self-cure is artistic production and activity. The person of the shaman, the metamorphosis which takes place in him when he begins to shamanize, and the result of shamanizing, are a form of artistic productivity."[27]

The specific mode of that productivity is *monodrama*, to adopt a term frequently applied to Whitman's ecstatic poems, and not least of the virtues of the shamanistic model is that it provides a paradigm for the blending of narrative, dramatic, and lyric modes that appears in Whitman's work and makes it so difficult to categorize his finest verse within the western traditions of genre. In the great ecstatic poems, as in shamanic performance, the dramatic situation is fundamental to the artist's discipline; this situation is triadic, involving relationships between the poet, the audience, and the spiritual world.[28] The poet holds the key position in this triad, mediating between the other two referents of the performance, attending to their diverse demands. Thus the poet's shifting sense of self and point of view are functions of his orientation toward the two primary worlds he joins as well as his internal state. The technique called for at any given moment will be chosen for its contribution to the dramatic matrix as well as the spiritual progression; therefore the form is open, active, an "energy construct," as Charles Olson would later call the projective poem. The poet surrenders his formal identity to transformative powers that break the traditional decorum of verse, until the central consciousness regains equilibrium through its very destruction and reconstitution amid the powers. Many of Whitman's most peculiar techniques—the catalogues, the shifting modes of address and transformations of the poetic "I," the changes in tone, the shifts and ambiguities in the relationship between soul and body, the breakthroughs in plane that allow leaps from the concrete to the abstract—are dependent for their success upon the faithful attention to a process of visionary experience that, however lawless it appears, is in fact rigorous in its discipline. The activity correspondent with each threshold of awareness prepares the groundwork for the one that follows until the climactic ecstasy integrates the sacred with the profane world, revealing prophesies, new meanings for life, and assurances about the enigma of death.

The fact that Whitman constructed many of his poems out of fragments written separately in moments of inspiration and that he revised incessantly does not affect the argument presented here. Regardless of the order in which different sections of a poem were originally written, their ultimate coherence is the subject at hand—their coherence in a process experienced by the reader, and perhaps by Whitman as he brought the scraps of his composition together with lyric concentration. As Mircea Eliade has pointed out, "It is a matter of indifference whether the epic content of . . . myths and legends [embodying ecstatic 'magical flight'] depends directly upon a real ecstatic experience (a trance of the shamanic type) or whether it is an oneiric creation or a product of pure imagination. From a certain point of view, the oneiric and the imaginary participate in the magic of ecstasy."[29] Moreover, the shamanic performance itself is not simply free-wheeling and unconscious; it follows patterns and alternatives that have been developed over time and passed down through a tradition according to judgments of effectiveness that are essentially aesthetic. Like jazz, in its very improvisation it is structurally coherent.

The concept of shamanism has been loosely applied to a great diversity of phenomena, evoking virulent denunciations from some anthropologists; previous applications of the concept to literature have been particularly sloppy, for which reason I have largely derived my conception of the functional, structural, and technical aspects of the shamanistic performance from the work of these who have studied it in its "classic" form in Siberia. However, my chief aim is not merely to indicate "correspondences," nor to point to a "universal" and schematic archetype abstracted from actual behavior. My analysis obviously proceeds from the position that the dynamics of the shamanistic process are adaptable to different historical circumstances; specific symbolism, technique, and environmental context may vary considerably. And yet, to analyze Whitman's ecstatic poems as shamanistic in nature is not to reduce their aesthetic texture or their functional and symbolic uniqueness, but rather to approach a more adequate understanding of that texture, that uniqueness, by showing the interrelations of these qualities with the inherent structure of the visionary experience as well as with the conditions provided by the world in which the poet lived—thereby, perhaps, also helping us to comprehend that world itself. An understanding of the shamanistic nature of Whitman's career will be most useful if it makes possible what Clifford Geertz has called "thick description"—description able to illuminate as never before the interrelations between the innumerable significant details that Whitman studies have unearthed.

To compare Whitman with the shaman is inherently to test the relation to American culture that he claimed for himself, for the shaman's function, like Whitman's, is central to his identity and his performance. To relate Whitman's poems to his culture we need a method that firmly links his mode of writing—and thus his mode of inspiration—to the cataclysms of his age. The usual "myth-symbol" approach of American Studies is insufficient for such a project; our chief concern is not how Whitman's choice of imagery reflects the myths and self-interpretations of his culture, but the connection between a cultural situation and the ecstatic calling. For surrounding the structures of any society and enclosing its myths and symbols is a larger environment that will not be tamed to that society's purposes. Culture finds itself repeatedly in the face of forces it cannot assimilate; it is called to transform itself, to resituate itself within its setting. Again and again, we must develop a new stance to reality that logic or technology alone cannot provide.[30] In what manner do we arrive at one? My belief is that creative processes are at the heart of the shift, that peculiarly sensitive individuals in every society—artists and prophets— indicate the transformations in the human sensibilities that are needed to cope with the threat of powers impinging from outside.

Focusing upon culture as a symbolic process unfolding dramatically through time, Victor Turner has modified the structuralist approach to anthropology. In addition to the cultural models embodied at various levels of communication as relatively static elements, Turner posits the existence of "anti-structure," a liminal element, free and unbound by structural norms. Thus a culture requires not only the paradigms of behavior and symbols of cosmic or social structure by which it defines itself, but the absence of structure in order to survive. Turner's approach is particularly applicable to visionary situations and should influence approaches to the myths and symbols of romantic literature:

> The vain task of trying to find out in what precise way certain symbols found in the ritual, poetry, or iconography of a given society "reflect" or "express" its social or political structure can . . . be

abandoned. Symbols may well reflect not structure, but antistructure, and not only reflect it but contribute to creating it. Instead, we can regard the same phenomena in terms of the relationship between structure and communitas to be found in such relational situations as passages between structural states, the interstices of structural relations, and in the powers of the weak.[31]

Among other things, the antistructural *limen* provides a society with the flexibility to adapt to cultural shocks or changes in its environment, just as the liminal aspect of initiation ceremonies—first examined by Van Gennep—aids the process of adaptation to a new role for the individual. The "passage between structural states" may occur to an individual in the course of his life or to an entire culture in critical periods of upheaval, and it is precisely here that we typically find the romantic poet. Turner points out that in periods of liminal transformation symbols from nature become particularly predominant as social-structural differentiations and hierarchy have been stripped away, including man's superiority to nature. Liminal moments are saturated with symbols relating to nature and biological processes, while two essential human traits are revealed and combined in enhanced ways as they could not be in the structured situation: "liberated intellect" (mythic and philosophical speculation) and "bodily energy."[32] Perhaps the romantic fascination with organicism is most closely linked to the process of transformation from one state of being to another. Thus a drama of subjective experience and personal initiation becomes fraught with significance for an age of upheaval. The boundaries between different forms of existence, typically guarded by established codes, break down as the antistructural experience overcomes the structural.

Here, Turner suggests, "communitas" is enacted—an "essential we" relationship, in Martin Buber's terms—whereby men confront each other as integral beings rather than social integers.[33] The communitas underlying all social bonds and achieved at certain points of ritual performance (the liminal normally being embedded in a stabilizing structural framework) is typically experienced in an antistructural landscape, the landscape of the road or of flux: "Society is a process which embraces the visions and reflections, the words and work, of religious and political mendicants, exiles, and isolated prophets, as much as the activities of crowds and masses, the ceremonies of the forum and marketplace, and the deeds of legislators, judges, and priests."[34] We would find Whitman, "the solitary singer," in the *limen,* in communitas. His very mode of address separates us from the mass and draws us into an intimate relation with the poet, who inhabits a status between or outside of structures, on roads, ferries, or the shores of ponds; the night and ocean, so important to Whitman's poetry, are particularly symbolic of the unstructured state. Yet in the liminal landscape the sense of true community underlying national and pan-human identity is to be found. It is here that Whitman always tries to lead us to reveal his most essential message.

The sense of communitas, closely associated with the most affective moments of ritual, finds one of its expressions in the shamanistic seance and perhaps its most extreme manifestation in ritual trance. It comes particularly in times of crisis, whether at a certain ritual moment exemplifying the passage between structural states or in the momentous "rites of passage" in history. The field of antistructure implicitly exemplifies the social flux in which human difficulties are explored to their roots. Therefore, the deeply antinomian and potentially chaotic nature of such moments renders them threatening to established systems, and priests have always embedded the liminal within highly stable social forms or churches. For instance, in the historic shift from nomadic hunting-and-gathering communities to more highly organized agriculturally-based civilizations, the spontaneous and individualistic religious practices of the shaman were often suppressed or absorbed and made "acceptable."[35] But in the great "liminal" moments of history, the individual visionary again grasps his opportunity and attempts to provide the solutions to community problems with which the "church" or "establishment" seems ill-equipped to deal. Such is the implication of Anthony F. C. Wallace's studies of "mazeway resynthesis" and revitalization movements, from which William McLoughlin has recently borrowed in a sweeping essay on the nature of "revivals, awakenings, and reform" in American history.[36]

Here a promising stream in the study of American civilization converges with Victor Turner's incorporation of the idea of the *limen* in his "social drama" approach to culture. In Wallace's analysis the moment of visionary awakening occurs during the passage between structural states—when a culture is in rapid disintegration and social flux. According to this model, a society is perceived as an organism made up of many communicative subsystems progressing from the cellular up to the national level. Each individual maintains a "mazeway" that represents the organization of potential inputs and responses *vis a vis* society and culture as well as one's own body and private experience of the entire outer environment. The mazeway reduces stress and maintains equilibrium within the organism, but under conditions that afflict the individual beyond the capacities of the mazeway to assimilate information appropriately and thus to prescribe effective adaptive behavior, the individual is forced either to endure continuous imbalance with respect to the environment or to change the mazeway. (The same holds true for an entire culture, I might add.) Such a mazeway "resynthesis," in Wallace's model, occurs as an inspired revelation during a trance brought on by the very psychological breakdown that previous imbalance with respect to the environment had caused. Certain individuals by nature (i.e., social position and neurological predisposition) will be most likely to undergo such experiences. During the visionary trance, the prophet being born manages to formulate the internally satisfying structure he needs to achieve equilibrium. If enough elements of this new structure attract the wider community and awaken cathartic responses through the charisma of the prophet and the account of his experience, a coterie of disciples forms to spread the word and found a full-fledged "revitalization movement."

Significantly, the pattern of the prophet's experience corresponds almost exactly to the shaman's "call"—as Wallace himself has recognized—and shamanism is widely understood as a protective response to extreme environmental hazards or socioeconomic instability and stress. I. M. Lewis calls it a means of replenishing the spiritual armory "against rapid and inexplicable social change."[37] The practice of shamanism developed adaptively, enhancing group survival. In fact, on the basis of the nearly unanimous testimony that shamans reinforce social unity while exploring social problems and proposing solutions and prophecies, it might be said that the shaman is the prototype of the prophet of revitalization. It is therefore not surprising that in many instances a shaman becomes the leader of a true revitalization movement. Whitman clearly perceived himself in this light.

That recent Whitman criticism casts doubt upon the idea of the poet literally undergoing an ecstatic conversion experience in the late 1840s or early 1850s does not pose a serious obstacle to my method of analogy. Indeed, the imaginative experience itself, taking place in the process of symbolization, had virtually the same importance to Whitman as the shamanic call does to the "genuine" shaman. Recent applications of hypnotic role theory to the practices and experiences of the shaman support such an equation, for they show us that the ecstatic acts out a part, develops the spiritual landscape and its denizens, and even controls the neurophysiological mechanisms of his performance according to traditional models of what is *supposed* to occur during the ecstasy.[38] Contrary to what several scholars have assumed in denouncing comparisons of Whitman's poetry to prophetic, mystical, or shamanic performances, there is no purely naive or "natural" form of ecstasy; every ecstatic performance is mimetic. Moreover, the fact that Whitman would choose to symbolize his revelations as ecstatic experiences, and that these symbolic experiences took on shamanistic patterns with corresponding psychological and social functions, tells us much about the nature of his creative processes. Perhaps, as Eliade suggests in the passage quoted earlier, there is a fundamental connection between the transformative psychological mechanisms of ritual trance and the oneiric or imaginative faculty, or the exercise of what Hayden White calls "metaphorical consciousness"—"a primitive form of knowing in the ontogenesis of human consciousness . . . and [the] fundamental mode of poetic apprehension in general." Psychoanalytic critics would term such modes of consciousness *regressive,* just as ritual trance is generally understood as an extreme example of regression; in either instance the essential benefit is either to reaffirm a concept of reality undergirding social life and endowing it with meaning or to help "resituat[e] consciousness with respect to its environment."[39]

The latter function strikes me as particularly significant, and it is directly related to the centrality of the death-experience in the shamanistic performance. The psychic danger that the shaman confronts in his self-sacrifice is that of being lost to madness and the underworld, the chaos gaping like a great maw beneath the power of symbolization and self-control. For at the moment when the "normal" structures of life are abandoned, the power of symbolization and of differentiation between phenomena disintegrates—binary oppositions collapse into the ineffable—and one is dissolved in undifferentiated being. All things are cut loose from their moorings in the old matrix of meaning that one has known as "life." Yet only from such a state of "death" and indeterminacy can a new symbolic structure emerge—the cosmic visions of Whitman, for example, and his capacity to name the world.

Victor Turner has speculated that tribalistic religions whose ritual today is systematized may have originated in times of severe social crisis (set off by either natural or human-caused catastrophes), "in the novel and idiosyncratic visions and deeds of inspired shamans or prophets."[40] In saying this he simply reinforces a view of Anthony F. C. Wallace and numerous religious historians. According to this line of thinking, the original experience of "communitas"—a heightened sense of union among group members coinciding with ritual or revitalization—is institutionalized and embedded in a routine. What the prophet did becomes sacred history, infused with mythical elements. Whether or not this theory is correct, it is precisely how Whitman believed religions and gods originated.[41]

For my purposes the shaman and the revitalization prophet can be distinguished upon two counts: (1) the revitalization prophet arises in rare instances, whereas the shaman may be called at any time, depending mainly upon his individual development, and (2) the revitalization prophet, if successful, attracts a coterie of disciples and eventually points toward the establishment of a new social organization, whereas the shaman remains an individualist and forms no "church." Other distinctions can be made, such as the contrast between the shaman's traditional training and mundane functions, and the prophet's lack of training and lesser interest in immediate "practical" matters, but these distinctions are not of major importance to the current discussion.

I wish to make the connections as well as the distinctions between the shaman and the revitalization prophet, because Whitman shared the qualities of both of them. His "call" was precipitated by historical crisis as well as by individual psychological conflicts. And whereas his poems may envision the revitalization of his culture, he always maintained his emphasis upon individualism and unsystematized religious experience (although late in his life the cult that grew up around him bore many resemblances to the cults of prophets). Perhaps this blending can be explained by the nature of his idea of American culture. Whitman seems to have perceived America as an experiment in antistructure; democracy for him was the absence of social forms, as he trusted in the flux of complete equality (for this Santayana branded him "barbaric"). He matured in the period when early Jacksonian egalitarianism was giving way to greater institutionalization and social hierarchy—particularly in New York City—and when the "slave power" was threatening the status of the white yeoman whom Whitman saw at the heart of American identity. His visions were partly responses, "regressive" ones, to these developments—the only effective alternatives to the direct political action by which he had already been disillusioned. Thus his visions were of a culture nearly nomadic in its formlessness and lack of social distinctions. He would not found a "church" of America—a contradiction in terms. His religion of "personalism" would lack any institutional trappings, specific rites, or prayers. His "revitalization" would lead to a nation "of prophets and cosmos en mass"—every man would be his own shaman.

Obviously, this is not the America we know today, and many would say that Whitman was a false prophet; but there is power in such a vision far greater than the apparent incongruity with current fact, and we would do well to ponder Whitman's insistence upon the social functions of his art. The culture Whitman envisioned inhabited the spiritual landscape in which there could be no solutions but the most primal ones to the chief quandaries of individual and social life: bodily existence, love, and death. These terms imply the more obvious social antinomies of unity in diversity, sexual difference, and the relation between the living and the dead. Whitman would have us understand democracy as simultaneously the most primitive and the most advanced of social conditions, requiring extraordinary faith and application to be realized; for he came, by 1871, to regard it as a mode of sociality that previously had existed only as spirituality, and to see its institution on earth as fundamentally a religious exercise. To understand the nature of his poetry, we must understand the role he attempted to play in that exercise. Ultimately we will find that Whitman's greatest verse depended upon the poet's intimate involvement with the identifying crisis of the Union. When that involvement was wholly genuine, his poetry was prophecy.

CHAPTER ONE

Backgrounds of Revitalization

*T*HE CRISIS of American identity that finally broke in 1861 came in the midst of a critical transformation of northern society, a transformation that deeply affected Whitman's personal development. Like many young men of his generation, the poet reached maturity intimately bound to the destiny of a country only beginning to move toward a distinct sense of "nationality."[1] During this era, in which American "civil religion" matured out of its Enlightenment roots, the chief means of establishing bonds of national "kinship" were sentimental glorification of the founding fathers and religious evangelism.[2] In the Whitman family, three members of which were named for presidents, Jeffersonian and Jacksonian views of democratic polity converged with an extreme version of the egalitarian "inner light" that grew to dominate popular religion throughout the country. Yet just as the democratic ideals embodied in the Declaration of Independence helped shape a national identity, they faced the challenge of socioeconomic transformations that ruined forever the possibility of realizing the Jeffersonian dream. This challenge had profound effects upon the psychology and civil faiths of Americans, effects that were expressed in ecstatic religious and reform movements as well as in literature. As the future of the Union came into doubt, regressive urges empowered the various romantic enthusiasms in a many-faceted movement for revitalization. Whitman's turn to poetry was one revealing example of the function of ecstaticism in an "American Renaissance" reaching far beyond the sphere of literature and finding its ghastly fruition in the Civil War.

The Legacy of the Fathers

In his study of the generation of Lincoln, George B. Forgie points out how the sentimental regression characterizing early nineteenth-century Americans' thoughts of the Revolutionary period intensified the emotional bonds joining Americans to each other and to their traditions by promoting "an extension of natural affections to the public realm." Imbuing the nation with human attributes through sentimental metaphors involving founding heros, patriotic writers, preachers, and orators developed a means by which unconscious (chiefly oedipal) conflicts in the individual "could be made public, made common by simultaneous repetition, and acted out, without necessarily becoming conscious in the process."[3] Ritualistic in nature, the process depended upon highly specific images to focus communal sentiment—images of key events and founders of the nation that condensed the mythology of cultural origins and mission. Founding figures and their experiences are especially important in "civil religion" because they are identified with the fundamental rationale of the cultural system, making it both intelligible and humanly appealing to the masses.[4] Forgie's intriguing hypothesis is that subconscious emotional conflicts also become entwined with the collective identity through the psychological drama that focuses upon founding figures and events. It is partly through such dynamics that the "mazeway" of national identity develops among citizens, as Whitman himself had intuited by the time he wrote "The Last of the Sacred Army" (1842). The emotions of individuals become partly organized around origins shared by the entire community, so that personal integration grows deeply attached to cultural integration.

Forgie has been criticized for failing to examine "actual childhood experiences and child-rearing practices" in support of his theory. Whitman's case, however, certainly helps validate those hypotheses that concern transference of private emotion to the public, patriotic realm. Indeed, such transference was of crucial significance to Whitman's growth and professional career. Nineteenth-century Americans, concerned about preserving the sense of unity they felt had cohered under the stress of revolution, employed images of the founders—particularly Washington—and of key events in the founding of the nation not only in public celebrations, but also in the nurturing of children. Models from history served as chief elements in home and school education, while changing socioeconomic conditions undermined the position of fathers as role-models for their sons.[5] Such factors were clearly important in Whitman's childhood development. Always ambivalent about his father, a taciturn man buffeted by the economic change and instability of the early nineteenth century, in 1888 Whitman told Horace Traubel, " 'It is lucky for me if I take after the women of my ancestry, as I hope I do: they were so superior, so truly the more pregnant forces in our family history.' "[6] Whether or not Whitman "got along" with his father, he clearly did not wish to "take after" him. On the other hand, as a youth he was always eager to hear about Revolutionary War days; he later thought himself fortunate to have fallen in with " 'superior men—the higher man of that past era. I remember Colonel Fellows . . . one of the finest of them all. He had been a bosom friend of Paine in his last days—Paine's last days. How good the stories he told! how well reflecting things as they must have been!' " In *Specimen Days* the poet points out how, as a boy apprentice for the Long Island *Patriot,* he learned to set type from William Hartshorne, "a revolutionary character, who had seen Washington," and with whom he often talked about the heroic past.[7] One suspects that Whitman's first role model in life was George Washington. His story of 1842, "The Last of the Sacred Army," insists that example carries more weight than exposition in moral development and suggests that all the youth of the nation internalize the behavior of the general: " 'Do not suppose, young man, that it is by sermons and oft-repeated precepts we form a disposition great or good. The model of one pure, upright character, living as a beacon in history, does more benefit than the lumbering tomes of a thousand theorists.' " In this opinion Whitman was not alone; Mason Locke Weems had applied essentially the same pedagogy in his best-selling biographies of revolutionary heroes—most notably his *Life of Washington.*[8]

One has to wonder, in fact, to what extent Whitman derived his early conception of Washington from the most popular rendering of the hero's life in the years of the poet's youth. In the effort to provide an image that a broad audience would respond to and internalize, "Parson" Weems imaginatively reconstructed the private and emotional side of the general's life. In the process he partly created and widely disseminated a series of legends that have dominated the popular conception of Washington down to our own day. In revolutionary scenes the general displays not only the necessary attributes of the warrior and strategist, but also the paternal concern and sensitivity appropriate for the father of a country. Weems's description of Washington telling the unpaid army to disband peacefully is pure sentimental fiction, but such hero-worship as might have stirred the young Whitman: "As he spoke, his cheeks, naturally pale, were reddened over with virtue's pure vermillion; while his eyes of coerulean blue were kindled up with those indescribable fires which fancy lends to an angel orator, animating poor mortals to the sublime of god-like deeds. His words were not in vain. From lips of wisdom, and long-tried love, like his, such counsel wrought as though an oracle had spoke [sic]."[9] As the troops depart, "shortly to disappear for ever [sic], then nature stirred all the father within him, and gave him up to tears" (p. 122). The same sort of exaggerated sentimentality pervades Whitman's journalistic references to Washington.[10] Repeatedly, Whitman harps on the general's parental sensitivity and refers to the American people as the charges over whom he has spread his mantle of love.

However, as important as Weems's portrait of Washington may have been to the poet's views, no single source provided Whitman with all of his knowledge and ideas concerning Washington; he undoubtedly heard and read several versions of important revolutionary episodes and various interpretations of the general's character. Sifting them through his own imagination he came up with the images most attractive to himself, those that left the deepest imprint upon his personality and later found their way into his journalism and poetry. By virtue of this process—including imaginative identification with heroes and meditation upon past events in the vicinity of his own upbringing—Whitman's involvement with the founding era became such that he created for himself symbolic "fathers" who were inextricable from national identity. The descriptions of Washington that appear in Whitman's antebellum writing are peculiarly complex and revealing of the inner dynamics of the poet's attachment to the American "family." In the fifth section of "The Sleepers," for instance, we find a subtle equivalence between Washington and Whitman's idealized view of himself. The patriot appears as an historic embodiment of both maternal and paternal concern—"a great tender mother-man," as Burroughs would later describe Whitman: "he cannot repress the weeping drops" at the sight of his soldiers dying in battle at Brooklyn. "He sees the slaughter of the southern braves confided to him by their parents."[11] Whitman apparently has taken John Marshall's more stoic version of the episode and infused it with a tone and imagery typical of

Weems, who did not describe the battle.[12] Significantly, the poet's personal landscape (Brooklyn) here provides the backdrop for a scene from the nation's family history; the sacrifice of "southern braves" is simultaneously a retort to sectional threats against the Union family of Whitman's day and an affirmation of aboriginal kinship. Moreover, as Stephen A. Black has pointed out, the death of young men by violence was one of Whitman's perennial subjects from his earliest fiction on, carrying a strong oedipal charge.[13] Here, as in the later *Drum-Taps* poems, the emotional current inherent in the suffering of sons is redirected toward affirmation of "family" bonds.

In the farewell scene at Fraunces' tavern, as the officers draw near one by one, "the chief encircles their necks with his arm and kisses them on the cheek, / He kisses lightly the wet cheeks one after another, he shakes hands and bids good-by to the army."[14] Like Weems and countless other hagiographers and artists, Whitman portrays the hero as a parent or elder companion; Washington's bearing resembles that which Whitman took on in the hospitals of Washington, D.C., during a later war, and his relationships with the soldiers are as tender as those depicted in *Specimen Days.* As an old man, Whitman claimed, " 'We . . . might say the United States came into existence not only with the Revolution of '76 but through our Rebellion of 1861–5. The blood, the fathomless experiences, emotions, of both, joined.' "[15]

A sort of "family romance" is implicit in Whitman's view of the national founders; whereas he often explicitly refers to his natural mother (for example, in the scene immediately following the officers' farewell mentioned above), he most frequently fills the paternal role with either a national hero or an element of his native landscape that reinforces his aboriginality. In the latter case, Indian placenames ("Paumanok") or hints of sanctifying blood spilled in the Revolution imply a lurking ancestral value. If, as E. H. Miller has said, Whitman generally perceived himself as an orphan,[16] he completed his family by appropriating the founding fathers and the land they fought for. The identification with Washington would have had a peculiar resonance for Whitman, who finally replaced the fathers and found his "sons" among the wounded of the Civil War. Lacking children of his own, Weems's Washington became a father-figure for his soldiers and the American people as a whole, the events of his life infused with the highly personalized aura of familial emotion. Moreover, Washington's own life was entirely absorbed by his country, the events of his biography bearing a mythic relation to the Union such as we will later find in Whitman's treatment of his own persona and, ultimately, in his view of Lincoln.

In fact, late in life Whitman could hardly speak of Washington without mentioning his own "cohort," Lincoln, in the same breath. When the Civil War proved the heroism of a new generation, Lincoln rose to a place with the father in Whitman's pantheon; both men had been perfectly constituted for leadership in emergency—patient in adversity, quiet, " 'and coming out at the end, victor.' "[17] Washington, the poet acknowledged, had been the representative of another era: " 'But Lincoln? Well, we are very near Lincoln. He is like somebody that lives in our own house.' "[18] Whitman kept on his mantlepiece in Camden a "strange little Washington-Lincoln photo" representing Lincoln entering heaven and throwing his arms around the founder, "who with a disengaged hand offers to put a wreath on Lincoln's brow." Horace Traubel found the picture "queer," to which Whitman responded, " 'Everybody seems of the same mind—everybody but me: I value it: yet I could hardly tell why: probably because it made a favorable impression on me at the start. When I was in Washington I had it on my desk.' "[19] For the reader with a knowledge of Whitman's attachment to the founders and his feeling of identification with Lincoln, it takes little psychological sophistication to see why such a piece would make "a favorable impression . . . at the start."

Although the significance of the paternal image of the founders may have been peculiarly intense for Whitman, it was typical of the age in which he was raised. Sentimental piety of a psychologically regressive sort was one of the important moods that gave birth to a national spirit and thus contributed to the emotional foreground of the Civil War. An important turning point in patriotic sentiment came as the heroes of the Revolution died off, intensifying anxieties about the maintenance of union and virtue. Lafayette's tour of 1824–25 was a peak collective experience in this sense, for he was one of the last surviving saints of the founding days; people turned out in droves to celebrate him: "The memory of this visit," writes Forgie, "as the century wore on, became a powerful factor in the growth of sentimental nationalism."[20] This was the visit in which Whitman, a child of six, met the hero—a particular favorite of Walter senior—and was allegedly kissed by him.[21] Whitman's memory of Lafayette (though not of all the details of the encounter) was yet clear in 1889. The poet and his hagiographers exploited the episode to improve his mythic stature, but their excesses should not blind us to the significance such an event may have had for Whitman's emotional attachment to the nation. Most of his writing before 1855 shows him thoroughly drenched in the national filiopiety of the age.

Whitman was one of many journalists who protested the demolition of national shrines that could bind his own and future generations to the early experience of the Republic, and in 1845 he wrote an article for the *American Review* calling for the salvation of St. Paul's Church.[22] At a funeral for a general of the revolutionary forces, he had met a former soldier who recalled being there with Washington to give thanks after the British had left New York: *"With Washington there!* Oh, hallowed be the spot where his footsteps fell! Thrice hallowed be the temple where the purest prayers ever breathed from a patriot's heart, went forth toward Heaven!"[23] Nostalgic for earlier days, Whitman laments the materialism of his contemporaries who are more impressed by the palaces of capitalists than by "that spot in an obscure street where the early days of an undying genius were passed."[24] Similarly, as editor of the Brooklyn *Eagle,* Whitman later fought for preservation of Fort Greene as a public park, objecting to the threat of "desecration" posed by commercial growth; and in 1847 he further campaigned for the construction of a monument to those who had died in the British prison ships during the Revolution, emphasizing that "the prisoners were from all parts of the Union, and their graves should be cherished as *national* graves."[25] Implicit in the attachment to Revolutionary shrines is anxiety that the nation has since strayed, that the days of heroes in the cause of the Union are gone. In fact, it was a pervasive anxiety of the period.[26] In the early 1840s Whitman masked that anxiety in hopeful prophecies that "kingcraft and priestcraft" were disappearing in a world-wide movement toward peace and perfection (see, for example, "The Last of the Sacred Army"). By the late years of that decade, however, and particularly after the failure of the European revolutions of 1848 and revocation of the Wilmot Proviso, his hopefulness became strained and gave way to bitterness and severe questioning.

When Whitman feared for the morality of the public, he fell back upon invocations of the founding days, the unity and heroism that had created a national purpose. This is precisely why critical events and figures reminiscent of the Revolution appear in his poems. In the context of the transformative vision, they are totems of the sleeping power of the citizenry, cathexes in the national subconscious. As the mid-nineteenth century brought fears of a loss of national virtue, Whitman, like others, looked for signs—signs that the postheroic generation retained the capacities for collective heroism implicitly identified with the Revolution. In "Song of Myself," scenes of heroism therefore provide concentrated episodes to reassert the virtues and unifying potential of the people. In an article of 1857, Whitman lauds the outpouring of public sympathy after the sinking of William Lewis Herndon's ship, *Central America,* with 426 aboard. Response to the crisis reassures him that the virtue of the early republic is not extinguished:

> Such great calamities as that which is just now occupying the public mind *serve as reminders, as warnings, as lessons.* They startle us from our paltry, apathetic selfishness, they elicit feelings better and higher than ordinarily moves us [sic], they link us together, for a time at least, *by the bond of mutual sentiment,* they teach us that poor frail human nature can deport itself bravely and well under circumstances the most appalling; they prove to us that *the days of heroic self-sacrifice are not yet passed;* that in these days, stigmatised [sic] as matter of fact and materialistic, the spirit still survives, serene, dauntless, undying, only awaiting the hour of development.[27] (my emphasis)

Fairly common editorial material, even in our own day, but in this passage we read a presage of the meaning of the Civil War for *Leaves of Grass.* In the *"Terminus"* of "The Centenarian's Story," one of the earliest of the *Drum-Taps* poems, a borrowed strain of "Crossing Brooklyn Ferry" accomplishes the ritual exchange of Whitman's ancestral landscape for sacred time:

> And is this the ground Washington trod?
> And these waters I listlessly daily cross, are these
>   the waters he cross'd,
> As resolute in defeat as other generals in their
>   proudest triumphs?[28]

Frustrations of
a Native Son

The socioeconomic trends of the antebellum northeast, of course, directly contradicted Whitman's inherited ideology. By the 1840s the Brooklynite found himself in a community becoming increasingly stratified, the workingmen with whom he most closely identified being victims of industrialization, urbanization, and specialization in both economic and social roles.[29] In fact, even as Jackson rode the crest of a Jeffersonian enthusiasm for the "uncommonness of the common man," the Jeffersonian world was dissolving.[30] This world Whitman, like other locofocos, had been raised to identify as his own.[31] The decline of social contacts between classes deeply worried Whitman and others in and near New York City. Moreover, citizens of the middle and lower classes suffered "relative deprivation," a condition in which people feel that legitimate expectations for status, power, or economic security are not being met, and a frequent precondition for revitalization movements, particularly in newly industrializing states.[32] Despite such developments, however, for some time Whitman did not recognize the severity of the threat to his concept of American community.

After a political altercation in 1840, he published a conciliatory poem, "The Columbian's Song," which exemplified his early optimism, portraying America as a Jeffersonian paradise and asserting democratic fraternity:

Nor let our foes presume
   That this heart-prized union band,
Will e'er be severed by the stroke
   Of a fraternal hand.
Though parties sometimes rage,
   And Faction rears its form.
Its jealous eye, its scheming brain,
   To revel in the storm:
Yet should a danger threaten,
   Or enemy draw nigh,
Then scattered to the winds of heaven,
   All civil strife would fly;
And north and south, and east and west,
   Would rally at the cry—

'Brethren arise! to battle come,
For Truth, for Freedom, and for Home,
And for our Fathers' Memory!'[33]

For Whitman, the legacy of the fathers had always been the socially fluid, egalitarian workingman's and farmer's republic. But by 1846 he had begun to perceive the danger posed by concentration of wealth and the "morbid appetite for money" that was infecting all classes.[34] His chief concern, of course, was the effect of the new capitalistic economy upon "the democratic averages of America"—the middle to lower classes of workingmen and farmers whom, when he wrote *Leaves of Grass,* he wished to endow with the "ranges of heroism and loftiness" of classical heroes.[35] Like most of his contemporaries, including reformers, he did not comprehend the profundity of the American socioeconomic transformation that was by this time already well under way. The massive urbanization that paralleled the poet's life and that he frequently glorified was helping transform the journeyman into a propertyless wage-earner.[36] As labor's dependence upon capital increased, the "community of interest" between journeyman and boss disintegrated, yet laborers resisted for some time the realization of this development; and Whitman, certainly, did not perceive the dimensions of it—although, with other locofocos, he opposed those aspects of the new industrial order that conflicted with his Jeffersonian conception of the democracy made possible by the Revolution.[37]

The self-reliance Whitman offers the reader in *Leaves of Grass* is thus in one sense an escape from, in another a transcendence of, the limitations and insecurities brought upon the common man by the new economy.

I bring what you much need yet always have,
Not money, amours, dress, eating, erudition, but as good,
I send no agent or medium, offer no representative of
  value, but offer the value itself.
. . . .
I do not know what it is except that it is grand, and
  that it is happiness,
And that the enclosing purport of us here is not a
  speculation or bon-mot or reconnoissance [sic],
And that it is not something which by luck may turn out
  well for us, and without luck must be a failure
  for us,

And not something which may yet be retracted in a certain
    contingency.[38]

The prophetic thrust of his message is psychologically regressive in its claims of omnipotence, of control over a situation that is not even completely understood. In this respect
Whitman's strategy bears comparison to that of the contemporary labor reformers whom Norman Ware has criticized: "They
were 'transcendental,' in that they proposed an appeal from
objective experience to some inner standard, an escape from
reality, a withdrawal into a specially created environment
where their ideas of perfection might be achieved; rather than
acceptance of the limitations always placed upon perfection
by reality."[39] Although Whitman's response was not the piece-
meal one of the humanitarian reformers, it bore a civil-re-
ligious charge similar to that of the evangelism behind most of
the reform movements. This charge was progressive in its millennial hopefulness, conservative and "regressive" in the way
it harked back to the days of the founding fathers. Together, the
millenarian and nostalgic qualities (typical of revitalization
movements) intensified rising expectations that the nation
would indeed be saved from corrupting influences.

    These expectations fed into Americans' fervent confi-
dence in the European revolutions of 1848, which Jacksonians
like Whitman saw as signs of a widespread democratic upheaval, evidence of the universal importance of our own revolution during a period when domestic developments threatened egalitarian democracy. But by 1850 the hopes for Europe
had been crushed; the prophetic view of the American experiment faced formidable obstacles on virtually all fronts except
that of continental expansion, which, ironically, ended up intensifying the controversy that would finally divide the nation.[40] In the period of disillusionment, Whitman gave up on
politics, putting his faith in a visionary program by which spiritual regeneration would overcome the mechanical forces he
could not control. Significantly, this is precisely the transformation Geoffrey Hartman has pointed out in the response of
English romantics to the French Revolution. The souring of
revolutionary hopes caused a turning away from millenarian
political expectations to the religious aggrandizement of art:
"The aggrandizement of art is due in no small measure to the
fact that poets like Wordsworth and Blake cannot give up one
hope raised by the Revolution—that a *terrestrial* paradise is

possible—yet are eventually forced to give up a second hope—that it can be attained by direct political action. . . . The 'failure' of the French Revolution anchors the Romantic movement, or is the consolidating rather than primary cause."[41] In the same way, the frustration of Whitman's political hopes for America—a whole series of defeats for the "free soil" faction of the Democratic party along with the failure of the European revolutions—ultimately forced him back upon a new strategy for sustaining and reinvigorating his faith.[42] Passages from "Resurgemus" (1850) remind us of *Drum-Taps* and some of Whitman's scenes from the American Revolution; a strident political tone bends into religious prophecy:

> These corpses of young men,
> Those martyrs that hang from the gibbets,
> Those hearts pierced by the grey lead,
> Cold and motionless as they seem,
> Live elsewhere with undying vitality;
> They live in other young men, O, kings,
> They live in brothers, again ready to defy you;
> They were purified by death,
> They were taught and exalted.
>
> . . . .
>
> Not a disembodied spirit
> Can the weapon of tyrants let loose,
> But it shall stalk invisibly over the earth,
> Whispering, counseling, cautioning.[43]

At the very moment that the European revolutionaries went down to defeat, the concern about American character that focused upon the average wage-earner and farmer was increasingly influenced by the controversy over the extension of slavery in which Whitman passionately embroiled himself.

Anxieties about the future of the Union had already reached profound psychological levels by the time the Wilmot Proviso was presented in 1846 and the Democratic party began to disintegrate.[44] The greater the threat to the Union, the more Whitman regressively drew upon materials from the nation's "family romance." In September of 1847 he called upon all free workingmen to fight the extension of slavery into the territories soon to be annexed as a result of the Mexican War—an extension that threatened to drag free laborers down to the level of slaves: "This it is which must induce *the workingmen of the North, East, and West, to come up, to a man, in defense of their rights, their honor, and that heritage of getting bread by the sweat of the brow, which we must leave to our children.*"[45] Reference to Americans' responsibility for a legacy, as George Forgie's book emphasizes, was typical of the postheroic age and linked to the sentimental memory of the founders that had played so large a role in binding people psychologically to the nation. After a long catalogue of the different categories of free laborers, Whitman claims that the founders themselves had wished to limit slavery: "For this the clear eye of Washington looked longingly; for this the great voice of Jefferson plead, and his sacred fingers wrote. For this were uttered the prayers of Franklin and Madison and Monroe."[46] An earlier editorial had made the same point, claiming that the issue of extension involved

> the question whether the mighty power of this Republic, put forth in its greatest strength, shall be used to root deeper and spread wider an institution which Washington, Jefferson, Madison, and all the old fathers of our freedom, anxiously, and avowedly from the bottom of their hearts, sought the extinction of, and considered inconsistent with the other institutions of the land. And if those true and brave old men were now among us, can any candid person doubt which "side" they would espouse in this argument?[47]

The tug upon familial instincts and natural sentiment is strong and intimate here, creating an exchange of involvements across time that puts the reader contemporaneous with the founding fathers and the revolutionary cause into the mid-nineteenth century.

Developments subsequent to the defeat of the Wilmot Proviso, which would have prevented extension of slavery into the territories acquired by the Mexican War, continued to call forth Whitman's bitterly personal wrath. "The House of Friends," which appeared in the New York *Tribune* on 14 June 1850 (after Whitman's being fired from the Brooklyn *Eagle* and the Democratic party's movement to the right), exemplifies the extent to which national and personal betrayal were conjoined. Moreover, it pointedly indicates the isolation into which Whitman had been forced:

> If thou art balked, O Freedom,
> The victory is not to thy manlier foes;
> From the house of thy friends comes the death stab.
>
> . . . .

> Virginia, mother of greatness,
> Blush not for being also mother of slaves.
> You might have borne deeper slaves—
> Doughfaces, Crawlers, Lice of Humanity . . .

Whitman's erstwhile allies, the northern Democrats, had bartered the promise of the fathers. The poet called upon the few sons left to renew the legacy:

> Arise, young North!
> Our elder blood flows in the veins of cowards—
> The gray-haired sneak, the blanched poltroon,
> The feigned or real shiverer at tongues
> That nursing babes need hardly cry the less for—
> Are they to be our tokens always?
> Fight on, band braver than warriors,
> Faithful and few as Spartans;
> But fear not most the angriest, loudest malice—
> Fear most the still and forked fang
> That starts from the grass at your feet.[48]

At the heart of the poem is a frustration not only with the political process and the Democratic party, but with the influence of money and concentration of power that have fostered betrayal. Moreover, Whitman feels the danger is of nearly cosmic proportions. In 1889 he expressed the opinion that extension of slavery could have destroyed not only American democracy, "but for ages at least, the cause of Liberty and Equality everywhere."[49]

The writing of 1848 and 1850 indicates a man ripe for the sort of transcendence of difficulties typical of revitalization movements. Continually harking back to the memory of the nation's origins and a primeval unity that reflects his idealization of the past, Whitman's thoughts turn to martyrdom and apocalyptic fantasies, tirades against those who "would quench the hopes of ages for a drink," whom,

> The shriek of a drowned world, the appeal of women,
> The exulting laugh of untied empires,
> Would touch . . . never in the heart,
> But only in the pocket.[50]

It is worth noting that "The House of Friends" and "Resurgemus" were the first poems in which Whitman's prosody broke the traditional standards of verse under the power of inspiration.[51] At this time Whitman's personal life was also in flux—his political orientation having made him unfit for editorship on the traditional Democratic papers. His general disgust with the direction of public life led him to a major vocational crisis. Politically, the break-up of the free-soil faction of the Democratic party after Zachary Taylor's 1848 election triumph had set him adrift, as Asselineau has explained:

> What was Whitman to do? He could not follow the opportunists and return to Democratic orthodoxy. He was too proud to recant and too much convinced of the justice of the cause to which he was devoted. . . . Since there was no question of his becoming a Whig, he found himself without a party, completely left out.[52]

This is precisely the sort of dilemma out of which, according to A. F. C. Wallace, a group moves toward "revitalization" behind the catalyzing influence of the religious prophet. The group is caught between "two other threatening or competing groups, with one of which . . . it would like to identify" in an alliance against the other. But the traditional or potential ally has effectively rejected alliance and might even appear to have joined the "enemy." "This dilemma can only be solved . . . by a revitalization movement which redefines the situation. This redefinition must include a new image of the group which is so satisfying, in a nativistic sense, that the group is confident of its ability to 'go it alone,' without identification or alliances with either of the other two groups."[53] In *Leaves of Grass*, Whitman finally set out on his own to renew the legacy of the founders— for the ancestral spirit was one of the sources of his power and self-confidence—and to create a hypothetical audience, the group of true "Americans" to join him. George Rosen gives us insight into why ecstatic expression would be an appropriate resource in such a situation, insisting that behavioral extremes of trance and spiritual "vision" are not necessarily psychotic or neurotic in the normal sense, but part of an attempt to alter "circumstances where . . . there is a contradiction between cultural goals and the institutional means to attain them."[54] The psychological regression of ecstatic states allows not only an immersion in infantile fantasies, but a reformulation of symbolic resources in the face of impending defeat.

It was a sure intuition that guided Whitman toward his visionary program in the late 1840s, and the process by which that intuition drove him toward ecstatic expression both proved the depth of his belief and reinforced it, so that he could say of himself as "the poet" in supreme self-confidence in 1855—while the Union disintegrated around him—"The time straying toward infidelity and confections and persiflage he withholds by his steady faith."[55] The comic naïveté of such statements—when the discrepancy between the meaning of America and her apparent condition becomes most obvious— has been alternately the wonder and a chief target of American poetry ever since.

Religion and Revitalization

Six years after the poet's death, John Jay Chapman, belittling Whitman's achievement, compared him to the prophets who had proliferated on the "ultraist" wing of the broad religious and spiritualist awakening during the first half of the nineteenth century:

> Brigham Young and Joseph Smith were men of phenomenal capacity, who actually invented a religion and created a community by the apparent establishment of supernatural and occult powers. The phrenologists, the venders of patent medicine, the Christian Scientists, the single-taxers, and all who proclaim panaceas and nostrums make the same majestic and pontifical appeal to human nature. It is this mystical power, this religious element, which floats them, sells the drugs, cures the sick, and packs the meetings.
>
> By temperament and education Walt Whitman was fitted to be a prophet of this kind. He became a quack poet, and hampered his talents by the imposition of a monstrous parade of rattle trap theories and professions.[56]

Since Bliss Perry turned Whitman criticism away from the tone established by "the hot little prophets" who surrounded the poet, Gay Wilson Allen and others have labored hard to dispel the aura of cosmic influence that early hovered about him. And yet, eschewing the thought that Whitman was divinely appointed in an absolute sense, we may find it worthwhile to think of his prophetic claims within the context indicated by Chapman. The revival and reform movements, the new religions and prophets, and such fascinations as spiritualism and communitarianism mediated a passage between social structures at the same time that they called for a renewal of the American mission. Whitman's relationship to popular forms of religious enthusiasm can be set in a new light by considering these phenomena—along with *Leaves of Grass*—as different means of reorienting or simply reinforcing the symbolic systems of American culture.

Only recently have historians begun to see the Second Great Awakening and associated chiliastic religious movements as part of a broad social movement to revitalize American democracy. Applying A. F. C. Wallace's model, William McLoughlin, in particular, has argued that disharmony between the pervasive images of American identity and the social environment stood behind the revivals of the early nineteenth century, which in turn spawned perfectionist reform.[57] Donald G. Matthews, from a different direction, has claimed that the Second Great Awakening "in its social aspect was an organizing process that helped to give meaning and direction to people suffering in various degrees from the social stress of a nation on the move into new political, economic and geographical areas."[58] Although Matthews avoids discussing the specifically religious aspects of this movement, deemphasizing its "intellectual" side, and McLoughlin emphasizes the religious with little attention to changing social, political, and economic structures, the relevance of Wallace's insights to both views is clear: "The stabilized coexistence of mutually contradictory beliefs and customs in a society is the prior condition for a revitalization movement, which—with more or less success—breaks up existing structures, conserving some of their component elements and rejecting others, and combines the materials selected for preservation into a new structure." Causes of cultural dissonace may include "uncontrolled innovation, segmentation resulting from factionalism, class and caste differentiation, age and sex distinctions, regionalism, or even individual differences."[59] McLoughlin emphasizes the intellectual dilemmas behind the evangelical movement partly because of his view of the centrality of its New England phase and his focus upon the period 1800–1830, when the disintegration of traditional religious structures began as a result of social and ideological changes fomented by the Revolution. This, it might be argued, was in fact the context of Emerson's vocational transformation, but it was less significant for Whitman and others of the urban revival era, particularly in New York City. We must make room for regional and chronological differences in the origins of cultural disarray—certainly the variety of changes on the intellectual, economic, and expansionist fronts can accommodate diversity in this respect better than uniformity. According to Charles C. Cole, Jr.: "The 1830 revivals differed markedly from those of the 1740's and 1800's in that previously salvation of the unconverted was the end in view, whereas in the 1830's the objective became the saving of the world through organized movements. Consequently, the converts of the 1830's were led to concern themselves with the great social questions of the day and to bring about a better world."[60] The social and institutional orientation of New York intellectuals is what most troubled and alienated Emerson when he went to New York to lecture in 1842 and when Whitman probably first encountered his ideas on "the Poet."[61] Indeed, the differences in age and regional background as well as social status should be remembered when we compare Whitman and his so-called "master." A chief period of enthusiasm in Whitman's region was 1830–60, when socioeconomic transformations and anxieties about maintaining a unified, egalitarian republic provided the major challenges to the "mazeway" of the common people.

The class whose habit Whitman donned for the frontispiece of his first edition was undergoing a deeply-resented loss of status and filling the ranks of nativism and revivalism. Because few people understood the fundamental problems that came with industrialization, urbanization, and the transportation revolution, the underlying causes of "mazeway disintegration" could not be directly faced.[62] Religious immediatism, beginning in the anxious hinterland (where a total lack of social cohesion provided the impetus for revivals) and among the relatively deprived, spread from the peripheries of the nation to its urban centers—becoming a subliminal rebellion, a millenarian warning of the carnage that finally broke, appropriately, over the issue of slavery. Particularly in New York City, socioeconomic transformation and the failure of the political order created rising anxiety about social cohesion and morality; this anxiety, in turn, helped fuel nativism, Christian reform, and splinter religious movements such as spiritualism.[63] As a newspaper editor and Jacksonian Democrat, Whitman naturally found himself in the thick of the Yankee turmoil, often attracted to movements that wedded ideals of health, spiritualism, science, and reform. Hence, to gain perspective upon the poet's visionary apprenticeship, it is instructive to analyze other religious responses to the "social drama" in which Whitman was also engaged.

The function of religious trance and ecstasy is to reassure us that the powers that control the world are near and can be invoked. By nature, "peripheral" possession cults tend to have the most extreme manifestations because the members of such groups are generally in greatest need—perhaps as a result of social disintegration, oppression, relative deprivation, or feelings of anomie brought on by uncontrolled change. Possession, I. M. Lewis maintains, is a subliminal retort to such stressors. It is a means of manipulating a situation in which one feels relatively powerless.[64] Shamanism itself makes particularly intensive use of possession trance, but trance phenomena of varying levels of intensity are widespread among some Christian sects as well.

The Second Great Awakening, preceded by such early religious "ultraists" as the Shakers and Jemima Wilkinson, initiated a general revival of spiritual immediatism that divided in several directions. Central to all the religious movements of the period was the experience of divine inspiration, exemplified by a wide range of physiological responses ranging from decorous conversion to trances and visions. The most extreme of the peripheral movements, and the most revealing, were those in which trance and possession phenomena became common and acquired a positive valuation. For these phenomena were merely the most obvious manifestations of a general sense that direct communication could be established between sacred and profane realities, the most graphic illustrations that the supernatural is *in* us, as Emerson would say.

Because it claims divine authority, the unmediated ecstasy can threaten established religions in stable societies, which must demote or control it if they are to preserve the codes of behavior and religious dogma from continual alteration and individual reinterpretation.[65] Thus, as peripheral enthusiasms are carried toward the center of a society, their ecstatic tendencies are downplayed or controlled by "accredited officers."[66] This has been particularly true of established Christian churches, which have traditionally disdained the mystical interpretation of trance visions, emphasizing instead a less flamboyant emotional and spiritual illumination as evidence of religious experience. However, "outside [the] rigid framework of established religion, fringe cults have increasingly taken over a mystical interpretation of trance as the sign of divine inspiration. This is certainly the manner in which trance is overwhelmingly understood in revivalist movements like those of the 'Bible Belt' of the USA."[67] During the Second Great Awakening, as religious evangelism and "ultraism" moved from the peripheries to the center of American religious life, their ecstatic features were channeled and muffled to reduce the inherent antinomian dangers to Christianity itself. Leaders like Charles Grandison Finney, though known for their charisma and flamboyant emotionalism, restrained their missionaries from excessive use of the "New Measures" that were designed to control at the same time that they facilitated religious enthusiasm.[68] Nonetheless, we should not ignore the obvious connection between the extreme manifestations of trance, possession and soul-journey, and the more controlled emotionalism of a Finney or a Lyman Beecher. Finney's "anxious bench," for example—one of the most effective of his theatrical "new measures"—served as a cathartic focus of spiritual engagement; "anxious" sinners would experience conversion, the prime influx of divinity known to Christians, while surrounding neighbors of high and low status prayed for their deliverance. Paul E. Johnson calls the "anxious bench" "the most spectacular of the evangelist's techniques, and the most unabashedly communal."[69]

As Finney's success grew and he mounted his assault upon the urban centers, the more radical products of the revival—men like John Humphrey Noyes—came more and more to put faith in visionary states as evidence of divine interaction with humanity. The ability of mesmerized persons to undergo soul-journey was one of the important factors that prepared the ground for spiritualism and Swedenborgianism.[70] The latter, according to Whitney Cross, presented "a new hypothesis for the attainment of millennial happiness" for those who had given up hope on earlier social nostrums.[71] Swedenborg's work benefited from the popularity of mesmerism and led into spiritualism, which made deliberate use of the trance experience. It should be remembered that most of the early mesmerists and spiritualists gave a religious valuation to the experience of trance or soul-possession and soul-journey even if they *also* believed that these phenomena could be deliberately induced and studied scientifically.[72] Moreover, many clairvoyants acquired what was known as an "associate spirit," curiously reminiscent of shamanistic elements, which, during the trance, was supposed to be able to leave the body and contact other spirits.[73]

One practitioner who perfectly illustrates the progression from mesmerism to spiritualism is Andrew Jackson Davis, who discovered as a youth (from a deprived background) his peculiar susceptibility to mesmeric trance and eventually became the most famous spiritualist medium of the mid-nineteenth century. Davis first learned to control his trances to cure disease, but in 1844 an illuminative experience (the result of a self-induced trance as he wandered in the countryside), in which his soul visited the spirits of Swedenborg and Galen, conferred religious insight, and he became a prophet, accompanied—significantly—by a priest and a physician. Davis's spiritualist messages are some of the best examples of the connection of contemporary trance phenomena to social conditions, for his "lectures"—delivered from a state of spirit possession—were a patchwork of reform ideas and religious (chiefly Swedenborgian) speculations. His book, *The Harmonial Philosophy,* went through thirty-four editions in thirty years. "Somehow," Alice Felt Tyler writes, "Davis had managed to express the aspirations and social needs of the inarticulate and to voice their protest against the waste, the injustice, and the futilities of modern industrial society."[74]

The same period in which Davis acquired his powers witnessed an extraordinary "influx from the spirit world" among the Shaker communities, which John Humphrey Noyes considered precursors of modern spiritualism. Between 1837 and 1844 (also the period of the Millerite flurry), the increase of spirit possession episodes in Shaker communities led the elders to close their meetings to outsiders. The ostensible cause of the outbreak is peculiarly instructive. It was supposed that a revival was taking place among spirits in the "invisible world" occasioned by the fact that, as one observer said, "'George Washington and most of the Revolutionary fathers had, by some means, got converted, and were sent out on a mission to preach the gospel to the spirits who were wandering in darkness.'" Chief among these spirits were Native American tribes, whom Washington sent to the Shaker communities to receive religious instruction. At one meeting in Watervliet, New York, the human participants were actually possessed by the spirits of the "Indians"—a group that had become extinct *prior to Columbus's discovery* and had been wandering in darkness ever since.[75] The national symbolism represented in this event, I would submit, is as clear as it is in similar episodes of Whitman's poetry. As tenure of the continent had passed from the pre-Columbian Native Americans through the founders to the new generation, so the spiritual progression that makes Washington both a convert and a guide to the Native Americans ritualistically asserts an aboriginal continuity. Mediumistic conditions are a form of subliminal "goal-directed striving," the role-identification represented by spirit possession being a means of establishing contact with needed elements of the supernatural world.[76] In this case contact was made with spirits fundamentally identified with America and interpreted as evidence of the approaching millennium.

Another instructive case is that of Thomas Lake Harris, originally a follower of Andrew Jackson Davis, who received spiritual awakening in 1850 and thereafter began a prophetic career based upon revelations inspired by spirits. The poems he produced were supposed to be trance dictations. One of the important resemblances to shamanism in Harris's experience is his acquisition, in one of his initiatory visions, of a spiritual wife—the "Lily Queen"—whom even his earthly second wife recognized as his true mate, accepting celibacy in consequence. Such spiritual marriage is widespread in ecstatic religions. More significant, however, is Harris's concern for social issues—chiefly the condition of labor. Deeply outraged by the degradation of labor and corruption in politics, he believed he had been chosen to begin a movement for spiritual regeneration that would usher in "the reorganization of the industrial world."[77] The American millennium was central to his creed, as appears in one of his visions:

> "The Archetypal American Commonwealth is placed in the center of the new Heaven, because it is the will of Almighty God that the pivotal power of the earth shall descend through it, and that it shall become, through human obedience, the central power on earth, representing Divine harmony above. I saw the banner of this Republic, which represents the starry heaven, illumined with a cross of fire displayed in the sun, and emblazoned with the words, 'Christ conquers all.' "[78]

According to Harris's scenario, the prophet must go through a crisis, likened to death, in which he becomes a new person— "the pivotal man." One of the chief characteristics of the crisis is the prophet's isolation, which he is able to endure only "by becoming the center of a new solidarity" leading to a social order in precisely the pattern Wallace has outlined for revitalization movements. Harris's "pivotal man" would lead the movement toward a perfect egalitarian society in which all would have direct relations with God and in which social relations would achieve permanently the radical communality that Victor Turner calls "communitas."[79]

Significantly, his view of the Civil War was very similar to Whitman's. Harris saw the conflict as a struggle between those who would degrade labor, postponing the American millennium, and "'the Spirit that studiously and persistently liberates, enfranchizes, protects and ennobles Labor.'"[80] According to Harris: "The strife upon the North American continent is not merely the result of a determination of a slave-holding class to possess the absolute control of the subject colored millions. It involves the whole of America, for both colored and white. It is a war, in which the fundamental principles of Liberty are staked upon the issue."[81] Moreover, the war was expected to make the way clear for the millennium.

It is only when we recognize the social transformations to which such men as Andrew Jackson Davis and Thomas Lake Harris responded through the mechanism of the trance and its associated prophetic role that we come to understand their illustrative significance.[82] Without buying the specific creeds of Swedenborg or the spiritualists, Whitman could have found attractive their use of trance experience. (He once said in a note, "The Poets are the divine mediums—through them come spirits and materials to all the people, men and women.")[83] Of broader significance, however, is the fact that the types of experiences exploited by the spiritualists and given religious valuation are typical of liminal periods. The correspondence between Whitman's use of religious trance and ecstasy and that of the spiritualists (even if we partly attribute that correspondence to "influence") becomes most interesting when we consider the social drama to which both Whitman and the spiritualists testified.

More important than spiritualism in terms of the general development of American society, of course, was evangelical Christianity, and the years 1857–58 saw a new climax of the revival in cities such as New York as the nation teetered on the brink of Civil War. Timothy Smith points out that pastors and lay leaders hoped a national Pentecost at this time would "baptize America in the Holy Spirit and in some mystic manner destroy the evils of slavery, poverty, and greed."[84] The reform movements supported by evangelists and certain Transcendentalists tried to reinvigorate the millenial promise by bringing a perfectionist ethos of spiritual immediatism and individualism to bear upon problems rooted in socioeconomic conditions.[85] Many believed that the American experiment would work only if all opened themselves to the Spirit as old creeds and usages fell away.[86]

The revitalizing nature of the religious awakenings and splinter enthusiasms so prevalent in the antebellum period throws light on the relation between Whitman's social purposes and the shamanistic nature of his aesthetic, as well as revealing the link between his new form of poetry and other socioreligious phenomena of his era. Our understanding of Whitman and of his broadest cultural significance should link the poet to the widespread religious movements of his age by referring to the social conditions in which trance and possession phenomena associated with religious immediatism arise throughout the world. By moving into this interdisciplinary, cross-cultural arena, one would hope to suggest a direction for understanding American romanticism as part of a broad "social drama," to use Turner's phrase, taking place as Americans underwent several major transformations in their collective life. The link between the character of romanticism *as a mode of consciousness* expressed in cultural artifacts and the drama of social transformation can help provide a larger field for interdisciplinary synthesis than has previously been applied in studies of this period of American literature.

Fundamentally, the individualistic spiritual immediatism that swept the United States in a number of religious, political, and cultural forms was a subliminally-directed response to structural transformations of ambiguous origins. Victor Turner notes that "the world over, millenarian movements originate in periods when societies are in liminal transition between different social structures."[87] The bonds formed between participants in such movements are "anti-structural in that they are undifferentiated, equalitarian, direct, nonrational (though not *ir*rational), I-Thou or Essential We relationships, in Martin Buber's sense."[88] It was precisely this sort of reconciliation of spiritual unity with an egalitarian, individualistic ethos that many Americans hungered for in the years before the Civil War.[89] George Forgie, upon whom I depended heavily earlier in this discussion, sees the ritualistic filiopiety directed toward the founders as the chief means of asserting a sense of unity and nationality in this period. That may well be true, but the larger field within which filiopiety acted was strongly affected by the spiritual awakening, which complemented filiopiety as Americans felt themselves drifting farther and farther from the state of the mythic republic of the founders.

Robert Bellah calls the Second Great Awakening the "second American revolution, inward and spiritual," indicating its contribution to national sentiment: "By the same token that neutral deistic language warmed the hearts of none by itself and unaided, it could hardly have provided the imaginative basis of a national consciousness without which the new nation could easily have shattered into the divisions and fragments that continually threatened it. What civil religion unaided could not accomplish became possible with the help of a burgeoning revivalism."[90] To Whitman, certainly, deistic thought likewise gave way to romantic spirituality as he grew increasingly worried about the direction of the nation and turned from journalism to the idea of becoming an orator or a poet. To the social and patriotic function of revivalism we can compare one of Whitman's ambitions of the 1850s—to travel and give addresses "directly to the people (admission 10 cts.) North and South, East and West—at Washington, at the different State capitols, Jefferson (Mo.), Richmond (Va.), Albany, promulgating the grand ideas of American ensemble, liberty, concentrativeness, individuality, spirituality, &c. &c. . . . Washington made free the body of America for that was first in order. Now comes one who will make free the American soul."[91]

Behind the later revivalism, antebellum spiritualism and related movements, as well as *Leaves of Grass*—perhaps behind much of the American Renaissance—is the fear of failing the promise of the Revolution during a passage between structures, a great anxiety that the nation is not turning out as it was supposed to and that the only answer to national problems is spiritual revitalization. For Whitman and his generation, the Civil War was the crisis toward which all of this anxiety tended, the historical substitute for the millennium that so many Americans were expecting in the middle of the century. And in the same movement by which it sacrificially replaced the millennium as counterpoise of the Revolution, it confirmed the religious underpinnings of democracy.[92]

CHAPTER TWO
Sorcerers'
Apprentice

AS MUCH AS historical interpretation can help situate
Whitman among the movements and transformations of his
age, it cannot explain how he adopted a new vocation and
brought the materials together for ecstatic poems. The "long
foreground" of *Leaves of Grass* has been painstakingly recorded by such scholars as Floyd Stovall, Joseph Jay Rubin,
and Harold Aspiz.[1] Their work, along with that of the psychoanalytic critics, has made more accessible than ever the intriguing drama of Whitman's role change. Yet the realms of his
reading and of his inner needs remain largely distinct in the
critical literature, as if evidence of influence through reading
would compromise theories of unconscious motivation. If,
however, the main activity of Whitman's life in the 1840s and
1850s was the search for and the creation of a role, then the
record of what he studied mirrors a psychological process. If
the role he finally settled upon focused his self-integration,
then the process of his role-creation must be the hub of biographical inquiry for each new interpretation of his work. The
pose Whitman finally adopted peculiarly suited his situation;
yet it bore certain necessities and rested upon secrets that have
an archaic heritage. He would learn the secrets and master the
necessities before he shaped the utterance that survives him,
transcending both influence and personal circumstance.

The Prophet's Affliction

From the psychoanalytic point of view, religious ecstasy is
a form of "regression in service of the ego" through which
infantile fantasies of omnipotence help mediate tensions between the id and the superego—a process Albert Gelpi finds
important in Whitman's poetry.[2] The similarity of poetic fantasy to ecstatic religious vision—along with the resemblance

of these phenomena to certain forms of madness—has, of course, long been recognized. Freud implicitly acknowledged this similarity (and its alleged roots in neurotic fixation) when he characterized the "primitive," "magical" mind as locked in the narcissistic stage of over-valuing psychical acts, transposing the structural conditions of one's own mind upon external reality.[3] Indeed, one might say that all artists—and particularly poets termed "romantic"—are peculiarly able to regress to "earlier" levels of development while keeping the regression subservient to the needs of the ego.[4] Such regression can be psychologically healthy. Regarding omnipotence of thought in poetry, Barbara F. Lefcowitz has pointed out that "the more [the poet] is able to allow the metaphor to function as a microcosmic object, with its own contours and attributes, its own locus in a new 'environment' of rhythm, language, and tone, the more he has transcended pathology."[5] Certainly this should be particularly true if the "microcosmic object" reflects upon social structures and historical events, thus fusing the private emotional struggle with public symbols. Moreover, the product of the artistic process may have a healthy influence upon the audience by helping fulfill their regressive needs (as E. H. Miller believes *Leaves of Grass* does).[6]

In Whitman as in the shaman, the social nature of the creative process enfolds its individual psychological nature. Unlike the hysteric, the ecstatic can control his experience, and his trance is central to the performance of a role extending beyond his own imaginative life. That role may help the shaman maintain psychic equilibrium, but the content of his performance derives from materials with important cultural values.[7] Shamans guard, transmit, and occasionally transform cultural tradition; much of their training involves mastering materials derived from the community's belief system, reflecting both inward upon personal emotional dynamics and outward upon the surrounding environment.

I have tried to show in chapter 1 how strongly Whitman's private emotional state had been fused with the state of the nation as he grew to maturity. His development of an ecstatic role and the symbolic processes associated with that role would serve both public (national) and private (often sexual) functions simultaneously. Like most transcendentalists, of course, Whitman tended to read his entire world symbolically, and he connected the symbolism of nature with an ethos and a view of the cosmos that were radically egalitarian. At the same

time, his powerfully sensuous response to the world, intimately connecting him with nature and (though not often
enough) with other men and women, he interpreted as indispensable to the new American personality; he thus projected
his own attributes onto the ideal image of the democratic man.

Incidentally, these two fused aspects of his character—
reading the world "transcendentally" and responding to it sen-
suously—also reveal how well-suited he was to an ecstatic
role. For psychological tests indicate that the shaman maintains a "symbolic attitude towards his surroundings" and is
continually alert to his relationship with the powers fundamental to his role—a sign of " 'deep anxiety connected with strong
and totally unrefined impulsive sensuous reaction.' "[8] Many
readers have argued that Whitman's anxiety and acute sensitivity to sensual stimuli (exposed especially in "Calamus")
derived from the repression of his sexual desires, an interpretation that calls to mind the frequency of shamanic transvestism
and the large proportion of shamans who are homosexual in
some cultures. No doubt the erotic component of ecstasy (not
only in shamanism, but in other religious complexes as well)
answers the special contact difficulties of people whose desires for sensual fulfillment are frustrated in daily life. There is
an interesting twist, however, to the shaman's attitude toward
the symbolic materials and psychic processes essential to his
role, for although the engagement of repressed urges is indispensable to the performance of the role, the individual does
not feel himself (i.e., his waking ego) responsible for those
urges; thus the threat to the self such urges represent is con-
tained by the mask.[9] Likewise, Whitman expressed abhor-
rence in actual life for many of the sexual escapades in which
he could indulge in his poems. Stephen A. Black makes a
similar point with regard to Whitman's associational technique, claiming that "free association" and "symbolization"
allowed the poet to face troubling aspects of his psychic life
(including powerful oedipal conflicts) without disrupting his
conscious image of himself or of his environment.[10] Whitman's "furtiveness" derived from this ability to exercise in
poetry the urges he must keep under hat in everyday life.

Proponents of psychopathological views of shamanism
(which were widely accepted until recently) encounter difficulty in using evidence from the shaman's role behavior to
infer his usual personality dynamics.[11] Although he commonly
suffers severe psychological or psychosomatic affliction prior

to learning the techniques of ecstatic performance, members of the community do not consider the practicing shaman neurotic. In fact, he must be the epitome of good health, both mentally and physically. His personality suits him to act as a religious intermediary. Eliade quotes Wenceslas Sieroszewski's observation that among the Yakut of Siberia the shaman " 'must be serious, possess tact, be able to convince his neighbors; above all, he must not be presumptuous, proud, ill-tempered. One must feel an inner force in him that does not offend yet is conscious of its power.' "[12] These are all qualities that Whitman had developed in himself (after a long, hard-fought struggle) by the time he began writing *Leaves of Grass*. Stephen A. Black correctly points out that Whitman's "characteristic role in the family drama was mediator during periodic crises," and George Whitman's testimony that he came to act as a sort of guardian and advisor—not only for the family, but for many neighbors as well—remaining cool in every crisis, confirms the fact that he had developed the demeanor of a shaman: "We all deferred to his judgment—looked up to him. He was like us—yet he was different from us, too. These strangers, these neighbors, saw there was something in him out of the ordinary."[13] In later life the "personal magnetism" on which Whitman prided himself was evident to practically all who met him, and it spawned fantastic legends.

His awareness of having an unusual emotional constitution appears in the early fiction, which frequently features protagonists modeled after the author and given to brooding, with special tendencies to dreaminess and rapt moods. Of course, the dream motif was a popular device at the time, but contemporary observers have testified that the young Whitman was a chronic daydreamer, and many details of his stories refer to materials important to his emotional life—for Whitman even more than for most authors, creative writing seems to have been another form of daydreaming and working out personal difficulties. In one fragment apparently from the 1840s, during his period of moody and troubled self-consciousness, he describes a character of about his own age who on the surface seems "normal" but hides a peculiar sense of himself:

> This singular young man was unnoted for any strange qualities; and he certainly had no bad qualities. Possessed very little of what is called education. He remained much by himself, though he had many brothers, sisters and relations and acquaintance. He did no

work like the rest. By far the most of the time he remained silent. He was not eccentric, *nor did any one suspect him insane.* He loved in summer to sit or lean on the rails of the fence, apparently in pleasant thought. He was rather less than the good size of a man; his figure and face were full, his complexion without much color, his eyes large, clear and black. He never drank rum, never went after women, and took no part in the country frolics.[14] (my emphasis)

Other than the deliberate masking of physical appearance (the mask is in fact precisely the opposite of the author's appearance), this description fits perfectly what we know of Whitman as a young man, including the fact that he was not eccentric or "suspected" insane. The implication of a hidden nervous abnormality or emotional pressure is indeed suggestive. In *The Solitary Singer* Gay Wilson Allen quotes Ellen O'Connor's testimony that Whitman told her much of *Leaves of Grass* " 'was written under great pressure, pressure from within, he felt that he must do it.' " After several years of "accumulation," says Allen, the pressure became so great that Whitman abandoned other occupations to work full time on his poetry.[15] Prior to their role change, most shamans suffer similar psychological pressure, often for a period of several years. Their behavior marks them as "different" from others; wandering alone, often dreamy and emotionally withdrawn, the potential initiate suffers depression and self-doubt—in some cases even severe illness (possibly psychosomatic)—which finally give way to seizures of trance and hallucinatory experiences. Such affliction can be a sign of "election" to the shamanic calling and must be followed by professional training if the individual intends to escape recurrent attacks; the taking on of the new role heals the affliction as the initiate learns to control his regressive episodes.[16]

Whitman was certainly depressed about his fortunes in life prior to beginning work on *Leaves of Grass,* and he connected his bad luck with a weakness in himself as well as with the conditions in which he lived. One woman with whose family he lodged in the early 1840s described him as feeling he had been badly used by the world: " 'My impression has always been of a dreamy, quiet, morose young man, evidently not at all in tune with his surroundings and feeling, somehow, that fate had dealt hard blows to him. I never heard him spoken of as being in any way bright or cheerful.' "[17] Many of Whitman's early stories feature a young protagonist with great gifts but no arena in which to exercise them and acquire deserved recognition. Two stories in particular, "Lingave's Temptation" and "The Shadow and the Light of a Young Man's Soul," can be cited in this connection.

"Lingave's Temptation," of unknown date and publication but certainly of the late 1840s, confirms the interpretation that a crisis of political conscience played a key role in Whitman's decision not to continue as an editor but to seek a new calling. The story concerns a "poet" who is poor though brilliant, who suffers in neglect while people of lesser talents gain wealth and renown. A man named Ridman (a *"money-maker"*) offers him "magnificent and permanent remuneration" for his services, but "the poet was to labor for the advancement of what he felt to be unholy—he was to inculcate what would lower the perfection of man."[18] (There is a clear correspondence here to Whitman's situations as editor of the New Orleans *Crescent* and the Brooklyn *Eagle*.) As conscience and fortune compete in Lingave's mind, one night "the spirit of poesy" approaches him in a dream that "seem'd conscious to the soul of the dreamer," to assure him that virtue is the "sinew of true genius. Together, the two in one, they are endow'd with immortal strength, and approach loftily to Him from whom both spring" (p. 334). This use of the dream would later evolve into the visionary motif of *Leaves of Grass;* in framing the spiritual visitation that announces a promise of moral triumph, it helps the author vicariously to surmount emotional affliction stemming from unsavory circumstances. The "spirit of poesy" counsels Lingave to continue poor, " 'while others around you grow rich by fraud and disloyalty. Be without place and power, while others beg their way upward. Bear the pain of disappointed hopes, while others gain the accomplishment of their flattery. Forego the gracious pressure of a hand, for which others cringe and crawl' " (p. 334; one is reminded here of the "cringers" and "crawlers" in "The House of Friends" and the 1855 Preface). Convinced by the spirit visitation, Lingave finally declines Ridman's offer of a position, "and then plod[s] on as in the days before" (p. 334). Obviously, at the time he wrote the piece Whitman was floundering in a vocational limbo but disdained editing any longer. "Lingave's Temptation" shows how the literary use of the dream-vision serves Whitman when he is suffering "relative deprivation"; moreover, it links this deprivation to his loyalty to national ideals and faith in virtue, qualities he associated with the "divine average." The author's problems, like the protagonist's, can be solved in one of three ways: the betrayal of principles, the ascension through virtue itself to a higher potency that the "spirit" promises, or a highly improbable change in the social order that will resurrect the principles of the founders.

"The Shadow and the Light of a Young Man's Soul," published in the *Union Magazine* in June of 1848, also features a young man oppressed by poverty and checks upon his ambitions. Archibald Dean must search for employment in the country to help support his mother and brother (a sickly younger child, reminiscent of the epileptic Eddie Whitman, whom the poet provided for throughout life and in his will). The mother worries about Archie because he is " 'unstable as water,' " wanting energy and resolution; she fears that he will not excel as he should. The protagonist's dandified dress also indicates an undue regard for popular opinion.[19] "Moreover, Archie looked on the dark side of his life entirely too often; he pined over his deficiencies, as he called them, by which he meant mental as well as pecuniary wants."[20] However, he is honest, benevolent, candid, very loyal to his mother, and "not indisposed to work, and work faithfully, could he do so in a sphere equal to his ambition" (p. 327). Ultimately, Archie undergoes a transformation—due partly to open-air exposure and exercise and partly to the influence of an exemplary old widow whose story, framed within the tale as a whole, corresponds structurally to the dream vision in "Lingave's Temptation." Again, the relationship of the transformation to models of conversion after "relative deprivation" appears in the resolution of the story, which indicates an advance from the hopelessness of "Lingave's Temptation" and perhaps Whitman's determination to forge a new role for himself:

> [Archie] found a novel satisfaction in that highest kind of independence which consists in being able to do the offices of one's own comfort, and achieve resources and capacities "at home," whereof to place happiness beyond the reach of variable circumstances, or of the services of the hireling, or even of the uses of fortune. The change was not a sudden one: few great changes are. But his heart was awakened to his weakness; the seed was sown; Archie Dean felt that he *could* expand his nature by means of that very nature itself. (P. 330)

The virtues Archie shares with the apparently earlier Lingave, concentrated and applied, would bring the freedom and self-reliance he needs. Willfully replacing despondency with cheerfulness and action, Archie finally provides his mother a good home. Furthermore, "never did his tongue utter words other than kindness, or his lips, whatever annoyances or disappointments came, cease to offer their cheerfullest smile in her presence" (p. 330).

The fact that Archie Dean's conversion "was not a sudden one" would seem to confirm the opinion of most students since Gay Wilson Allen's biography that Whitman underwent no sudden transformation in a mystical experience. However, both "Lingave's Temptation" and "The Shadow and the Light of a Young Man's Soul" indicate Whitman's sense of deprivation, which finally reached such a point that he made a concerted effort to imagine a new vocation and improve his temperament. The type of role that he imagined—a charismatic one—and the importance to that role of the regressive urge for omnipotence are revealing in this context.

The charismatic prophet's initiatory role-change is considered "cathectic" on the individual level—that is, it helps him regulate his own "psychomental complex," as Shirokogoroff has said of the shamanic initiate.[21] In the most successful and spectacular instances, self-cure leads, through the assumption of prophetic leadership, to social revitalization: Lingave triumphs. Insofar as cultural disturbances have contributed to the psychological pressure upon the potential prophet, and to the extent that the spirits afflicting the potential shaman have a cultural signification, the initiatory experience is a model of a much broader cathectic experience for the community as a whole. Thus the shaman, or the charismatic prophet, becomes what Lévi-Strauss has called a "professional abreactor" for his society.[22] Not only does he lead others through the process of psychological disturbance and re-synthesis, but his experience is necessarily symbolic, and he maintains a symbolic attitude toward the world in the manner that Freud terms "infantile." The role and the personality complex (described earlier) are perfectly suited to each other.

The ecstatic or visionary mask became an aid in Whitman's shift to a new role. His emotional predisposition and desire for that role were the initial and fundamental facts. In shamanism itself the performer's means of establishing an interaction with the spiritual world "is fundamentally an ecstatic role-taking technique."[23] For the shaman the new role has already been defined by the culture and is semi-institutionalized; Whitman essentially reinvented the role for himself, although there were plenty of other spiritualist prophets and the like around from whom he might have borrowed ideas. Chiefly, however, Whitman came to a definition of his role through a gradual process of "studying" opera, oratory, literature, and world religion.[24] Without tracing all of his "sources" in detail, I shall examine crucial influences upon Whitman's development of a shamanistic aesthetic. At the same time, we must remember that for Whitman reading was an actively creative rather than passively absorptive process. His own needs and interests determined both what he read and how he chose to make use of it.

The Dawn of Religion

While compiling the "Notes and Fragments," Richard Maurice Bucke came across one fragment, "the paper torn and almost falling to pieces from age," that he felt must have dated from when Whitman was on the first track toward *Leaves of Grass*.[25] The note concerned Whitman's desire to combine the thoughts of all religions, to locate their common denominator, and thence to develop the personal charisma to imbue his work with the pure transparency of nature, the immediacy of green life:

> For example, whisper privately in your ear . . . the studies . . . be a rich investment if they . . . to bring the hat instantly off the . . . all his learning and bend himself to feel and fully enjoy . . . superb wonder of a blade of grass growing up green and crispy from the ground. Enter into the thoughts of the different theological faiths— effuse all that the believing Egyptian would—all that the Greek— all that the Hindoo, worshipping Brahma—the Koboo adoring his fetish stone or log—the Presbyterian—the Catholic with his crucifix and saints—the Turk with the Koran. (*CW*, 10:17)

The ability to participate in nature's creative power, which appears to be the dream articulated here, Whitman perceives as encompassing all religious experience. Conversely, to encompass the thoughts of all religions by finding their common basis and "effusing" the essence of their worship may be one pathway toward matching the "superb wonder of a blade of grass." To find the root of the sacred is to approach union with natural processes and thus increase one's living force.

Others have mentioned Whitman's "rich investment" in the study of ancient and comparative religion, but the significance of his early reading of Volney's *Ruins* has been insufficiently elucidated.[26] This was one of the books, Whitman told Traubel, "on which I may be said to have been raised."[27] Allen claims that as a youth, due to the influence of Volney and such other thinkers as Paine and Frances Wright, Whitman came to see all religion as superstition.[28] Indeed, Volney does hold priestcraft up to ridicule, but an important thesis of the *Ruins* is that all religions have common features and a common origin. Volney's book provides the foundation for a religious primitivism even as it rejects traditional myth and religion in favor of reason.

In the chapter "Problem of Religious Contradictions," Volney parades the religious functionaries of all the cultures of the world in order to show how superficial differences have split them into factions.[29] The "Lawgiver" of Volney's book (somewhat of an Epicurean wise man in the manner of Frances Wright's hero in *A Few Days in Athens*) attempts, as a central project, to discover the "physical model," or origin, upon which all religions are based: "in a word, to find out from what source the human understanding has drawn these ideas, at present so obscure, of God, of the soul, of all immaterial beings, which make the basis of so many systems: to unfold the filiation which they have followed, and the adulterations which they have undergone in their transmissions and their ramifications" (pp. 166–67). Whitman would be exploring this problem for nearly his entire life.

Interestingly, Volney does include Chinese "Chamans" in his group of religious functionaries, linking them (as Eliade has more recently) to the Lamaist "Samaneans," and finding their religious system "the same as that of the sectaries of Orpheus, of the Essenians, of the ancient Anchorets of Persia and the whole eastern country" (p. 159 n). Furthermore, according to Volney the chamans "give a complete representation of the whole system of the Stoics and Epicureans, mixed with astrological superstitions, and some traits of Pythagorism" (pp. 163–64 n). This statement is fascinating, given the fact that the other book Whitman said he "grew up on"— Frances Wright's *A Few Days in Athens* (which his father owned)—was a fictional account of Epicurus himself, dramatizing his principles, and stoicism was an important influence throughout the poet's career. Volney gives no clue to the chamans' methods of gaining divine wisdom. He does, however, portray the chamans as the most reasonable and tolerant of all the "priests," for they would accept the idea that they might be in error if the other priests would do the same. They demand immediate evidence because only the senses can transmit spiritual truths (p. 164).

The chamans would have us looking for Whitman literally under our boot-soles, for according to their idea of immortality

> the moral metempsychosis is only the figurative sense of the physical metempsychosis, or the successive movement of the elements, of bodies which perish not, but, having composed one body, pass, when that is dissolved, into other mediums, and form other combinations. The soul is but the vital principle which results from the properties of matter, and from the action of the elements in those bodies where they create a spontaneous movement. (Pp. 162–63)

As Volney's book is, by Whitman's admission, one of the earliest literary influences upon the poet, I suggest that it was here Whitman first was attracted to the ideas of immortality which scholars have traced to so many different religious heritages he might have read about later on. Volney's ultimate thesis concerning immortality is precisely that of the chamans. The idea of transmigration of the soul, says the "Lawgiver," derived "from the real transmigration of the material elements. And behold, ye Indians, ye Budsoists, ye Christians, ye Mussulmen, whence are derived all your opinions on the spirituality of the soul; behold what was the source of the dreams of Pythagoras and Plato, your masters, who were themselves but the echoes of another, the last sect of visionary philosophers" (p. 228). The implied materialism of this statement can be misleading, however, for Volney considered the "vital principle"—sometimes called the "soul"—of matter to be electricity, which in turn was energy in the form of physical particles. Hence the apparent ambiguity—or perhaps contradiction—in both his and the chamans' spiritualism. In effect, Volney does not deny the existence of the soul or its immortality, but rather supplies quasi-scientific support for these archaic conceptions. And although he does not explain the widespread belief in "phantoms" and "spirits," his own narrator is led on a flight over the earth by a phantom "Genius."

Diane Kepner's elucidation of Whitman's view of the relationship between matter, spirit, and "energy" reveals that the
poet's views were virtually identical to Volney's: "Materialists
may speak about an atom as being the smallest component of
matter, but Whitman thinks the reality of that atom is that it is
as much nonmatter as it is matter. It is completely fused with
energy (electricity)."[30] This energy inhabits every object we
can perceive. In effect, Kepner's idea matches Gay Wilson
Allen's much earlier formulation: "In his notebooks Whitman's
thoughts about the soul were in the main abstract and imper-
sonal: soul was equal but not superior to matter, yet it perme-
ated all matter, and was eternal. At times his thinking about the
soul seems clearly . . . to anticipate Bergson's *élan vital,* the
life impulse that propels each generation of plant or animal
through the cycles of existence, from the first crude germs to
the most complex organism."[31] At times, Allen adds, Whitman
seems to hold to a "physical pantheism"—"that is, the chem-
icals of the body going into plants and thus continuing to be a
part of life. But the process involves more than this, for the
beneficent soul or spirit of the departed still lives and influences or enters other persons."[32] As the contradiction between
the poet's "physical pantheism" and his use of "phantoms"
implies, Whitman did not consistently and literally espouse a
particular view of the relation between spirit and matter; rather,
he believed that the views of this relation which could be found
in virtually all religions indicated a profound mystery that was
essential to the greatest poetry. Basically, however, Volney
stamped his mind with the conviction that matter and spirit
could be reconciled to each other and that, in the deepest
sense, each partakes of the qualities of the other—perhaps
because spirit is "electricity." (Whitman avoided pinning his
beliefs to specific scientific theories, which he realized are
ephemeral.)

In his understanding of the origin of belief in the soul,
Volney seems to have been influenced by current theories
concerning electricity which were also the basis of much of
Mesmer's thinking and practice. Thus, Whitman's first exposure to such ideas may have been not through the writings
and lectures of actual homeopathists, mesmerists, and spiritualists, as scholars have previously supposed, but sec-
ondhand, by way of Volney.[33] When he did come across the
various quasi-scientific theories in phrenological journals and
such, he would have found ideas merely amplifying Volney's

speculations about the origin of mankind's belief in the soul: "The more I consider what the ancients understood by ether and spirit, and what the Indians call *akache,* the stronger do I find the analogy between it and the electrical fluid. A luminous fluid, principle of warmth and motion, pervading the universe, forming the matter of the stars, having small round particles, which insinuate themselves into bodies, and fill them by dilating itself [sic], be their extent what it will. What can more strongly resemble electricity?" (Volney, p. 221 n). This theory implies a kinship between the spirit of a man and the spirit of all matter; it allows for transformation and a form of transmigration we find in Whitman's early notebook jotting entitled "Dilation": "I think the soul will never stop, or attain to any growth beyond which it shall not go.—When I walked at night by the sea shore and looked up at the countless stars, I asked of my soul whether it would be filled and satisfied when it should become god enfolding all these, and open to the life and delight and knowledge of everything in them or of them; and the answer was plain to me at the breaking water on the sands at my feet: and the answer was, No, when I reach there, I shall want to go further still."[34] Reminiscent of "Circles" and certain statements of *Sartor Resartus,* this passage indicates that Volney's ideas prepared Whitman for the ideas of Emerson and Carlyle as well as the quasi-scientists of "animal magnetism." Moreover, the apparent contradiction between the spiritualism of the passage and Whitman's frequent statements that the body *is* the soul—or, even more immediately puzzling, the contradiction between the latter belief and his consciousness of himself "as two—as my soul and I," with the accompanying knowledge that his body will decay and free the soul—is precisely the contradiction we find in Volney and his view of the chamans' soul-concept. It was also part of the spiritualist creed, no doubt, but Volney's formulation would have been particularly attractive to Whitman because of its attachment to a democratic ideology and its supposed ancestry in ancient religion.

Volney's bent is ultimately as primitivistic as it is rationalistic: he believes that sects and priests have corrupted the original religious ideas that were based upon pure observation of nature. Contemporary scientific discoveries, Volney feels, illuminate the kernel of truth in the unclouded perception from which all religion emerged. Most significantly, the idea of the soul has deviated from the original understanding that spirit resides in the "genius," *mana,* or electricity that all material necessarily holds. From the original "architypes" [sic]—forces and principles of nature that the earliest nomadic men revered as genii—have developed symbols, idols, and finally the modern religious concept of God: "a chimerical and abstract being, a scholastic subtility [sic] of substance without form, a body without figure, a very delirium of the mind, beyond the power of reason at all to comprehend" (Volney, p. 231). To return to the earlier concept of the soul would be to achieve a more intimate knowledge of the original "architypes" behind religion and even symbolization, to return to a condition less alienated from nature. Though couched in the terms of "Reason," this view embodies a mythic hope— one that we can trace to Rousseau—but it is a mythic hope embedded in virtually all religious quests: the return to *illud tempus,* the paradisal situation at the dawn of time that pre- ceded profane disintegrations. The priests of all religions, whom the common people have foolishly allowed to monopo- lize relations with the "divine," have fostered the entire pro- cess of degeneration. Thus the ultimate blame rests not only upon the arrogance and chicanery of religious functionaries but also upon the servility and credulousness of the people (p. 273). Volney's analysis perfectly suited Whitman's ideological convictions. It proved that the spirit of priestcraft in every age is fundamentally antidemocratic (p. 271 n), and it contributed to the aspiring poet's ambition to achieve direct "rapport" with nature.

Nonetheless, Whitman clearly believed that some people develop greater spiritual knowledge than others; what he de- nied the priests was that such knowledge and insight (or, more precisely, *experience*) was not available to all who would ear- nestly seek it. That he was such a seeker from an early age is evident from a piece he wrote for the Long Island *Democrat* in 1840, which seems to be an imitation of Volney. Number eight of the "Sun-Down Papers—From the Desk of a Schoolmaster" features a narrator who is troubled by the squabbling among different creeds. Although he yearns to know more about "Truth and Religion," one day fatigue from work and self- questioning overpowers him; falling asleep, he is possessed by the "spirit of dreams" and wanders all over the earth, among many of the peoples represented in Volney's book, without gaining new insight. Finally the voice of a guiding spirit in- structs him to ascend a mountain of rocks that reaches into the clouds, from there to observe the "holy altar of Truth." Ultimately, after crossing a desert and ascending yet another precipice, he looks down upon an edenic setting, "more beautiful than was ever before revealed to mortals."[35] In the distance, on an elevation, rests a temple. The voice cautions him not to approach it, for his eyes, "covered as they are with the dark web of mortality, would be unable to comprehend the awful mysteries which Nature veils from [his] mind."[36] (This advice represents a distinct difference from the message of *Leaves of Grass*, in which the poet would gain immortal powers in ecstasy.) In an earthlike landscape below him, the narrator sees human beings continually gazing upon the temple through weirdly-shaped "optical glasses"; anyone attempting to look upon the altar of Nature with the naked eye is persecuted by the rest. The voice leaves the dreamer with the advice to be humble and adore "with voiceless awe" the power he cannot comprehend. Clearly the theme of the tale is the worthlessness of creeds; but in other important respects—particularly the narrator's inequality to divine Nature—the message is vastly different from that of *Leaves of Grass*. Some transformation would have to take place in Whitman before he could pretend to walk with gods, to transcend death and peer into the mysteries of all creation. To chronicle this transformation and "explain" it has been one of the chief conundrums of Whitman scholarship.

The Techniques
of Ecstasy

The transformation arrived simultaneously with a new ecstatic quality in Whitman's writing and confidence in the human ability to withstand the experience of divinity. In the third of his "Letters from Paumanok" for the New York *Evening Post* (14 August 1851), Whitman adopts the familiar address to the reader, the voice of trust and the promise to "divulge secrets" that the fashionable crowd knows nothing of. Here the soul is almost richer than apparent nature itself; it measures the altar of sky and water at sundown as Whitman gazes from Brooklyn Heights:

> Rapidly, an insatiable greediness grew within me for brighter and stronger hues; oh, brighter and stronger still. It seemed as if all that

eye could bear, were unequal to the fierce voracity of my soul for
intense, glowing color.

And yet there were the most choice and fervid fires of the
sunset, in their brilliancy and richness almost terrible.[37]

The greater ability to withstand nature's power is linked to the
ecstatic note in an oft-quoted passage from the same article:

> Have not you, in like manner, while listening to the well-played
> music of some band like Maretzek's, felt an overwhelming desire
> for measureless sound—a sublime orchestra of a myriad orches-
> tras—a colossal volume of harmony, in which the thunder might
> roll in its proper place; and above it, the vast, pure Tenor,—identity
> of the Creative Power itself—rising through the universe, until the
> boundless and unspeakable capacities of that mystery, the human
> soul, should be filled to the uttermost, and the problem of human
> cravingness be satisfied and destroyed?[38]

The answer to the "cravingness" mentioned here is a sacralization of the self, a form of sacralization hinted at in the passage
that takes the "superb wonder of a blade of grass" as its model
for encompassing all forms of religious reverence. Whitman's
mode of approaching his model matches nature's power with
his own and then allows the transfer between the poles
"nature" and "man"—a transfer that his view of the soul could
accomodate. Only this exchange could suffice Whitman's voracity; it is also the exchange that Victor Turner locates in ritual
and Eliade finds in the paradisiac state achieved through
shamanic ecstasy. The end of the aesthetic purity Whitman
reaches for is implicit in the shaman's transformational
powers and in his ability, like Orpheus's, to speak with animals. Without this power of transformation, there can be no
success in either the poem or the rite; with it, the performer
demonstrates his equality with God, his total union with
nature.

Such is the distinction between dream and ecstasy, which
may be partly attributable to a physiological property of trance
by which opposites are united, paradoxes overcome.[39] Justus
Lawler has considered this experience of transcending contradictions the "central poem" behind all lyric, rooted in our
ontological status.[40] In shamanism this aesthetic purity is the
tool to a social end, the achievement of harmony (which in
itself is a fusion of the one and the many—Whitman's "One's
Self" and "En-Masse"). Social harmony, moreover, depends

upon cosmic harmony, which is why, from a functional point of view, the shaman must be able to ferry between worlds and mediate with the supernatural powers.

As I indicated in the last chapter, the transformation in Whitman between 1840 and 1851 is connected with the revitalization process that had gripped many other northerners in varying ways. Just as American "civil religion," rooted in the Enlightenment, was deepened and transformed by the revival impulse, Whitman outgrew early deistic influences (including Volney) and waxed ecstatic as his pessimism about the state of society grew, as he became increasingly sensitive to the corruption of national purpose and distraught over the frustration of his own ambitions. His response to the crisis of national identity initially was political and rhetorical rather than religious and aesthetic, but in his early notebooks we see the shift in his emphasis from the political / discursive (of a bitter tone) to the religious / charismatic. At the same time, he continually harps upon the theme of health in both the personal and the public senses. The ideal of magnetism in the orator blossoms into the charisma of the prophet as Whitman moves more confidently toward his final pose. And when he reviews literature, he continually applies the standard of "originality" in the sense of a gushing forth of prophecy from inspiration, as opposed to the manipulation of literary tradition.[41] Looking for clues to the type of role that would suit him, Whitman was consistently attracted to charismatic expression with religious and moral effects—the entrancing and otherworldly aria of Italian opera (which, says one historian, used the voice to produce a "hushed, neurotic ecstasy"),[42] the lightning oratory of Elias Hicks, and the ecstatic pronouncements of ancient poets and prophets.

Although Whitman consistently criticized Milton and the romantics for copying the antique, he continued to study primal religion long after his first exposure to Volney's work. The problem of discovering a common denominator of all religious traditions remained his most engrossing interest, and Volney's idea of the relation between soul and body would be amplified by other reading and experience. In his study of inspired states, visionary experience, and sorcery, Whitman could not help but notice how often communication with "familiar spirits" informed such phenomena. He read extensively about the possible uses and importance of spiritual "messengers" to prophecy and "unconscious" poetry by the time he began writing *Leaves of Grass*, his early fiction and verse attesting to his fascination for the subject. Moreover, the numerous references to phantoms and spiritual visitation in Whitman's latest prose and verse prove the persistence of his belief that such motifs were indispensable to visionary expression. Whitman never precisely defined his concept of the spiritual "helper" or of the phantom, for he associated them with the general mystery of immortality and the nature of the soul—aspects of being that would forever elude definition and "statements to mortal sense." Yet he made use of spiritual agents repeatedly to dramatize communications between the earthly and the supranormal worlds.[43] Among the early influences upon him in this respect, Walter Scott ranks among the most important.

At the age of about sixteen, Whitman acquired *Minstrelsy of the Scottish Border,* apparently in an edition that included Scott's "Letters on Demonology and Witchcraft."[44] In a later interview for *Harper's Weekly,* Whitman claimed, " 'The only poetry that had nourished him was Sir Walter Scott's Border Minstrelsy, particularly Sir Walter's memoranda of interviews with old Scotsmen and Scotswomen respecting the folk-lore of their earlier days. The folk-lore of witchcraft was especially interesting to him.' "[45] Scott's may well have been the first extended discussion of "eidolons" with which Whitman came in contact. In the "Letters on Demonology," Scott uses the term "eidolon" synonymously with "phantom" and concludes that the term expresses an archaic concept born out of the consciousness of a spiritual world and of immortality.[46] He further links the appearance of these spirits to certain types of crises: "Sometimes our violent and inordinate passions, originating in sorrow for our friends, remorse for our crimes, our eagerness of patriotism, or our deep sense of devotion—these or other violent excitements of a moral character, in the visions of night, or the rapt ecstasy of the day, persuade us that we witness, with our eyes and ears, an actual instance of that supernatural communication, the possibility of which cannot be denied."[47] Whitman probably not only accepted Scott's rationale but saw the metaphorical possibilities and inherent power of a concept that had caught the imagination of humanity in all ages.

Scott's letters also contain numerous references to witches and sorcerers who professed to commune with familiar spirits which gave them the ability to journey to the supernatural world, to prophesy and to cause illness. He even mentions American Indian "powahs" in this connection, but he assigns them far less potency and more transparent charlatanism than the pagan priestesses of ancient Europe and Asia: "It was no unusual thing to see females [in Europe], from respect to their supposed views into futurity, and the degree of divine inspiration which was vouchsafed to them, arise to the degree of Haxa, or chief priestess."[48] Scott finds that evidence from Scandinavian sagas on the lore of scalds and of Othin (Odin) correlates with evidence in classic mythology of the practices of mystic rites and prophesy. In more recent times, Nora K. Chadwick has spoken of Odin as the inspired poet and seer among the gods, having closest affinities "with the Siberian shamans whom he resembles in a remarkable degree. He is, in fact, the divine shaman of the Norse pantheon, and his affinities are to be sought in Northern Asia."[49] That Whitman found Odin an attractive figure is certain; whether he knew much of Odin's practices and abilities I do not know, but if he did, then he would have had some idea of how classic shamans practiced their profession. He apparently did find Scandinavia particularly significant as the "nursery" of much Anglo-Saxon legend and folktale, and he noted the word "rune" as referring to "Poems, traditions of the ancient northern Europeans." (Runes were in fact Scandinavian charms and incantations.)[50] As regards a related tradition Whitman occasionally mentioned, Chadwick points out that Celtic literature is quite specific about methods of inducing inspiration and the adventures of the soul.[51]

Many of the ideas and theories Whitman was developing with the help of Volney and Scott he found amplified, extended, and partly altered by the work of other thinkers. Hugh Blair's prefatory "Critical Dissertation" on the *Poems of Ossian* held the spiritual machinery of the works supposedly translated by Macpherson to be essential and "sublime," connected with universal religious and epic motifs.[52] Carlyle similarly praised the way in which supernatural beings, "skyey messengers," contributed to the spiritual depth of the *Nibelungen Lied* without diminishing its aura of lived experience. Carlyle respected the metaphorical significance of "ghosts" and spiritual presences as embodiments of the belief that we are all derived from spirit, shaped into bodies, and later resolved to spirit again. He further supposed that "the fiction of the Nibelungen was at first a religious or philosophical Mythus" later integrated with traditional accounts of historical events and gradually developed into the current epic form.[53]

The theory that the oldest of Germanic "epics" was based upon sacred chants, historical legends, and the "mythus" of spiritual experiences corroborated Whitman's prior suspicions about the origin of epic forms and matched Carlyle's thesis concerning Odin in the first of his lectures on *Heroes and Hero-Worship*.[54] Ironically, the antidemocratic Scotsman's works—particularly *Sartor Resartus, Heroes and Hero-Worship,* and the essay "Characteristics"—were probably Whitman's most important sources with regard to prophetic expression. Carlyle provided Whitman not only with a theory of poetry as prophecy but with a theory of the role of prophecy in periods of historical crisis that perfectly suited the journalist's unhappy situation in the late 1840s. In the essay "Characteristics," which Floyd Stovall believes influenced Whitman most deeply,[55] Carlyle connects the need for inspired, "unconscious" expression of the prophetic type with the need for a new object of faith and loyalty. Acknowledging the decay of the feudal, Catholic order, Carlyle predicts that a new order, to be announced by a heroic prophet, is on the horizon. (In *Sartor Resartus* he even has Teufelsdröckh point to newspaper editors as harbingers of the new era—"idol-breakers" who prepare the ground for the coming prophet.)[56] The new, "unconscious," and inspired Poet will awaken men to loyalty and faith in a new "Idea," a new religion that absorbs what is good of the past but moves beyond it in freedom and "unconscious" moral action, more deeply rooted in cosmic laws than the popular panaceas of reform (such as Whitman also criticized in newspaper editorials).

According to Carlyle the "revitalization" scenario, as we might call it, follows a pattern as old as the most ancient religion. First the prophet awakens, inspired with his message; then he receives the assent of another:

> a mystic miraculous unfathomable Union establishes itself. . . . The lightning-spark of Thought, generated, or say heaven-kindled, in the solitary mind, awakens its express likeness in another mind, in a thousand other minds, and all blaze up together in combined fire. . . . By and By, a common store of Thought can accumulate, and be transmitted as an everlasting possession: Literature, whether as preserved in the memory of Bards, in Runes and Hieroglyphs engraved in stone, or in Books of written or printed paper, comes into existence, and begins to play its wondrous part.[57]

Whitman broke ranks with Carlyle only when the latter went on to say, "Politics are formed; the weak submitting to the strong;

with a willing loyalty, giving obedience that he may receive guidance." Here, Whitman would object throughout his life, Carlyle's feudal prejudices—his resistance to egalitarianism and his almost perverse fascination with the singular hero— prevented him from moving on to the great discovery of the age: that Democracy was the new "Idea," the faith and political order of the future. "Altogether," Whitman would say in *Specimen Days*, "I don't know anything more amazing than these persistent strides and throbbings so far through our Nineteenth century of perhaps its biggest, sharpest, and most erudite brain, in defiance and discontent with everything; contemptuously ignoring . . . the only solace and solvent to be had." Indeed, "the bearings [Carlyle] ignored were marvelous."[58] Had Carlyle emigrated to America in 1835—as he nearly did, following the critical failure of *Sartor Resartus* and at the urging of Emerson—he would have avoided his "grim fate . . . to live and dwell in, and largely embody, the parturition agony and qualms of the old order, amid crowded accumulations of ghastly morbidity, giving birth to the new."[59] Carlyle's misfortune was to suffer from the same Old World decrepitude he could so brilliantly diagnose.

Whitman bridged the historical chasm from which Carlyle, in his stubborn "dyspepsia" and "feudal" prejudices, had withdrawn. That chasm Emerson had also bridged in emphasizing the potential divinity of the common man (although, in his early work, Carlyle did not ignore that divinity and Whitman thought him very nearly a "democrat"); there is no doubt that Whitman found in Emerson certain natively "modern" elements Carlyle lacked, although the American "master's" influence has been overdrawn on the whole. From Whitman's point of view, Emerson was strong where Carlyle was weak, and vice versa. What Whitman claimed he did not find in Emerson or the German metaphysicians to whom Carlyle introduced the Anglo-American intelligentsia—"the lightning flashes and flights of the old prophets and *exaltés*, the spiritual poets and poetry of all lands (as in the Hebrew Bible)"—he did find in Carlyle.[60] This is not the place to debate the relative value to Whitman of what one might call his two chief "masters"; such a debate would be fruitless in any case, but if (as many scholars have alleged) Whitman desired in his later years to "cover up" his indebtedness to Emerson, he felt no such impulse with relation to Carlyle, of whom he thought as " 'more significant than any modern man—as in himself a full answer to the cry of the modern spirit for expression.' "[61]

Whatever specific sources influenced him in addition to Volney, Scott, Carlyle, and Emerson, Whitman came to believe that all gods had once been enlightened mortals: "Back to ten thousand years before These States, all nations had, and some yet have, and perhaps always will have, tradition of coming men, great benefactors, of divine origin, capable of deeds of might, blessings, poems, enlightenment. From time to time these have arisen, and yet arise and will always arise. Some are called gods and deified—enter into the succeeding religions."[62] Whitman moved increasingly toward a theory of the ecstatic seer as he browsed through many books, "pursuing some clue or thread of his own."[63] As he did he gained his shamanic training: "The primitive poets, their subjects, their style, all assimilate. Very ancient poetry of the Hebrew prophets, of Ossian, of the Hindu singer and ecstatics, of the Greeks, of the American aborigines, the old Persians and Chinese, and the Scandinavian Sagas, all resemble each other" (*CW*, 9:96). Yet Whitman was not interested in the "epic" mode that frequently chronicled the adventures of heroes, gods, and shamans; he wanted the direct inspiration, the "subjective" or "lyric" mode that registered the ecstatic adventure in the first person.[64]

The evidence shows that Whitman had absorbed the ideological foundations and prerequisites of ecstatic practice by the time he began to work on *Leaves of Grass;* but he did not simply attempt to imitate a role—he hoped to live one. In this sense precisely, he differentiated himself from Milton and the European Romantics. Goethe's poems, for example, he found "competitive with the antique . . . because he has studied the antique. They appear to me as great as the antique in all respects except one. That is the antique poems were *growths— they* were never studied from antiques." Goethe had not the faith of the masters because he never allowed himself to be "carried away by his theme" as the old ecstatics had (*CW*, 9:112). Similarly, Keats's poetry "is imbued with the sentiment, at second-hand, of the gods and goddesses of twenty-five hundred years ago" (*CW*, 9:120).

Whitman's notes on oratory reveal his attempts literally to train himself as a charismatic—an effort that did not succeed, but that was important in the development of his verse. Indeed, C. Carroll Hollis has shown that the 1855 edition of *Leaves of Grass* "had a speech base and a rhetorical intention in a far more direct and literal sense than we have heretofore realized, with a consequent imperative for a large-scale reassessment of our first native poet."[65] He goes on to argue, in greater linguistic detail than any previous scholar, how Whitman apparently did think of his shaman-like persona in "Song of Myself" as delivering an ecstatic oral performance. Years ago F. O. Matthiessen pointed Hollis's direction when he stated that in the notes on oratory the poet made use of words as a "primitive conjuror" would, and by now many of the passages supporting such an interpretation are fairly well-known, such as the one that advises, "The great thing is to be inspired as one divinely possessed, blind to all subordinate affairs and given up entirely to the surgings and utterances of the mighty tempestuous demon."[66] In another passage Whitman emphasizes the essentially lyric and ritualistic nature of his conception, "Counterparting in the first person, present time, the divine ecstasy of the ancient Pythia, oracles, priests, possessed persons, demoniacs &c."[67] In the "agonistic arena" of the oration, the great speaker "wrestles" with his hearers—"he suffers, sweats, undergoes his great toil and extasy" (*WWW*, p. 37). These notes date from before and after the 1855 edition, indicating that as late as 1857 the poet was still thinking of his vocation in physical terms as recreating the mode of ancient rites.[68] He trained himself in charismatic gestures and posturings to convey his magnetism, at the same time that he stressed the need for an absolutely perfect physique to radiate inner power (*WWW*, pp. 37–38). It goes without saying that shamans are masters of charismatic performance. Their charisma helps strip the audience of profane thoughts and feelings to mold them into a unified body. Such is Whitman's ambition: "Notwithstanding the diversity of minds in such a multitude, by the lightning of eloquence, they are melted into one mass, the whole assembly actuated in one and the same way, become as it were but one man, and have but one voice" (*WWW*, p. 38).

The dramatic situation as Whitman describes it is also instructive, for the orator must act with relation to the spiritual as well as the human world. The role context is triadic, with the speaker in the third, intermediary position, requiring incredible mimetic abilities. In one passage Whitman imagines an oratorical process that moves through several different moods and scenes, starting out calm and easy for the induction stage, giving way to an almost imperceptible stirring in the body; the head shakes hair away from the eyes with the grace of a horse or an athlete:

"now perhaps a silent pause, then that voice again, with vigor, but now the body co-operates, as a lover; soon a passage that seems to force its own way through every limb . . . and anon a stern and harsh passage crackling and smashing like a falling tree, many other passages of many different tones, but all converging sooner or later into the clear, monotonous voice, equable as water— sometimes direct addresses made to you, the hearer, without a pause afterward, as if an answer was expected, then perhaps for many minutes total abstraction and travelling into other fields, the vocalism limpid, inspired, no account made of the material place, the audience, but only of that other more spiritual world in which the speaker is now roaming."[69]

Whitman obviously sees the inspired state as literally abstracted and trance-like; moreover, his exercises for states of abstraction cultivated a natural propensity he already had. The triadic dramatic situation, the shifting nature of the address to the audience, the ventriloquistic uses of the voice, and the fluid manipulations of space exemplified in the passage above show that Whitman had substantially reconstructed the shamanic rite situation. Impelled by an inner necessity, he had taught himself the secrets normally passed from master to initiate.

The Healing Way

Perhaps the shaman's most common function is to heal disease, which he is peculiarly qualified to do according to the concept of illness as soul-corruption or soul-loss. Thus it is fascinating to find that in the same early notebooks that document Whitman's interest in comparative religion we find him continually harping upon the theme of health—health both personal and national. Other scholars have noticed this—particularly Harold Aspiz—but they have not considered how conditions of health and sickness function as somatic "tropes" for equilibrium and disequilibrium at every structural level, from the cellular right up to what Wallace identifies as the public "mazeway." When the public equilibrium is closely connected to the individual—as Forgie claims it was in Whitman's generation and as nearly all students agree it was for the poet—the trope "health" reaches across the entire axis of individual and society. It becomes the prime metaphor for cultural equilibrium; societies that are under stress frequently spawn charismatic and spiritualistic curing cults that can be connected with reform and even develop into full-fledged re-vitalistic religions.[70] The concern for "health" at the public level reaches through the individual's consciousness to his internal state. Conversely, the visionary who has first cured himself by spiritual integration gains the capacity to cure others, and his curing is a deeply social event. Thus it is not surprising that Swedenborgianism, Transcendentalism, and reform develop side-by-side with such health fads (temporarily espoused by Whitman) as homeopathy and hydropathy.[71]

Images of affliction virtually dominate Whitman's earliest verse notebook. Most of the people he mentions or identifies with are afflicted in some sense; the poet is to restore their *souls* to health so that they can participate fully in the perfection of the cosmos. "Wickedness," claims the poet, "is most likely the absence of freedom and health in the soul."[72] "The mean and bandaged spirit is perpetually dissatisfied with itself." Therefore the poet's chief function is to heal the soul that other influences have corrupted. Whitman thus arrived at a view matching the shaman's theory of disease.

Beyond the healing of individuals Whitman extends his metaphor and his program to the nation as a whole, which he believes is borne by a "current . . . broadly and deeply materialistic and infidel": "I do not believe the people of these days are happy. The public countenance lacks its bloom of love and its freshness of faith.—For want of these, it is cadaverous as a corpse." Established religions and political reforms are unequal to the task Whitman has taken on since his awakening, to give "the entire health, both of spirit and flesh, the life of grace and strength and action, from which all else flows."[73] That the idea of soul- and body-corruption was connected with Whitman's political disillusionment is evident in another note that bears the stamp of the late 1840s or 1850s: "? seems perpetually goading me—the soul—If all seems right—it is not right—then corruption—then putridity—then mean maggots grow among men—they are born out of the too richly manured earth" (*CW*, 9:145–46).

The connection of social corruption with the state of the soul may have occurred to Whitman when he read Carlyle's essay "Characteristics," which can be seen as an earlier European response to a social drama similar to the one that occurred in Whitman's America. Carlyle saw his own society staggering in a state of decrepitude reflected not only in literature but in medicine and reform: "The whole Life of Society must now be carried on by drugs: doctor after doctor appears with his nostrum."[74] The outward diseases (such as class antagonism) to which reform is a response originate, according to Carlyle, in an inward disease of the spirit that the genuine prophet must address in a more profound and encompassing, though "unconscious" and "inspired," manner. Meanwhile, reformers argue about politics, churches argue about religion, philosophers argue about metaphysics, and "spontaneous devotedness to the object, being wholly possessed by the object, what we can call Inspiration, has well-nigh ceased to appear in Literature. Which melodious Singer forgets that he is singing melodiously?" Literature, philosophy, theology and politics— indeed, all sorts of moral action and thought—reflect the relative health or sickness of society in their tendency to either "unconsciousness" or artificiality and "consciousness."[75] Furthermore, in addition to being "healthy," the authentically inspired poet is a great healer. Thus Carlyle provided Whitman with the stance from which the latter criticized even Goethe, who was Carlyle's early idol. Goethe's work was too studied and self-conscious; moreover, it failed the "Test of a poem": "How far it can elevate, enlarge, purify, deepen and make happy the attributes of the body and soul of a man."[76]

The extolling of "unconsciousness" as a sign of health may have had something to do with Whitman's habit, beginning in the late 1840s, of avoiding "sophisticated" attachments and going "with powerful uneducated persons." Above all, it helped convince him to avoid argument and self-conscious depression as he moved toward a prophetic role. However, Whitman came to both his theory of disease and his change of demeanor not simply by absorbing the ideas of Carlyle and others, but by sublimating the bitterness he felt over social developments, using a strategy Carlyle helped him to find.

We have seen in "Lingave's Temptation" and "The Shadow and the Light of a Young Man's Soul" how Whitman bore his frustration and finally decided to quit complaining. *Leaves of Grass* similarly turns away from the bitter notes of "The House of Friends" of 1848, certain statements of which are embedded in a proclamation of faith and optimism in the 1855 Preface. The poet had decided that it was "unworthy [for] a live man to pray or complain no matter what should happen"; he would no longer "pronounce his race a sham or swindle," but he would adhere to a higher faith in the democratic future (*CW*, 9:139–40).

The healthy, "affluent souls" may be found in all strata of

life; "Their centrifugal power of love . . . makes the awfulest forces of nature stand back. Its perennial blow the frost shall never touch; and what we call death shall go round outside it forever and ever" (*CW,* 9:144). With some revision this thought would appear in a highly revealing sentence of the 1855 Preface: "The most affluent man is he that confronts all the shows he sees by equivalents out of the stronger wealth of himself."[77] We might compare this statement with the sentiment expressed in the "Letter From Paumanok" cited earlier—that in which Whitman shows his soul's voracity and equality with Nature. The metaphor of affluence—in a passage contrasting the profanely rich with the man of wisdom—underlines the fact that Whitman surmounted his feelings of deprivation through the ecstasy that allowed him to match and surpass Nature's power. Through this acquisition of force, Whitman vastly overleaped the meager wealth of the politically powerful, attaining at the same time to the utterance with which he hoped to lead the "democratic average" away from the "morbid worship of money" that threatened the national identity itself. Such an interpretation is further supported in the 1855 Preface by Whitman's contrast of "the prudence of the mere wealth and respectability of the most esteemed life" with the great poet's prudence—"wisdom spaced out by ages" (of which Whitman is confident, having studied the prophets and exaltés of the ages)—a prudence that "answers at last the craving and glut of the soul."[78]

The Shamanic Persona and Ecstatic Achievement

Recent interpretations of shamanism show how the apparent automatism and sudden ecstaticism in shamanic initiation and practice are more akin to Whitman's conscious creative processes than we might initially expect. Borrowing from interpretations of a dissociative practice familiar to the West and very popular in Whitman's day—hypnotism—Anna-Leena Siikala has analyzed the shamanic experience as an "ecstatic role-taking technique." She builds upon Sheila Walker's analysis of possession as a form of hypnotic regression in service of the ego, pointing out that the important factor in hypnotism and in possession is the creation of a new subsystem in the ego through adjustments made in the course of trance-induction. Personality traits conducive to these adjustments include particularly " 'the need for *love*, . . . the tendency for *passive compliance*, . . . and the wish to participate in *omnipotence.*' "[79] E. H. Miller's interpretation of how Whitman's role-taking related to his emotional needs might well serve as an illustration: "The deeds he performs and the adulation he enjoys are the long-suppressed daydreams of an unhappy youth who envisages himself as a hero in order to gain attention and to alleviate his feelings of impotency. In short, the poet in maturity supplies the affectional needs of the emotionally frustrated child."[80] The new ego subsystem created during hypnotic or shamanic trance induction represents the personality of the possessing force or role. In hypnotism the professional serves as the object upon whom the patient transfers responsibility for his actions; the patient's behavior depends chiefly upon his idea of what a hypnotist *is supposed to be:* " 'The hypnotist, in effect, is a culturally approved authority or sanctioning figure upon whom many fantasies involving omnipotence are projected' " (Siikala, p. 48, quoting Van der Walde). Siikala extends this analysis to shamanism by arguing that the hypnotist's role is fulfilled by a fusion of many factors derived from the cultural complex: symbols, spirits, and ancestors that control the progress of the spiritual experience. Thus the shamanic initiate learns, under the tutelage of an elder shaman, to control his trance experiences according to the culturally conditioned idea of how a shaman is supposed to act and of how spiritual agents behave. Whitman's method of study indicates quite clearly that he created the model role-figures necessary for his visionary program out of his reading and experience.

The written medium, on the other hand, gave the poet a certain freedom not allowed the shaman, for he would not have to perform in a literal state of dissociation. This advantage was offset, however, by the poet's loss of the dramatic context that would have allowed a more direct participation with the audience than print allows. As C. Carroll Hollis shows, Whitman artfully developed a language and style to convey illocutionary force and thus compensate for the loss of the *actual* "agonistic arena." In expressing his position, Hollis rejects thinking of Whitman as a prophet or shaman because such performers are allegedly less "artful"—they do not "play" at their roles but have complete sincerity and confidence in their performances. Whitman, on the other hand, created a literary "illusion" of prophecy and shamanistic healing.[81] Siikala's and Walker's analyses indicate that Hollis's distinction dissolves upon close inspection of the ecstatic experience, although his discussion of "speech acts" in *Leaves of Grass* remains significant—even supports the interpretation presented here. If shamanism is essentially a form of role-taking, then it can serve well as an analogue for such poetic activity as Whitman engaged in. The state of dissociation simply represents the most complete adoption of a role, requiring the greatest possible organismal involvement (Siikala, pp. 51, 64). Whitman certainly strove to convey such involvement in his poems—in part through the "illocutionary style" Hollis analyzes. The shaman is an artist who willfully manipulates physiological and aesthetic techniques to perform a religious role, just as Whitman manipulates techniques available to him as a publishing poet. In their own communities, shamans are basically judged for the completeness of the "illusion" they create and its effect upon the audience. The "ecstatic role-taking technique" is crucial to the "illusion" (in which the shaman normally believes, although he "knows what he is doing"); to communicate between the "sacred" and "profane" worlds demands a far more fluid sense of self than ordinary consciousness allows. Hence, even the physiological phenomena of the trance must be considered as part of a "language" controlled by the shaman's role-process, contributing to the drama of intercourse with an order of reality known only by virtue of the shaman's creativity. This experienced "reality" works reciprocally back upon the role-process in turn; for the ecstatic, "consciousness changes as reality takes shape according to the new role" (Siikala, p. 64).

We thus come to one of the most significant contributions that the analogy of shamanism provides for students of Whitman and the American Renaissance because it gives us an intercultural paradigm for the sort of narrative and even generic discontinuity so distinctive of America's greatest romantic texts. Ecstaticism shows us the connection between the speaking persona's fragmentation, his ferrying between worlds, and those transcendent moments in which antagonistic elements mate with each other on the bridge of the unspeakable. It thus gives us a model from outside of (and probably prior to) the Aristotelian tradition to account in a new way for the "unity" of such radically resistant texts as "Song of Myself," revealing the coherence of the poet's transformational performance and tying that performance to both personal and social intentions.

In shamanism certain requirements adhere to the role-taking process; these requirements are remarkably constant in different cultures, apparently because of the manner in which the autonomic system must be engaged to allow such transformations as one finds in "Song of Myself." The successful performance improvises upon a recognizable structure of transformation. First of all, a preparatory stage signals the performer's change of status, his adoption of the mask. Then comes a period in which the visionary state is induced, usually through the help of spiritual aids and technical devices (chiefly rhythmic)—the shaman's senses are often powerfully wrought upon at this point, and it is here that one might find erotic episodes with spiritual agents. This threshold—in which oppositions such as those between "sacred" and "profane," "animal" and "human," "self" and "other," or "past" and "future" dissolve—is a form of death, even a dismemberment in some cases, that allows the soul to undergo phenomenal transformations incident to possession or to the spiritual adventures of an ecstatic journey. Eventually the shaman obtains an answer to the originating problem and then returns to the normal state of consciousness, which marks a triumph insofar as the shaman has once again surmounted the life-threatening dangers of the performance and gained the necessary insight. Joyousness and reassurance mark this final stage of the performance.

From the narrative standpoint, the performance is somewhat like a frame tale; but here, instead of one narrator's story being framed within another's, the single narrator adopts different roles as he changes consciousness at recognizable transition points. The lyric progression is of course implicit in the narrative progression, as the performer's subjective experience, which determines musical properties and is reciprocally aided by them, corresponds to the various thresholds of consciousness.[82] From the dramatic standpoint, one notes the interaction between the performer and spiritual agents as well as between performer and audience. Not all seances follow precisely the same pattern, but they all adhere to the same underlying structure. The intensity of the experience will be reflected throughout the narrative, lyric, and dramatic properties.[83]

Siikala finds essentially three paradigms for the shaman's

role-taking *vis-a-vis* the audience and the supranormal world: (1) a situation of lesser ecstasy and light trance, in which the shaman is very aware of his audience and minimally immersed in the supranormal; (2) a situation demanding varying depths of involvement, in which the trance comes and goes as the shaman is alternately keyed to the audience or to the supranormal, but generally identified with his spiritual role; and (3) deep trance, sometimes leading to unconsciousness, with the greatest concentration upon the spiritual world and very little on the audience. The curve of ecstasy is simplest (and most purely "lyrical") in the latter situation, constituting a rise, climax, and fall in fairly clear order, as in "The Sleepers." If, as in situation two, the shaman must attend more to audience response, and if the spirit-identification and audience groups interchange repeatedly as objects of orientation, then the ecstasy is wave-like, with several climaxes, as we find in "Song of Myself." These climaxes, of course, build in intensity toward the ultimate resolution. The more the poet is oriented toward the audience, the less he experiences altered consciousness or symbolic death and spiritual intensity, notwithstanding the fact that that intensity comes as the gift of a socially-directed role.

The epistemological significance of the shaman's transformative capability cannot be overestimated, and I would suggest that those who would like to refine our view of the American search for origins, for the ground or abyss beneath the beginnings of symbol-making where binary oppositions collapse (and man ceases to be estranged from himself and his products), could do no better than to consider the ecstatic achievements of the shaman. In the shamanistic arena Poe's vortices, Melville's whirlpools, and Thoreau's ponds appear as figures for the same landscape of transformation.[84] The hieroglyphic quest of which John Irwin has written appears as merely one mode of the ecstatic adventure by which a human voyager penetrates the opposition between the one and the many, history and eternity, subject and object—thereby accepting dismemberment to enter upon cosmogenic beginnings.[85] (In the figure of dismemberment, we read the multiplicity of the narrative voice.) But even here, where the antipodes spiral within him as within a god and he shape-shifts to the rhythm of pure accomplishment, his people hold him to his promise to return (in some seances literally begging him to come back while enchanting spirits detain him below), for it is only by virtue of his return that we get the prophecy, the cure, the reassurance, or the knowledge of the underworld.

If such a scenario seems to argue against the historicity of the literature in question, we should remember that historical particulars both precipitate the spiritual adventure and determine, to a large extent, its symbolic content. History is the ground of ecstasy. In fact, neurological evidence suggests that the awareness of death and the capacity for transcendence developed at the same turn of our evolutionary spiral, the latter perhaps in response to the former cognitive ability. In "Out of the Cradle Endlessly Rocking," Whitman would dramatically attest at least to the poetic validity of that evolutionary view.

CHAPTER THREE

Healer and Prophet, 1855

OVER THE YEARS scholars have come to regard "Song of Myself" and "The Sleepers" somewhat as companions in the 1855 *Leaves of Grass*—not only because they are the finest poems in that book, but also because they seem to lie at the heart of Whitman's conception, revealing the source of his awakening as a poet. Both represent experiences of religious inspiration of a very similar, sensual sort, precipitated by existential riddles that lead to trance-like absorption, symbolic death, spiritual "vision," achievement of equilibrium, and an assumption of prophetic power. Called *monodramas* by Howard Waskow, both have dramatic-narrative structures and point to American community, incorporating scenes from the national past in visionary episodes, but also moving beyond that community to global prophecy in a typically millennial fashion. Like "Song of Myself," "The Sleepers" is one of the most powerful ecstatic poems in American literature, and it illuminates, more clearly and simply than "Song of Myself," the process of inspiration and insight upon which *Leaves of Grass* depends.

The differences between the poems derive chiefly from the different tasks they perform. "Song of Myself," as the opening poem in the 1855 edition, had to create its subject and audience even before it could concentrate toward the climactic spiritual process that was its reason-for-being.[1] It shows the making of the mask—the first half of the poem being largely concerned with absorbing the diversities and contradictions of a nation, distilling them into the dualities of existence (combined most succinctly in the symbol of the leaf of grass), and building up the context within which the poet's project must be understood. Furthermore, the speaker of the poem must repeatedly take note of his audience to help lead his readers through his strange new script—a necessity that complicates the visionary nature of the poem. "The Sleepers," on the other hand, does not face these challenges and is therefore far simpler in structure, more concentrated, if less bold in its aspiration.

Like a great many other critics, I have chosen the 1855 texts of both "The Sleepers" and "Song of Myself," and for two reasons: (1) reading the 1855 texts brings us closer to the chronological "birth" of the poet—an asset in a study that is in part historical, following the poet's development; and (2) the earlier versions contain certain important episodes that were cut later on, to the detriment, nearly all critics agree, of both "Song of Myself" and "The Sleepers"—and that bring us closer to Whitman's initial urges and indecorums than he would later allow.

"The Sleepers"

This is the poem that Emory Holloway said "gives us a clue to the whole poetic mentality of Whitman"—a view seconded by Gay Wilson Allen's judgment that "The Sleepers" reveals, more than any other composition, "the methods by which he sublimated his life into the universal symbols of poetry."[2] Such evaluations have naturally made "The Sleepers" an important text for psychoanalytic critics, most notably Edwin Haviland Miller, who believes the poem concerns maturation, the entrance into manhood and society. Although there clearly are such psychological resonances in the poem, the piece manifestly has nothing to do with a "puberty rite."[3] Rather, the protagonist performs the functions of a healer and prophet. The first section of the poem indicates his curative intentions and that he is troubled by the suffering of others; the last two sections represent the accomplishment of his curing as well as a religious vision. When we read the poem with this in mind, its structure and intent stand out unmistakably. Instead of a playing-out of oedipal conflicts, we read the clear progression of an ecstatic performance (which may, indeed, be energized by unconscious conflicts, like any ritual, but is not primarily concerned with them). The surface texture of the poem comes to make far greater sense than before, and the connection of that texture (with all the oddities that make this one of Whitman's most difficult poems) to Whitman's deepest intentions as a poet becomes clear. In short, we are able to take the poet "at his word" to a greater extent than in the past. The poem exemplifies how Whitman came to indicate "the path between reality and [our] souls" by directly "communicating" with the spiritual world and manipulating the manifestations of that world.[4] Specifically, "The Sleepers" dramatizes an ecstatic spiritual descent through which the forces of the underworld are brought into use for healing and the discovery of an expanded context for human life.

The poem occurs entirely in the present and, like a shamanic seance, opens with the seer at the threshold of descent, speaking his thoughts and actions so that he is "overheard" by the reader, who seems to be nearby, attentive. With the many sleepers who are wounded, crippled, ill, or dead, the poet is at first "confused," "ill-assorted," "contradictory."[5] He is most concerned about the "worst suffering and restless," passing his hands soothingly over their faces until they drop into a fitful sleep that allows him to begin his soul-journey.[6] Through identification with them and passage beneath their dreams he can descend to the underworld in search of the causes of illness—which in the world-views of peoples who employ shamans are usually regarded as corruptions or alienations of the soul (Eliade, p. 217).

A fit of dance curiously akin to possession takes place just as Whitman crosses the threshold of a deeper immersion in the trance: "I am a dance . . . . Play up there! the fit is whirling me fast" (1.32). Precisely at this point in shamanic ritual, it is said that the healer takes possession of his "helping spirits," and is himself transformed into a similar being so that he can begin his "ecstatic journey" to the hidden realms (Eliade, p. 92). Emerging from the dance into "new moon and twilight," Whitman calls himself "the everlaughing"; he sees "nimble ghosts" whichever way he looks, and with those helping spirits descends toward the underworld, "cache and cache again deep in the ground and sea, and where it is neither ground or sea" (1.35). From this point on, the deepening shades of darkness noted by Sister Eva Mary correspond to the descent of the poet by degrees through the graded levels of his trance, leading to the "blank" darkness of ritual death in which his visions of loss arise.[7]

The love scene by which section one comes to a climax is comparable to a shaman's sexual ecstasy with a celestial being, serving to deepen the poet's immersion in a state of trance (Eliade, p. 79). The preliminary tryst of the "expectant woman" and her "truant lover" is only a prelude to a more significant union with the darkness, which emphasizes the spiritual character of the ecstasy continuous with its physical nature—suggesting a "surrender to the world of spirit, a loss of identity in an all-encompassing spirituality" precipitated by the sexual act.[8]

Erotic consummation was most important for Whitman in its function of transporting the participants to a unified spiritual and physical plane, where the awareness of a conjunction of soul and body is most acute. In fact, it seems to have been his model for the "trance-like suspension of acitivity" out of which poetic inspiration came. He described the state of creative power as " 'a trance, yet with all the senses alert—only a state of high exalted musing—the tangible and material with all its shows, the objective world suspended or surmounted for a while, and the powers in exaltation, freedom, vision—yet the *senses* not lost or counteracted.' "[9] The same words might be used to describe the shamanic experience, in which the erotic elements contribute to the "possession" or "journey" of the soul.

The poet's unification with the darkness through a feminine persona serves his descent to an awareness more primitive than gender differentiation, where the personal feminine point of view is dropped for a complete intermingling of the sexes in consummation. The folded "cloth" of the woman

> laps a first sweet eating and drinking,
> Laps life-swelling yolks . . . . laps ear of rose-corn,
>   milky and just ripened:
> The white teeth stay, and the boss-tooth advances in
>   darkness,
> And liquor is spilled on lips and bosoms by touching glasses,
>   and the best liquor afterward.
>
> (1.67–70)

The fact that masculine and feminine identifications are interchanged throughout the poem indicates that the significance of the erotic experience exceeds its physical nature in the common sense, by which a sexual encounter can be known only from one side or the other, male or female. The darkness is masculine at the beginning, but feminine (a mother) at the end. The narrator is first masculine, then feminine, then masculine again. He is not merely "omni-sexual"; his identity is fluid. This transformational ability agrees with the sexual equivalences of shamanic experience, and the passive role taken by the poet in this as in other poems—even when he is the male partner—matches the shaman's relation to the spiritual companion.[10]

"Healer and psychopomp," the shaman can confront the dangers of the underworld because his ecstatic techniques enable him to "venture into a mystical geography" and emerge unharmed (Eliade, p. 182). Prepared by the sexual experience of section one, Whitman daringly enters the world of the dead by covering a body as a shroud and lying underground. Such a descent is not recommended for everyone, as he intones in a skaldic basso: "It seems to me that everything in the light and air ought to be happy; / Whoever is not in his coffin and the dark grave, let him know he has enough" (2.79–80). This experience is crucial for the poet's progress toward the base of those conflicts he hopes to cure—corresponding to the ritual death of a shaman, it is a passage to the visions out of the past that recover buried aspects of the soul-life. A fragment that at one time followed the two lines just quoted would seem to support such a view: "The retrospective ecstacy [sic] is upon me, now my spirit burns volcanic; / The earth recedes ashamed before my prophetical crisis."[11] In shamanism "magical flight," such as that implied in relation to the receding earth above, is an expression "both of the soul's autonomy and of ecstasy"; "shamans and sorcerers can enjoy the condition of 'souls,' of 'disincarnate beings,' which is accessible to the profane only when they die."[12]

In section three we witness the danger of the poet's situation as he "retrospectively" observes his own death in the sea through a projection from the state of visionary trance within the coffin. The "courageous giant" "in the prime of his middle age" suggests the grand bard Walt Whitman, who prided himself on his robust physique at the time the poem was written and achieved a gigantic identity in the prime of his life. "Swimming naked through the eddies of the sea" like the naked poet in the deep waters of the unconscious, the hero is finally dashed on the rocks and killed. We shall find in the end, however, that he is restored to become an example of the regenerated identity.

Depicting encounters with loss in experiences of the past, in the middle sections of the poem Whitman emphasizes the continuity of the individual identity with our deepest ancestral roots and the spiritual world. He suggests a link between the suffering of the sleepers, events with national significance, and demonic disequilibrium. Sections three through six, the visions of loss, are characterized by a progressive personalization of point of view, paralleled by a gradual generalization of existential import, until the scene depicted from the most personal perspective is that which has significance for all of life. Rather than describing this process in detail, I will simply point out that the speaker's point of view moves gradually from that of a distant onlooker in section three to identification with Lucifer's "heir" and the final transformation into a whale who embodies the power of destruction. The significances of the scenes move from the very personal one of the poet's individual death through the more generalized shipwreck scene, thence to episodes from the early years of the national identity that suggest, as R. W. Vince has put it, "a tie between the poet's personal experience and the experiment of the American nation itself."[13] Section six (narrated from the selective omniscient point of view) reports the bridging of opposed racial identities through love between an Indian woman and Whitman's mother, extending the American identification to affinities between the conquerors of the land and its aboriginal peoples.

The poet's intention gradually to generalize his message can be highlighted by analyzing the development of the lament of Lucifer's "heir," which was deliberately abstracted in the course of revision from a detailed description of a slave's condition to a more archetypal drama of demonic rebellion. An early version, noted as "Item 38" in Dr. Bucke's edition of the "Notes and Fragments," did not mention Lucifer, but had specific reference to the internal slave trade. A later version (Item 40) reduced the description of the slave's condition, called him "Black Lucifer," and heightened his rebellious function.[14] Finally, in the verses that appeared in 1855, the opening reference is to "Lucifer" (the word "Black" being dropped from the name) and the allusion to slavery reduced to the point that one might easily read the passage without recognizing Whitman's heir to Lucifer as a black slave. The steamboat, machinery of the oppressor that carries away his woman, renders him effectively sterile but also particularly dangerous (a fact not without significance for the antebellum Union). Passing from slave to "God of revolt," thence to Lucifer's heir, the figure becomes an emblem of both the evil impulse and Satan's "righteousness," which must be integrated in the poet's mind to bear seed. Whitman's identification with him is a mode of recovering demonic potency to the healing way. Similarly, in shamanic practice "the recovery of physical health is closely dependent on restoring the balance of spiritual forces, for it is often the case that the illness is due to a neglect or an omission in respect to the infernal powers, which also belong to the sphere of the sacred" (Eliade, p. 216). Furthermore, the shaman's own capacity for evil must often be activated before equilibrium can be established and the unifying vision achieved.[15]

In the final two lines of section six, ending the images of loss, Whitman identifies absolutely with the whale who lies "sleepy and sluggish" in the spiritual ocean, a "vast dusk bulk" embodying the fatal power that underlies many of the losses described in the preceding verses. This acquisition of the whale's identity, following immediately upon the identification with Lucifer's heir, signals the end of the poet's descent into the underworld and his attainment of power. He has completely balanced the "antipodes" in acquiring the spiritual potency of the phallic whale for both generation and destruction (in the underworld it appears in its destructive aspect only).

In fact, we perceive that each episode of the underworld vision dramatizes loss, martyrdom, or destructiveness in an ancestral landscape, for psychic integration that serves the regeneration of life in the concluding sections. Scenes associated with national identity prominently enhance feelings of union—and hint that the suffering of the sleepers is connected with a straying from the communal ideal. In the scene of Washington's defeat at Brooklyn, the poet specifically mentions the slaughter of the "southern braves" on northern soil, defending the poet's native ground. Similarly, the officers' farewell scene in Fraunces' Tavern is an affecting reminder of Revolutionary unity that was dearly bought and painfully parted with. The visit of the red squaw in section six invokes longing for indigenous bonds and aboriginal continuity deeper than political identity and schism, and the image of the enslaved demon who will either be released or will destroy his oppressor makes for an interesting premonition of the Civil War. (Indeed, these lines are not simply the "Lucifer in harness," but the *Benito Cereno* of American verse.) With regard to white American racial consciousness (and subconsciousness), the position of the slave in this poem is of perdurable significance, with parallels reaching through our literature to the present day. When

Whitman cut "Lucifer's heir" out of the poem in 1876, he cut out the phallic and destructive whale at the same time, as if in his own imagination they were somehow connected to each other. He thus left a gap at the very climax of the poem; it is as if Dante had cut the fourth round of Cocytus—Canto 34—out of his Inferno.[16]

In becoming the whale, Whitman has penetrated to the seat of destruction. In the next moment, the landscape inverts, as if he has crawled down Satan's side and suddenly found himself in a reversed gravitational field. The phallic connotations of the death-tap of the whale's "dusk bulk" echo in the sunlit gamesomeness of the "unseen something" that richly showers at the opening of section seven. The result of Whitman's transformation into a whale is an ecstasy likened to sexual climax, "a show of the summer softness . . . . a contact of something unseen . . . . an amour of the light and air," and emergence into a daylight world returning to edenic origins (7.135).

In sections seven and eight it becomes apparent that the "illness" that is a sense of physical or psychic imbalance is cured by a return of souls that makes possible a unification of the "diverse." Such return is outlined in the long catalogue of section seven, which culminates in the "waiting" of all that is "arrived" and "in its place" for the healer's announcement: "The diverse shall be no less diverse, but they shall flow and unite . . . . they unite now" (7.178). I have previously stated that the purpose of a shaman's ecstasy is the retrieval or purification of the soul, since the practitioner regards illness "as a corruption or alienation of the soul" (Eliade, p. 217). Through the underworld journey in ecstasy and dream, Whitman has, by the beginning of section eight, effected the return of the souls of the sleepers while undergoing a psychic integration of his own which has resulted in a realization of peace and a profound power of cosmological insight to serve the poet and his community. The soul that "is always beautiful" has been found and restored to the poet and the sleepers in an edenic condition, through the merging and return of the suffering and the dead within the seer's trance:

> The consumptive, the erysipalite, the idiot, he that
> is wronged,
> The antipodes, and every one between this and them
> in the dark,

> I swear they are averaged now . . . . one is no better
>   than the other,
> The night and sleep have likened them and restored them.
>
> . . . .
>
> Peace is always beautiful,
> The myth of heaven indicates peace and night.
>
> The myth of heaven indicates the soul;
> The soul is always beautiful . . . . it appears more or
>   it appears less . . . . it comes or lags behind,
> It comes from its embowered garden and looks pleasantly
>   on itself and encloses the world.
>
> (7.158–69)

Subsequently, the "myth of heaven" that "indicates" peace, night, and the soul is laid out to view in section eight.

The myth asserts the complementarity of all things, and the revelation within the rite is accompanied by miraculous remedies for the disease, oppression, and incompleteness of each of the sleepers. The correspondence is clear: "There is always a cure, a control, an equilibrium brought about by the actual practice of shamanism" (Eliade, p. 29). Conflicts in the psychic life of the shaman and his people are reflected in grievances or afflictions among the spirits and the dead (such as the feelings of loss in the middle sections of Whitman's poem), which are resolved periodically in ecstatic seances for the healing of others (in this case, the "sleepers"). These seances are simultaneously "safety valves" that liberate the community from spiritual conflicts.[17] We can see that the healing of the shaman-like poet is coincident with that of the human community depicted as the "sleepers." The sleepers are all the people on the earth: "They flow hand in hand over the whole earth from east to west as they lie unclothed; / The Asiatic and African are hand in hand . . the European and American are hand in hand" (8.180–81). Whitman's vision is thus global in its implications, but distinctly grounded in his democratic American idea of the millennium. One of the purest examples in our literature of prophecy; it exposes the cutting edge of contemporary history on the ground of mythological time.

Although the process dramatized in "The Sleepers" has powerful resonances at the subconscious level and, as critics have long seen, exemplifies the associative versatility of the dream state, the poem does more than awaken subconscious feelings and images.[18] Though cathartically exercising the psyche, its end is profoundly social and religious, and may be differentiated from merely psychic phenomena since it overcomes personal crisis in an exemplary, transpersonal manner with explicitly social intent: "It is by the exemplary character of the religious solution that one can best judge the distance that separates the universe of the unconscious from the universe of religion. The religious solution lays the foundation for an exemplary behaviour, and, in consequence, compels the man to reveal himself as both the real and the *universal*. It is only after this revelation has been assumed by man in his entire being that one can speak of religion."[19] With this thought in mind, we can turn to "Song of Myself."

"Song of Myself"

In the past decade, interpretations of "Song of Myself" as a form of religious exercise or testimony of spiritual experience have declined along with analyses of its formal structure or attempts to define its narrative "phases." Yet linguistic and stylistic studies of recent years have increasingly revealed how Whitman experimented with language to convey visionary experience and simultaneously to engage his audience in a ritualistic communion.[20] Perhaps a new approach from the perspective of the shamanistic ecstatic process (exemplified more simply by "The Sleepers") can help us to address both the form of the poem and its religious character, accommodating the linguistic discoveries but countering recent tendencies to ignore Whitman's religious orientation or to assert that he suspected immortality to be an illusion, that in fact all of his statements of conviction about the "real reality" are sly evasions of "reality." Although it may be true that the poem, in a certain aspect, springs from the poet's need to control symbolically forces that threaten the meaning of his existence, to argue that Whitman did not "believe" in his religious message is overly reductive. A crisis of faith does not necessarily imply its hollowness. Similarly, a recognition of the regressive, womb-like destination of the poem—where a principle might be found to harmonize the disparities of life—is inadequate to the poem's full intentions.[21] Even a reading of the poem as an example of Vedantic or Western mystical experience is inadequate, for, as Helge Normann Nilsen points out, "'Song of Myself' is also a poem about America in a social, geographical, and historical sense, and its mysticism appears to be of a different nature than that of the old hermits and ascetics."[22] At the threshold where the mystic would normally present a vision of the spiritual world, Whitman delivered catalogues of America, while fusing self, subject, and audience to project a transformation of all three in the ecstatic performance.

The major critical problems in approaching "Song of Myself"—truly the inkblot test of American literary interpretation—have to do with genre, function, structure, the nature of the experiences represented, and technique; in other words practically everything we normally look for in a piece of literature is problematic here.

One of the most popular approaches to the problem of genre has been to regard the poem as some new form of epic.[23] According to this view, Whitman transformed the traditional genre to suit American conditions (as he himself once claimed). The chief distinction between his "epic," "democratic epic," "proto-epic," or "personal epic" and the traditional form are the democratic treatment of persons and events, and the focus upon the *process* of the quest. As Roy Harvey Pearce put it, "This new kind of poem was more a process than a form."[24] But once we talk about process rather than form we have already left the domain of the epic and the term no longer serves. James E. Miller, Jr., avoids this difficulty by providing and defining his own term, "personal epic":

> A long poem whose narrative is of an interior rather than exterior action, with emphasis on successive mental or emotional states; on a subject or theme not special or superior but common and vital; related not in a literary, measured, and elevated style but in a personal, free, and familiar style; focusing not on a heroic or semi-divine individual but on the poet himself as representative figure, comprehending and illuminating the age; and whose awareness, insight, being—rather than heroic actions—involve, however obliquely, the fate of the society, the nation, the human race.[25]

Miller's definition fits "Song of Myself" well, but I am not sure we need a new version of the "epic" designation to go with it; in fact, Miller's term might equally fit the shamanic rite, a 'genre' that has profoundly influenced many postmodern poets in the Whitman tradition.

What Pearce and Miller do not mention in their descriptions of the poem as an "epic" (but what Miller recognized in his earlier article on "'Song of Myself' as Inverted Mystical

Experience") is the dramatic quality of the piece. Again, this quality stretches the "epic" designation out to something we no longer recognize. Thus a few critics have come up with ideas of "drama" to fit Whitman's poem—"dramatic monologue," "monodrama," and "dramatic representation of a mystical experience" (James E. Miller's original idea of the poem).[26] Indeed, when we recall that many epics and episodes in epics are based upon the spiritual adventures of shamans, Roy Harvey Pearce's designation of "Song of Myself" as a "proto-epic," together with a recognition of lyric and dramatic qualities, brings us very near whatever genre we might use to classify a shamanic performance. This understanding can also meet Mutlu Blasing's objection that "because Whitman's narrative situation remains fluid, 'Song of Myself' cannot be considered a narrative or a recording of an experience. . . . Since a continually changing speaker precludes a particular narrative order, then, 'Song of Myself' cannot be considered an epic, even though it is a mimesis of direct address."[27]

Another quality of the poem that indicates its similarity to the rite is the poet's peculiar relation to his audience. In yielding to the poem, we are expected to be caught up in a process of self-realization analogous to the one the hero has experienced. Whitman's main end in "Song of Myself"—more than merely defining himself or undergoing transformation—is to effect the conversion of his audience to the democratic form of identity he exemplifies in his own person. Indeed, the climactic ecstasy of the poem can be regarded as initiatory only in the sense that it initiates the poet *into his new function* in the community and initiates the audience's self-realization.[28] When the speaker addresses us in the first lines of the poem, he speaks as a man sure of his ground and of his power. What he does not yet have is an audience or a role recognized by others.[29]

One would expect the structure of the poem to suit the poem's function, within the constraints of the genre. There have been numerous attempts to divide the poem into various phases of realization but few general agreements about its total structure. One agreement concerns the wave-like progression by which the poem modulates from one subject to another through various "peak" experiences interspersed with didactic interludes. That the poem builds in intensity toward a climax between sections twenty-four and thirty-three is also generally agreed; and the hint of a completed cycle between the first and last sections of the poem, brought to attention by the symbol of the grass, is widely regarded as evidence of Whitman's organicism. Yet to go any further requires a greater understanding of the performance itself than has previously been achieved.

Perhaps the most common problem found in the "mystical" interpretations of the poem's structure is the view that section five records an experience in the present, although it is clearly a reminiscence.[30] Frequently connected with such a reading of the fifth section is the view that the poem as a whole enacts the poet's initiatory self-creation. This is an attractive interpretation to make, because the creation of the self and subject for the audience reads much like a self-initiatory creation. In fact, nearly the first half of the poem is concerned with absorbing the subject matter's diversity and contradictions into the prophet's self while gradually engaging the audience and "educating" it. In "Song of Myself" Whitman had to create the field within which his poems would work. The poet's awareness of audience is one of the factors that makes the poem more than what, for instance, James E. Miller, Jr., and Malcolm Cowley have found it to be. Mystics of the Vedantic and Western traditions do not concern themselves with live performances and audience support. The presence of the audience also complicates the "phasal" progression, for advances in the persona's engagement in his visionary process alternate with momentary suspensions in that process, during which the poet addresses the audience discursively. In these addresses paradoxical messages are conveyed that can only be *"understood"* through the ecstatic experience that all of Whitman's technical innovations are intended to support and spread to the reader.[31]

The superiority of the shamanistic model to the "inverted" model offered by James E. Miller, Jr., and the Vedantic models suggested by others can be supported by reference to the two contrasting modes of inducing transcendent consciousness: (1) through meditation associated with deprivation of the senses, and (2) through bombardment of the senses in ritual activity accompanied by "a repetitive motor, visual, or auditory driving stimulus," such as drumming, chanting, or dancing.[32] Cognitive elements (verbal or symbolic content and meaning) can also help "drive" brain functions toward a climax that sets off the trance experience. The superiority of the shamanic model does not end here, however. The ecstatic state achieved through meditation can be maintained over a prolonged period of time, but only after years of practice and discipline (such as the "five steps" outlined by James E. Miller, Jr., which he once believed Whitman had compressed into one dramatic representation). On the other hand, the ecstatic state induced through exercising the senses is usually brief and may be repeated "at numerous focal points during the ritual." Finally, the ecstatic state is available to "many or most participants" in the ritual rather than being exclusive and attained through years of private practice. In the shamanic seance, although participants are not all expected to fall into trances, the driving rhythms and singing accompanied by verbal and symbolic forms elevate them from the profane state and change their awareness so that they can both support the shaman's performance and believe in it.

Whitman's catalogue technique, in particular, is a form of driving stimulus intended to induce a special state of awareness through which the poet engages us in the process of his theater. Everything in the catalogues contributes to this effect—the rhythm, which is in effect "polyrhythmic," composed of several different base rhythms overlaid on each other through the interplay of larger and smaller units of stress as well as phonic modulation and syntactic virtuosity (the closest approximation to this effect in our own culture, outside of certain religious sects, is found in jazz); the kaleidoscope of images that runs before our vision, our smell, our hearing, our touch; and the symbolic or emotional associations evoked by those images. By the time we get through one of Whitman's magnificent catalogues, as in section thirty-three, the "whirling and whirling" is not only elemental in *him;* it has us in a dizzying gyre, as well. Whitman was always pushing against the limiting membranes of his medium, seducing the tympanum of an ear to believe in miracles.[33]

The speaker's occasional exits from the primary spiritual orientation to address the audience or "explain" what he has learned only help emphasize the participatory nature of his performance and throw in relief the superiority of the state of mind induced by the experience over the discursive consciousness. For when Whitman addresses the reader prosaically and "explains" things, he expresses paradoxes and riddles that cognition cannot overcome. The ritualistic techniques and libidinous seductions then help us bridge the incongruities that confound "verbal," "analytic" processes.[34]

This alternation is the foundation of that "bipolar unity" that Howard Waskow sees, and the "curious triplicate process" posited by Marki, as the essence of Whitman's view of the world, the fusion of antagonistic elements.[35]

We can now broadly outline the structural foundations of "Song of Myself." The poem begins by introducing poet, subject matter, and method while also posing riddles and paradoxes. The subject matter and audience—or, from the American audience's point of view, "objective" and "subjective" referents (identical in many respects)—present diversity and "contradictions" that the poet absorbs into himself, gradually concentrating them toward the central riddles of life and death, "good" and "evil," subject and object, and unity and diversity—all of which dualisms are joined in the dominant symbol of the grass, a riddle in itself. At the peak of this concentration, the poet's central ecstasy erupts and solves the riddles experientially: diversity merges with unity, subject with object, good with evil, life with death. At the same time, the foundations of the culture are identified and integrated, the audience itself caught up in this integration and unified. The performance congeals them and, as becomes evident at the end of the poem, begins their realization—which is also a democratic revitalization grounded in the solution of the riddles of life.

The structure, however, is not merely "phasal," as this outline would suggest. Rather, it is *convective,* if you will, made up of many cycles intermeshed into the grand cycle broadly suggested. For the general process of the poem is mirrored in the smaller units of the repetitive, ever-building process of accruing diversity, absorbing dualities, breaking into ecstasy, and then trying to "explain" the resultant insight that inevitably must congeal to a riddle (specifically, "grass")—which in turn begins the cycle all over again. The cycles build in intensity until the climactic one that begins in section twenty-six (following direct identification of the mask—"Walt Whitman"). In the heart of each ecstasy the poet is unaware of audience, whereas his audience-orientation can be identified with the poet's discursive moments and his riddles. After the grand visionary journey, the speaker emerges from the state of transcendence, oriented most fully to the audience but with his expression again relegated to discursiveness, riddles, paradoxes, and encouragement. As he bequeaths himself to the dirt, the next cycle must be performed by us; his seed is spread across the nation. As this final image suggests, it is important to see the symbol of the "leaf" of grass as embracing the entire process of the poem and embodying its nature.[36] Moreover, this symbol stands both for the complementarity of life and death and for democracy—rooting democracy in the existential condition. Extending Whitman's cycle beyond the text, its aim is a much larger convection by which all of America, and ultimately the world, moves toward ecstatic triumph, by endless cycles of creation. If the shamanic analogue does not fully contain Whitman's achievement, it provides us with the most comprehensive method yet for analyzing "Song of Myself" in terms of genre, structure, function, content, and technique. And it helps give definition to what we mean when we call the poem "visionary," "ecstatic," and "prophetic"—against those who would strip the poem of these dimensions.

The first section of the poem establishes the importance of the relation between poet and reader, while also embodying the "invitation" of the soul that indicates the beginning of a spiritual process. The poet is quite sure of himself; he has already been initiated into the mysteries upon which his power is based, and what hostelry he offers is meant for our benefit, as becomes clear in section two:

> Stop this day and night with me and you shall possess the
>   origin of all poems,
> You shall possess the good of the earth and sun . . . .
>   there are millions of suns left,
> You shall no longer take things at second or third hand
>   . . . . nor look through the eyes of the dead . . . .
>   nor feed on the spectres in books,
> You shall not look through my eyes either, nor take
>   things from me,
> You shall listen to all sides and filter them from
>   yourself.[37]

This message and that which closes the poem frame the piece as a whole to indicate its prime function: to initiate a process of realization in the reader which is in effect an "Americanization" of the deepest stamp.

At the same time, section two continues the movement begun in the invitation to the soul by making of nature an intoxicating agent. The established way of reading these stanzas is to concentrate upon the superiority of nature and the open air to the artificial "perfumes" of literature and closed rooms as settings for Whitman's message. The uses of nature are more specific, however. In his *Letters on Demonology and Witchcraft*, Walter Scott mentions that intoxicating gases and "perfumes" were employed by ancient sorcerers to call up spirits and induce an altered state of consciousness.[38] Whitman clearly has this model in mind as he invites his soul— aided by the pure intoxication of the atmosphere, the wood, the smoke of his own breath—and achieves the first mild ecstasy of the poem, "undisguised and naked":

> A few light kisses . . . . a few embraces . . . . a reaching
>   around of arms,
> The play of shine and shade on the trees as the supple
>   boughs wag,
> The delight alone or in the rush of the streets, or
>   along the fields and hillsides,
> The feeling of health . . . . the full-noon trill . . . .
>   the song of me rising from bed and meeting the sun.
>
>   (2.18–21)

Next, in a pattern typical of the poem's many ecstatic episodes, the poet turns to his audience again with messages in the form of riddles: "Have you reckoned a thousand acres much? Have you reckoned the earth much?" he asks, to follow with his promise that if we stop with him we shall "possess the origin of all poems."

Section three introduces the constant principles of the poet's project: the idea of immortality and perpetual procreation, the unification of contraries, the necessity and divinity of all things, even the most despised. The gift that comes of an erotic ecstasy with God, "a loving bedfellow," is then contrasted with merely discursive knowledge and the intellectual searching of the "trippers and askers" of section four. We have some hint now of how Whitman would have us learn his secrets.

Section five becomes more specific in this sense by reporting the poet's own initiatory experience. Before reporting this experience, however, he continues the motif of "inviting" his soul, which Harold Aspiz has compared to the "associate" spirit in spiritualistic seances.[39] The famous "mystical experience" follows, rendered as a reminiscence and a further introduction of the sort of inspiration with which Whitman must familiarize his audience. By reminding the soul of this earlier loving encounter, the poet also continues his "courtship." Psychological resonances of the episode (perceptively analyzed by Edwin Haviland Miller), important as they are, are subordinate to the fact that this is represented as a *spiritual* coitus and a model of inspirational experience.[40] The knowledge that has come from it is a condensed version of the poem's democratic-religious message, which we cannot yet fully comprehend, but which will become ours as we respond to the possessing force of the poem. The last line of the section, in a manner typical of Whitman's "hypnagogic" (Pearce's term) modulation from movement to movement, turns the poem toward the dominant symbol—the grass.

The manner in which Whitman introduces his symbol again indicates his ritualistic intentions, for he presents it in the context of a riddle. As Lévi-Strauss has pointed out, the function of ritual is commonly to overcome the contradictions underlying a given social system and expressed in myth. The fact that the question "What is the grass?" is posed by a child only highlights our own ignorance, and the poet's answer is so multifarious we cannot hope to fully absorb his meaning. The beautiful verses linking grass to death have been interpreted, incredibly, as evidence of the poet's terror of death, but Whitman produced no lines more tender. The riddle of the grass and the riddle of death are fully entwined in Whitman's conception, binding all the other riddles of "Song of Myself" together and, with the recurring ecstasies, providing a basal rhythm for the poem's wave-like movement. To get to the bottom of the riddle of the grass is to get to the bottom of death and democracy, and to be renewed with supreme power. The dead are absorbed into the earth, their bodies broken apart to feed the grass, which in turn feeds us—as Whitman would feed us after he departs at the open end of his poem, "and filter and fibre [our] blood" (52.1333). Thus "the smallest sprout shows there is really no death, / And if ever there was it led forward life" (6.117–118). The way in which Whitman leads us toward a solution of the riddle of the grass by enacting its germination (and, metaphorically, his own) is the process of the poem. In that process he also solves the riddles of democratic culture—including the problem of unity in diversity, the conflict between individualism and communal bonding, and the relationship between the living and the dead. The poem revitalizes and cures the nation, for the grass is the totemic symbol of the nation's people, its prolific sprouting an emblem of cultural renewal. Furthermore (to jump ahead of myself a bit), the answer to this riddle is to be had only by becoming part of the very life-force that is beneath all and that always survives.

The grass exemplifies the three properties of "dominant" ritual symbols enumerated by Victor Turner:

(1) *"condensation"* of "many things and actions . . . in a single [symbolic] formation."

(2) *"unification"* of a wide variety of ideas and phenomena having apparently "trivial" or "random" associations with each other.

(3) *"polarization of meaning":* "At one pole is found a cluster of *significata* that refer to components of the moral and social orders . . . , to principles of social organization, to kinds of corporate grouping, and to the norms and values inherent in structural relationships. At the other pole, the *significata* are usually natural and physiological phenomena and processes" (Turner terms these two poles the "ideological" and the "sensory").[41]

The obvious multivalence of the grass symbol and its association with disparate phenomena (enumerated in the catalogues) need not be elaborated, but Turner's third property seems to me particularly important, for the grass is associated with democratic values—"Growing among black folks as among white, / Kanuck, Tuckahoe, Congressman, Cuff, I give them the same, I receive them the same" (6.99–100)—but also arouses the most personal desires and feelings (dominated, according to E. H. Miller, by mother-child eroticism).[42] Symbols of this sort, says Turner, appeal at the sensory pole to "the lowest common denominator of human feeling" and may be "flagrantly physiological" even as they represent the social unity of the group (pp. 28–29).

The uniting of "high" and "low" qualities in the symbol helps make certain social values and modes of behavior desirable. Encapsulating "the major properties of the total ritual process," the dominant symbol "brings the ethical and jural norms of society into close contact with strong emotional stimuli. . . . [It] effects an interchange of qualities between its poles of meaning. *Norms and values, on the one hand, become saturated with emotion, while the gross and basic emotions become ennobled through contact with social values"* (p. 30; my emphasis). Understanding what the leaves of grass represent, then, helps us to understand "the major properties" of the process of "Song of Myself." A strictly psychoanalytic interpretation of the grass ignores the importance of the ideological pole of meaning. In fact, dominant symbols come to absorb "most of the major aspects of human social life, so that, in a sense, they come to represent 'human society' itself"— with all its tensions and contradictory qualities, the riddles that are impervious to mythic "explanation" (Turner, p. 44). The symbol can thus be invoked in many different circumstances for different purposes.

In addition to its symbolic function, however, the "leaf" of grass, as a page in Whitman's book, mediates between the poet and ourselves. Both symbol and mechanical device, Whitman's leaf is closer than anything else in our literature to the ritualistic symbol that is also a tool of performance—binding us to the poet while helping him penetrate dualities and achieve higher consciousness. It is another of Whitman's innovations intended to overcome the limitations of literary media. When Whitman asks his soul to loaf with him on the grass in section five, he implicitly alludes to the meeting of soul and body in the leaf of paper (a sort of meeting he will later attempt with the reader), just as the shaman's drum—symbol and mechanical device, its rim (in Buryat culture) constructed of wood stripped from the cosmic tree that joins the earthly and spiritual worlds—stands for the interface between the sacred and profane aspects of experience, soul and self, eternity and time.

Parallel to the grass's multivalence and unification of poles are the similar qualities of the poem itself in sections eight through approximately twenty-five. The mere diversity of America and of life settles gradually into polarities, all "tending inward" to the poet and building toward erotic union.

At the end of section six, the poet moves from addressing the grass to addressing the reader again with a discursive, didactic tone that carries over into section seven; here Whitman reassures the reader about death and birth before going on to say that he is "for" all people (presented in dualistic terms) and then suggesting a union with his audience, a "merging" that also resonates with the sense of the merging of death.

Who need be afraid of the merge?
Undrape . . . . you are not guilty to me, nor stale nor
    discarded,

I see through the broadcloth and gingham whether or no,
And am around, tenacious, acquisitive, tireless . . . .
and can never be shaken away.

(7.136–39)

The idea of the leaf of paper as interface for this seduction is important; the reader momentarily takes the position of the poet lounging on the grass, and the poet replaces the possessing "soul" for the reader. The poet will not be satisfied until he has poured his meaning into us.

The hint of eroticism gives way to the first catalogue of "Song of Myself" in section eight—one beginning with a synopsis of the life cycle but otherwise various and largely "disordered." Section nine reinforces the symbol of grass—the correspondence between the hay the poet rolls in and the people with whom he identifies being deliberate without calling attention to itself—while continuing the catalogue sequence. But here, "rolling" in the "leaves" of hay, the poet enters the field of the experiences described. He maintains this orientation in section ten, which concentrates a series of American types in short dramatic scenes: a hunter (as opposed to the farmer boy in section nine), a sailor in a Yankee clipper, a clam-digger, a guest at the marriage of a trapper and a "red girl" in the far West, and a comforter of a runaway slave. The gallery of American types continues through sections eleven and twelve, broken only when, in the middle of section thirteen, the poet stops to describe himself before shifting into the observation of animals:

In me the caresser of life wherever moving . . . .
    backward as well as forward slueing,
To niches aside and junior bending.

(13.226–27)

Even these animals are carefully chosen as characteristic North American fauna.

The connection of grass with the objects of Whitman's catalogues is reinforced by the statement that "the press of my foot to the earth springs a hundred affections, / They scorn the best I can do to relate them" (14.246–47), and again in the line, "What is commonest and cheapest and nearest and easiest is Me" (14.252). Indeed, section fifteen, immediately following, is a list of citizens, each allowed only one line—like blades of grass. Whitman never refers to his own presence or attitude in the midst of this list, but he ends it on a summary note of identification and absorption: "And these one and all tend inward to me, and I tend outward to them, / And such as it is to be of these more or less I am" (15.324–25). Moreover, section fifteen begins a movement from mere diversity of types to contrasting types, a movement that continues in the subsequent section.

The speaker is still absorbing the diversities and contrarieties he must actively merge through the ecstatic process while establishing his subject and audience, his field of action. The diverse and apparently contrary elements are virtually all American; although in two lines the poet extends his identification to include other nations and continents, the chief subject of absorption is America, and only through the identification with his own country can his democratic self extend to embrace others.

Turning to address the audience more directly, the poet, as he often does in this attitude, summarizes the nature of his message in discursive terms, reinforcing several paradoxical motifs that have dominated the poem to this point: the antiquity and universality of his "modern" and "local" insights, the mutuality of poet and reader, the all-inclusiveness of his message, and the fact that he presents a "riddle" and the "untying" of a riddle:

> These are the thoughts of all men in all ages and lands,
>   they are not original with me,
> If they are not yours as much as mine they are nothing or next to
>   nothing,
> If they do not enclose everything they are next to nothing,
> If they are not the riddle and the untying of the riddle
>   they are nothing,
> If they are not just as close as they are distant they are
>   nothing.
>
>   (17.353–57)

To emphasize that his thoughts are "of" and "for" all people, ages, and lands the poet refers to the dominant symbol: "This is the grass that grows wherever the land is and the water is, / This is the common air that bathes the globe" (17.358–59). To demonstrate his democratic sense of audience and his communicative versatility he draws upon the associations of hearing, taste, and touch—his "music" in section eighteen intended not only for victors but for the "conquered and slain"; his "meal pleasantly set" for the wicked, the "sponger and thief," "the heavy-lipped slave," and the "venerealee"; the touch of his lips for each one of us. These characterizations of his song end on a note echoing the recurrent pattern of Whitman's realization: "This is the thoughtful merge of myself and the outlet again." And his "merge" "lets out" to a riddle addressed to the reader: "Do you guess I have some intricate purpose? / Well I have . . . . for the April rain has, and the mica on the side of a rock has" (19.381–82). Confounding logical discourse, such riddles are always posed in order to catch the reader up in the process of the poem, and section nineteen ends with a promise that the poet will tell us his secrets "in confidence."

Section twenty begins with another riddle that leads back to the resonance of the dominant symbol: "How is it I extract strength from the beef I eat?" (answer: because the cattle eat grass, which grows from soil well-manured by death. Notice that this hidden "answer" only implies an endless succession of further insoluble questions unfolding from the symbolism of grass.). The poet suggests that we are to match him in largesse and divinity; he announces that he is deathless before, in section twenty-one, bringing to a head the dualities he encompasses: body and soul, heaven and hell, woman and man. For some time now, the poet has shown no progress in his *own* experience, but a consideration for his audience. However, the congealing of the dualities into cosmic "antipodes" leads to two amorous apostrophes, growing directly out of the awareness of contrary elements in nature. "Walking" with the night the speaker "calls" to the earth and sea "half-held by the night" (and, we interject, half-held by the day). A tryst with the night gives way to a tryst with the earth and, in section twenty-two, with the sea. We can imagine the intersecting axes of night-day, sea-land. The sexual episodes show directly how the poet unifies contraries. Underlying all polarities is that of life and death, which are present in everything—"Sea of the brine of life and of unshovelled yet always-ready graves." The poet, "integral" with his lover, is also "partaker of influx and efflux . . . . extoller of hate and conciliation," and of all other contrary terms. Through section twenty-three Whitman—now facing the audience—continues to suggest that he unifies contraries in his person. In the process he resurrects the buried poles of our dualisms (evil, death, the body, and vice), all of which are indispensable to his (and our) identity.

Finally, in section twenty-four the poet announces his name, identifying himself as American and "kosmos." As J. M. DeFalco has noted, this announcement marks an important culmination of all that has preceded, a climax of the poet's preparation for his central *agon*.[43] At the moment when he names himself, the speaker is positioned at the intersection of all the dualisms in which human consciousness is ineluctably caught, from the level of the most private experience to that of the most universal. Speaking "the password primeval" and "giving the sign of democracy," he brings his intention of representing even the despised to a head in a mediumistic revelation:

> Through me many long dumb voices,
> Voices of the interminable generations of slaves,
> Voices of prostitutes and of deformed persons,
> Voices of the diseased and despairing, and of
>   thieves and dwarfs.
>
> (24.509–12)

J. M. DeFalco comments that at this point in the poem Whitman proves his spirituality in terms "normally used to present man as a debased animal"—a technique we have also come to recognize in ritual.[44] Eschewing shame of the flesh, the poet dotes on his body, which is an "embodiment" of the geography of his native land. As the self is sanctified, it is universalized, as well, and made an emblem of the country's primary, "lowest" self—which thereby shares in the sanctification.

The ecstasy that follows beautifully complements the ecstasies of sections twenty-one and twenty-two. The trysts with the night and with the earth and sea "half-held by the night" are counterpoised with an ecstasy at daybreak:

> Seas of bright juice suffuse heaven.
>
> The earth by the sky staid with . . . . the daily close
>   of their junction,
> The heav'd challenge from the east that moment over
>   my head,
> The mocking taunt, See then whether you shall be master!
>
> (24.558–61)

The appearance of the horizon at sunrise marks the "daily close" of the junction of earth and sky, and sunlight mocks the darkness as perpetually renewed life mocks death. The climax here is the answer to and consummation of the earlier unions, and the precise moment of sunrise joins night and day. This cosmic mating Whitman matches with the sort of power I have identified (in chapter 2) as a gift of his first discovery of the ecstatic capability: "Dazzling and tremendous how quick the sunrise would kill me, / If I could not now and always send sunrise out of me" (25.562–63). Implicitly, this sunrise came after the immersion in night, death, and despair that Whitman has been accruing to himself continuously in the course of his poem. Thus section twenty-five shows the poet poised on the antipodes, untying the riddle, ready to launch the central process of his song. Whitman wants to free himself of logocentric distinctions, and yet he realizes that his very dependence upon language threatens to subvert his liberating project, for differentiation enters the field at the moment of language, which is also the moment of "thought." He returns to the dominant symbol to protest the inadequacy of speech for conveying his meaning:

> Do you not know how the buds beneath are folded?
> Waiting in gloom protected by frost,
> The dirt receding before my prophetical screams,
> I underlying causes to balance them at last,
> My knowledge my live parts . . . . it keeping tally
>   with the meaning of things,
> Happiness . . . . which whoever hears me let him or
>   her set out in search of this day.

(25.572–77)

What ensues, from section twenty-six on, exhibits the pattern of a classic shamanic ecstasy.[45]

If we ignore, for the moment, the passages in which Whitman addresses his audience and reconstruct the ecstatic process of sections twenty-six through thirty-eight, the pattern looks like this:

1. Section 26: Ecstasy induced by sounds, symbolic death and reawakening.

2. Sections 28 and 29: Ecstasy induced by touch—a sexual consummation expressed in metaphors of victimization; the

poet is "given up by traitors" to a kind of death that is also sexual orgasm.

3. Section 31: The poet's acquisition of a fluid identity; he has the power of self-transformation and of penetrating all things.

4. Section 32: He turns to live with animals in a prelapsarian condition, then mounts a horse that carries him to a higher spiritual state until the poet himself takes flight. (This passage strongly suggests the common shamanic motif of the horse that either carries the shaman to the spirit-world or is sacrificed at the beginning of the ecstatic ascent.)

5. Sections 33–38: The poet entirely engrossed in his spiritual journey and visions.

In the purely visionary phase, we find the longest lapse from concern with the audience, because the poet fully immerses himself in the spiritual world, where he encounters heroic suffering and touchstones of American identity, as in the parallel sequence of "The Sleepers." The attainment of his visions here exposes the historical and communal substructure of the performance.

When Whitman turns from the audience after deciding to "do nothing for a long time but listen," the everyday sounds he hears intensify until they become a "grand opera" of cosmic dimensions: "I hear the violincello or man's heart complaint, / And hear the keyed cornet or else the echo of sunset" (26.597–98). The opera that convulses the poet becomes the music of the universe:

> A tenor large and fresh as the creation fills me,
> The orbic flex of his mouth is pouring and filling me full.
>
> I hear the trained soprano . . . . she convulses me like
>   the climax of my love-grip;
> The orchestra whirls me wider than Uranus flies,
> It wrenches unnamable ardors from my breast,
> It throbs me to gulps of the farthest down horror,
> It sails me . . . . I dab with bare feet . . . . they are
>   licked by the indolent waves,
> I am exposed . . . . cut by bitter and poisoned hail,
> Steeped amid honeyed morphine . . . . my windpipe squeezed
>   in the fakes of death,
> Let up again to feel the puzzle of puzzles,
> And that we call Being.
>
> (26.600–610)

The passage owes something to Whitman's opera-going experience, but it uses such experience only to help express a true ecstasy of shamanic type, combining erotic climax, the speaker's passivity before the possessing forces, physical suffering and laceration, symbolic death in an entranced state ("amid honeyed morphine"), and finally reemergence. The astonishingly quick movement to cosmic and finally ontic awareness owes much of its success to the libidinal appeal of the language that joins the disparate qualities of the experience, for, as the final lines suggest, the ecstatic experience penetrates the riddles that cannot be fathomed in the ordinary state of mind.

In section twenty-seven the poet returns to the reader briefly, again with a riddle that has been suggested by the preceding experience: "To be in any form, what is that?" Rather than answer the question, he tells us he has "instant conductors" all over his body through which every object can pass. When they do so, they wring ecstasies from him that answer the riddle of form. The experience of sections twenty-eight and twenty-nine produces the insight and celebration offered in sections thirty and thirty-one.

The ecstasy of section twenty-eight is commonly read as onanistic, but surely Whitman's intention is confused by such an interpretation. The fact is, Whitman considered masturbation an unhealthy habit; at the beginning of "The Sleepers" he mentions "the sick-grey faces of onanists" in the context of those he would heal. Whatever masturbatory fantasies we read into the episode of section twenty-eight today must be subordinated to the more overt indications that spiritual agents induce the climax. "Prurient provokers" stiffen his limbs and "behave licentious" toward him, unbuttoning his clothes, holding him by the waist, "bribing" all the senses but touch to desert him, "fetching the rest of the herd around to enjoy them awhile," and gathering to "worry" him. These "provokers" correspond to the "gay gang of blackguards" that help induce the ecstasy of "The Sleepers," here described as demonic, aids to a "red marauder," because the poet resists the ecstasy (an understandable attitude, since the ecstasy demands a relinquishment of the normal identity and a form of death). The combination of loving and threatening imagery comes to a "point" at the moment of orgasm: "Blind loving wrestling touch! Sheathed hooded sharptoothed touch!" (20.641). Touch is both lover and executioner, janus-faced like Whitman himself.

Interestingly, the death / orgasm immediately leads to a reference to the dominant symbol of the poem; the "rich showering rain" feeds the seeds of grass: "Sprouts take and accumulate . . . . stand by the curb prolific and vital, / Landscapes projected masculine full-sized and golden" (29.645–46). This sprouting is an answer to Whitman's protest to speech (in section twenty-five) that it does not know how the "buds" beneath it are "folded." We have witnessed the process by which *Leaves of Grass* came into being.

Section thirty-one completes the address to the audience and introduces the poet's identification with objects and animals of the continent. Living with the animals in section thirty-two, the poet has entered a paradisal situation:[46]

> They do not sweat and whine about their condition,
> They do not lie awake in the dark and weep for their sins,
> They do not make me sick discussing their duty to God,
> Not one is dissatisfied . . . . not one is demented with the
>   mania of owning things,
> Not one kneels to another nor to his kind that lived
>   thousands of years ago,
> Not one is respectable or industrious over the whole earth.
>
>   (32.686–91)

The condition of the animals reflects Whitman's view of the American millennium and the new democratic temperament. The animals, in fact, become helpmates in the speaker's search for insight: "So they show their relations to me and I accept them; / They bring me tokens of myself . . . . they evince them plainly in their possession" (32.692–93). These "tokens" prove to be secrets he has dropped or forgotten and that are now, in paradise, restored to him. Like the messages traditional ecstatics receive from animals in the "spirit world," they have to do with the regeneration of the self and are related to the poet's visionary mission. "By entering into the condition of the animals, the shaman shares their secrets and enjoys their plenitude of life," for animals "know secrets of Life and Nature, they even know the secrets of longevity and immortality."[47]

The poet picks out a special friend among the animals, "a gigantic beauty of a stallion, fresh and responsive to my caresses," that carries him until he launches on the soul-flight under his own power:

Swift wind! Space! My Soul! Now I know it is true what I
 guessed at;
What I guessed when I loafed on the grass,
What I guessed while I lay alone in my bed . . . . and again
 as I walked the beach under the paling stars of the
 morning.

(33.709–11)

Whereas the previous ecstasies (to three of which these lines allude) all led to the posing of riddles, statements of paradox, now Whitman launches the journey that, carrying the reader along, transcends the riddles with accomplishment and proves the message to the audience without relying upon logic and argument. Whitman puts all his rhythmic skill to use in the catalogue of his journey—a journey he characterizes as a shaman might:

My ties and ballasts leave me . . . . I travel I
 sail . . . . my elbows rest in the sea-gaps,
I skirt the sierras . . . . my palms cover continents,
I am afoot with my vision.

(33.712–14)

The catalogue of section thirty-three, in which the poet flies the "flight of the fluid and swallowing soul," consists almost exclusively of American elements and modulates from a kaleidoscope of images to distinct scenes of martyrdom and heroism amid suffering that continue through section thirty-six. This vortex-like effect parallels a movement from the present into the past that ends with the fight of the *Bonhomme Richard*. Whitman's visionary technique here raises the consciousness of the audience—"entrains" our participation through the rapid, dizzying catalogue—and then immerses us, once prepared, in the sort of experiences that evoke feelings of union and patriotism. The scenes encourage further heroism and self-sacrifice, assuring one of the spirit's superiority to suffering. The origin of this technique is in Whitman's journalistic glorification of the founding fathers and his approval of contemporary heroics, which he viewed in the light of revitalizing Revolutionary values. But here the poet's identification with the suffering makes the abstract tangible by working directly upon the sensibilities of the people, enforcing feelings of catharsis and union as does a shaman's self-laceration or symbolic sacrifice in the realm of the ancestral dead. The intentions of the technique become clearest in the summation of the journey among the suffering heroes, part of a fit of possession:

> O Christ! My fit is mastering me!
> What the rebel said gaily adjusting his throat to the
> rope-noose,
> What the savage at the stump, his eye-sockets empty,
> his mouth spirting whoops and defiance,
> What stills the traveler come to the vault at Mount
> Vernon,
> What sobers the Brooklyn boy as he looks down the
> shores of the Wallabout and remembers the prison
> ships,
> What burnt the gums of the redcoat at Saratoga when he
> surrendered his brigades,
> These become mine and me every one, and they are but
> little,
> I become as much more as I like.
>
> (37.933–40)

What "more" he becomes is a shape-shifting sufferer, criminal, beggar, as he dances the dance of the possessed like a dervish or shaman: "I rise extatic through all, and sweep with the true gravitation, / The whirling and whirling is elemental within me" (37.953–54).

Many theories have been devised to account for what happens at the beginning of section thirty-eight, when the poet suddenly stops, as if struck by a spiritual force, and shifts the direction of his performance:

> Somehow I have been stunned. Stand back!
> Give me a little time beyond my cuffed head and slumbers
> and dreams and gaping,
> I discover myself on a verge of the usual mistake.
>
> (38.955–57)

It is important to recognize that Whitman sees himself "on a verge" of a mistake; the passage does not repudiate what has preceded it but marks a turn in the poet's role-process.[48] Thus it is hard to believe that the preceding vision is now recognized as "illusion," as "false," or even as unnecessarily pessimistic. The poet employs his suffering, as in "The Sleepers," to help effect cure. We can assume, furthermore, that the content of the possession passages that dramatize suffering is related to the "disease," and that some relation exists between the underworld figures or possessing forces and the community for whom the cure is intended. This relation is quite clear in "Song of Myself" if we recognize the immediate audience as America and her "disease" as the decay of union, heroic sacrifice, virtue, and democracy—the sacred values of the Republic that would be revived in the hospitals of the Civil War. When Whitman speaks, at the beginning of section thirty-eight, of a "usual mistake" after a catalogue of suffering to introduce an image of Christ, we can be sure he is about to "translate" the "pains of hell" into "a new tongue" (21.424–25). He "remembers" the contribution of evil, suffering and death to the "overstaid fraction" of transcendence, healing, and procreation:

> I remember . . . . I resume the overstaid fraction,
> The grave of rock multiplies what has been confided
>   to it . . . . or to any graves,
> The corpses rise . . . . the gashes heal . . . . the
>   fastenings roll away.
>   (38.961–63).

The prophetic vision of healing and the rising of the dead here is no different from what we have seen in "The Sleepers" after the underworld experience, and the poet comes from his "crucifixion" "replenished with supreme power, one of an average unending procession" (38.964).

More obviously than the parallel event in "The Sleepers," however, this replenishment is concerned with spreading a gospel.[49] The poet's "procession" extends throughout North America (Whitman believed the nation would ultimately take in Mexico and Canada), as the vision of the "numberless gangs" of the poet's "eleves" marks a turn in the poem toward a more direct exposition of its central aim, which is the conversion of the audience. Hence, the remainder of "Song of Myself" chiefly dramatizes applications of the power the poet has acquired through the ecstatic process.

The "friendly and flowing savage" of section thirty-nine, then, is not specifically the poet himself but the generic American ideal, referred to as "he" (not the "I" of the preceding and following sections) and associated not with Manhattan but with any region of the country—and, ultimately, abroad, as the

American message will become universal.[50] The poet is *such* a savage, but that is not the main concern at the moment; the concern is for providing the audience with an appealing "aboriginal" model.

In sections forty and forty-one, the poet returns to himself and boasts, tongue in cheek, of his new powers. But the humor here does not negate the poet's claims; it points to the comedy of cosmic potency suddenly inflating the average man.[51] Interestingly, Whitman first displays his healing powers and then expands to measure himself against the gods—mirroring the sequence commonly followed by prophets of revitalization. Section forty displays his capacity to cure with the aid of his spirits:

> To any one dying . . . . thither I speed and twist the knob
>   of the door,
> Turn the bedclothes toward the foot of the bed,
> Let the physician and the priest go home.
>
> I seize the descending man . . . . I raise him with
>   resistless will.
>
> O despairer, here is my neck,
> By God! you shall not go down! Hang your whole weight
>   upon me.
>
> I dilate you with tremendous breath . . . . I buoy you up;
> Every room of the house do I fill with an armed force
>   . . . . lovers of me, bafflers of graves:
> Sleep! I and they keep guard all night;
> Not doubt, not decease shall dare to lay finger upon you,
> I have embraced you, and henceforth possess you to myself,
> And when you rise in the morning you will find what I
>   tell you is so.
>
> (40.1003–14)

In the subsequent section of the poem, Whitman asserts the superiority of the new democratic god—everyman—to assure his followers that his "religion," tallying their lives and land, stands higher than any of the past and that each of his people is equally divine. The people he mentions in this context are all of the working class: a house-framer, a fireman, a mechanic's wife with her nursing child, harvesting farmers, and a hostler who gives up all he possesses to pay his brother's *lawyers* in a forgery case.

In section forty-two the speaker turns his gaze to a different class of people, the "weakest and shallowest," whom, not surprisingly, he associates with greed and slothfulness—the type of people whose success had galled the young Whitman. The motif of "possession" recurs explicitly to manage the transition from the previous class of persons. "Launching his nerve," the "performer" calls his "household and intimates" to him (apparently the virtuous Jacksonian followers compared to gods in the previous verses); he identifies his written verses as those of a possessed ecstatic:

> Easily written loosefingered chords! I feel the thrum of
>   their climax and close.
>
> My head evolves [revolves?] on my neck,
> Music rolls, but not from the organ . . . . folks are
>   around me, but they are no household of mine.
>
> (42.1055–57)

These "folks" are the shallow, the faithless, the greedy who, Whitman believed, were endangering the Republic; the poet has the "nerve" to accept even them and to see through their clothing to their purer souls:

> They who piddle and patter here in collars and tailed
>   coats . . . . I am aware who they are . . . . and
>   that they are not worms or fleas,
> I acknowledge the duplicates of myself under all the
>   scrape-lipped and pipe-legged concealments.
>
> (42.1074–75)

The sort of awakening that has come to the speaker "waits" for them; in fact, he would hurry it by "fetching" them "flush" with himself (anticipating a dominant concern of the 1860 edition).

Addressing another group of people Whitman had learned to distrust, section forty-three shows the poet accepting even the priests of all religions, though his worship encloses theirs and he takes leave of them to tramp his own greater journey, to take in the "excluded" atheists and doubters that most churches would excommunicate. To these unbelievers the poet initially can express his faith only in negative terms, naming those whom death "cannot fail." In section forty-four he tries a series of metaphors to convey the sense of eternity, but ultimately he returns to the root of his own faith, the experience of being "an acme of things accomplished" and "an encloser of things to be" (44.1148).

In a sort of mythic autobiography, we witness the life cycle of the poet—from "the huge first Nothing" to the planets and the ever-expanding "far-sprinkled systems" of stars. If the speaker's own history is representative, then an individual's life cycle partakes of the universal cycles of creation, a fact mimed in the ecstatic process and symbolized in the blade of grass. Adopting the familiar address to the reader, the speaker can then confidently say that we shall meet in eternity: "Our rendezvous is fitly appointed . . . . God will be there and wait till we come" (45.1197).

The motif of pilgrimage, dominating the following section, further unites us with the teacher in his liminal terrain, while his intimate mode of address banishes structural impediments to our meeting on terms of *communitas*:[52]

> I lead no man to a dinner-table or library or exchange,
> But each man and each woman of you I lead upon a knoll,
> My left hand hooks you round the waist,
> My right hand points to landscapes of continents, and a
> plain public road.
>
> (46.1203–06)

Bringing us to his American version of the cosmic road (an archetypal phenomenon in ecstatic and mythic expression), Whitman here takes on the role of master of our initiation. The page acts as the surface of the dream he penetrates to make contact. The sense of his being with us yet being dead, of his hiding in the leaf of paper as a timeless being emerging in time, controls the reader's experience from here to the end of the poem. As he is to his spirit, we are to him:

> This day before dawn I ascended a hill and looked at the
> crowded heaven,
> And I said to my spirit, When we become the enfolders of
> those orbs and the pleasure and knowledge of every
> thing in them, shall we be filled and satisfied then?
> And my spirit said No, we level that lift to pass and
> continue beyond.
>
> You are also asking me questions, and I hear you;
> I answer that I cannot answer . . . . you must find out
> for yourself.
>
> (46.1217–21)

The sense that he acts as an initiatory spirit recurs in an image that Whitman would later explore in a poem of a boy and a bird: "It is you talking just as much as myself . . . . I act as the tongue of you, / It was tied in your mouth . . . . in mine it begins to be loosened" (47.1244–45).

The poet consistently imagines his students as common working people, whom he removes to an antistructural domain to implant his message. That message he recapitulates in terms of the dualities he has merged, moving inevitably toward the underlying janus of life and death, a complex he reinforces in erotic imagery to convey through the libido his sense of eternal life and vegetal transformation:

> And as to you corpse I think you are good manure, but
>   that does not offend me,
> I smell the white roses sweetscented and growing,
> I reach to the leafy lips . . . . I reach to the polished
>   breasts of melons.
>
>   (49.1285–87)

In these lines, as throughout section forty-nine, the poet imagines his own death while he approaches the end of his poem. The experience upon which he bases his faith, the ecstatic death and resurrection, mimes natural cycles, but it is also man's way of magically immersing himself in those cycles to overcome the fear and alienation that produce infidelity and soul-corruption. There is no rendering of the passage through the portals of death more delicately and confidently accomplished than what Whitman has given us where he emerges from his trance:

> Of the turbid pool that lies in the autumn forest,
> Of the moon that descends the steeps of the soughing
>   twilight,
> Toss, sparkles of day and dusk . . . . toss on the
>   black stems that decay in the muck,
> Toss to the moaning gibberish of the dry limbs.
>
> I ascend from the moon . . . . I ascend from the night,
> And perceive of the ghastly glitter the sunbeams
>   reflected,
> And debouch to the steady and central from the offspring
>   great or small.
>
>   (49.1292–98)

As James E. Miller, Jr., observes, section fifty begins with the poet just returned from his experience: "Wrenched and sweaty . . . . calm and cool then my body becomes; / I sleep . . . . I sleep long" (50.1300–1301). This description matches well the exhaustion of the shaman after his performance and his need to sleep—often for hours on end—to recuperate from the fatigue of his heroic exertions. Unable to express the quality of his insight (such insights always being of a noetic nature), the poet gropes for "outlines," asks the audience for aid in this task, and finally settles for abstractions. His emphasis upon "happiness" need not be considered an example of the "inversion" of normal forms of mysticism, as "form," "union," "plan," "eternal life," and especially "happiness" are always the ends of the shamanic seance.[53] Nonetheless, these abstract terms are impotent compared to the communication afforded by the process of the poem itself. The poet has already outlined the riddles that provoke him and exemplified the experience by which he fathoms them; in doing so he hopes to have sparked a revitalization of his culture by bringing his audience into participation in his rite.

As "[t]he past and present wilt" in the penultimate section of the poem, the speaker shifts the frame of his audience-orientation somewhat, facing the "eleves" of the future. He addresses *us* as an ancestral spirit from Hades:

> Listener up there! Here you . . . . what have you to
>   confide to me?
> Look in my face while I snuff the sidle of evening,
> Talk honestly, for no one else hears you, and I stay
>   only a minute longer.
>
> (51.1311–13)

An American humor informs these lines, Whitman's colloquial "here you" brilliantly puncturing the usual formality in relations between the living and the dead as he plays the ancestor maintaining contact with those who earnestly seek him. One of the pleasures of Whitman's intimacy is his feigned nonchalance about the page that should be separating us from him, and that is why the last two sections of "Song of Myself" are a grand concentration of his wit.

The "metaphysic" underlying the final lines of the poem is one Whitman first found in Volney's account of the origin of belief in metempsychosis (one very close to that of the "chamans"), the material body diffused to continue existent in the universe while the vital principle, the spirit, also passes on to other spheres. To convey this final version of his immortality, Whitman draws upon the dominant symbol, grass, which "encapsulates the major properties of the total process" of the poem and implicitly reinforces the emotional complex now invested in the ethos of renewal.[54] Looking back to the creation of this symbol in section six, the riddle of the grass recurs here as a spur to perseverance. "What is the grass?" is echoed by "You will hardly know who I am or what I mean"; "How is it I extract strength from the beef I eat?" (20.389) by "I shall be good health to you nevertheless, / And filter and fibre your blood" (52.1332–33). Our cycle picks up where his disappears into the further fold of the future.

CHAPTER FOUR
"O What is My Destination?"

*T*HE NOTE on which "Song of Myself" ended in 1855 became even more pervasive by 1860; it provided the starting point not only for "Crossing Brooklyn Ferry" of 1856, but for the "Calamus" group as well. The relationship between poet and reader became increasingly important in Whitman's program partly because of the function he hoped his *Leaves* would serve in the salvation of American democracy.[1] By 1860 this hope was desperate. Whitman had passed through a trough of political bitterness, begun to rise on a crest of optimism, and then seen his dreams dashed as the nation approached its crisis.[2] Indeed, his editorials for the Brooklyn *Daily Times* show that in the spring of 1858, after the defeat of the "slave power's" Crittenden amendment to the Lecompton bill in the Senate, the poet was optimistic about the chances of free labor defeating the forces that threatened democracy and the Union. By the spring of 1859, this optimism had vanished, and the editorialist fully expected a "disruption of the Union."[3] For the second time in his life, Whitman quit journalism about this time (perforce, apparently, as before) and, with a new burst of inspiration, overhauled and vastly expanded *Leaves of Grass.* In the new edition, the poet tried to achieve erotic intimacy with his readers in order to infuse them with his meanings and spread his faith—a natural strategy, considering the fact that his own means of inspiration and of rejuvenating his faith were infused with eroticism. Thus the same volume in which "Calamus" is introduced also carries the most overt and sustained political charge of Whitman's poetic career while directly emphasizing a "Religion" of democracy as its over-arching theme. Indeed, the core of *Leaves of Grass* 1860 is religious; yet Whitman's religiosity is also a basis for national union and would be unthinkable without it. In millennial fashion all events in this edition are dated from the year 1776; the abbreviation "T. S." (for "These States") even appears as a time marker like "A. D." in the table of contents.

Biographical speculations centering on "Calamus" have

distracted attention from the main ends of Whitman's edition of 1860, which is not only the most personal, but also the most emphatically political of his volumes. More specifically, personal feelings, psychological threats and joys, have been integrated with the poet's prophetic role. Whitman nearly always enfolded his private longings in socially significant acts, and he studded his volume of 1860 with political pronouncements, many concerning specific historical events; although the political poems often may be weak, the prophetic utterances occasionally shrill and empty, our composite view of the poet should account for the connection of these neglected modes to the poems we now rank among the masterpieces of world literature. It will do no good to differentiate the "poet" from the "prophet" or to say that Whitman occasionally "forgot" what sort of poet he was, as Roy Harvey Pearce did in his very defense of this most political and prophetic version of *Leaves of Grass*.[4] In 1860 the longest cluster of poems (by far) is "Chants Democratic and Native American," which immediately follows "Proto-leaf" (later "Starting from Paumanok") and "Walt Whitman" ("Song of Myself") at the front of the book. Both "Enfans d'Adam" and "Calamus" follow and include overtly political poems. The final cluster, "Messenger Leaves," is largely political, including such pieces as "To a Foiled Revolter or Revoltress," "To The States, to Identify the 16th, 17th, or 18th Presidentiad," "Walt Whitman's Caution," and "To a President." The poem that closes the volume, *"So long!,"* prominently includes a prophetic announcement of the future of American democracy:

> When America does what was promised,
> When each part is peopled with free people,
> When there is no city on earth to lead my city, the
>   city of young men, the Manahatta city—But when the
>   Manahatta leads all the cities of the earth,
> When there are plentiful athletic bards, inland and seaboard,
> When through These States walk a hundred millions of
>   superb persons,
> When the rest part away for superb persons, and contribute
>   to them,
> When fathers, firm, unconstrained, open-eyed—When breeds
>   of the most perfect mothers denote America,
> Then to me ripeness and conclusion.[5]

In short the 1860 edition of *Leaves of Grass,* is, as Robin P. Hoople has insisted in a discussion of "Chants Democratic," "nothing short of a nineteenth-century poet-priest's attempt to bring about an evangelical conversion of the heretics of democracy."[6] The "healing" motif of 1855 has been relegated to the background as religious conversion has become even more prominent; the shamanic healer has become more and more of a messianic prophet.

To be more specific about the "democratic" structure of the 1860 edition, we should note two particular emphases: the "Many in One" and the personal relation of love between two people (the key to overcoming the paradox of individualism and union). The informing process of the 1860 edition is the merging of these two poles, which have become the foundations of the new democratic "religion" Whitman claims to "inaugurate" in "Proto-leaf." At the overtly political level is an emphasis clearly connected to the religious message: the problem of reconciling Union with the integrity of each state, which is now more prominent than concern about the effects of capitalism and corruption.

Framing and encapsulating the entire book, "Proto-leaf" and *"So long!"* reveal in integral fashion the full nature of Whitman's undertaking while displaying the ecstatic pattern we have come to regard as the sign of inspiration in his career. Moreover, in the finest new poem of the collection, the pivotal "A Word Out of the Sea" (later "Out of the Cradle Endlessly Rocking"), we find a clear analogue of the shamanic "call." A discussion of these three essential ecstatic poems can help us interpret the meaning of Whitman's volume as a whole and the book's relevance to our knowledge of his vocation. First, however, let us clear a space for interpretation by responding to certain vexing issues surrounding "Calamus."

"The Love of Comrades"

There are two respects in which the "Calamus" emotion chiefly has concerned students of *Leaves of Grass:* (1) the intentionally public, the importance Whitman perceived this emotion, once awakened and acted upon, could have in American society; and (2) the private, its relationship to Whitman's psychology, sexual nature, or personal state of mind. Neither strictly "political" nor "autobiographical" readings of the "Calamus" group (even when such readings associate sexual sublimation with its political thrust) can sufficiently address the connections between these realms of significance. The most recent homosexual approaches to the poems, while addressing both realms and illuminating possible connections, ignore, like the other readings, the religious dimension which is the "soul" of the 1860 edition. Hence, most attempts to interpret "Calamus" have amputated the cluster from the full body of Whitman's poetry, inhibiting a coherent approach to his "canon."

In a recent article, M. Wynn Thomas astutely examines the manuscripts and revisions of the original twelve "Calamus" poems (first collected as "Live-Oak with Moss") to show that Whitman intentionally increased the emotional drama of the pieces to achieve an effect he had decided upon in advance, apparently in the early summer of 1859 (at the same time he quit journalism and began shaping the 1860 edition): "It is clear from the manuscripts that what matters to Whitman is not fidelity to the facts of personal experience, but the fullest possible development of the poetic and the human possibilities of this material." If Thomas is correct, then it may be helpful to read the poems with relation to an overall scheme Whitman was developing for his third edition at about this time.[7] "Calamus" contributes an important theme to that edition, but the statements that Whitman would give up "singing" and "prophesying" for the States because of the jealousy of his lover, or because of some profound disappointment, must be regarded as part of a rhetorical strategy, not as direct autobiographical confession. A convincing dramatization of a fervent "adhesive" love would demand the portrayal of jealousy, anxiety, and overpowering attraction strong enough temporarily to supersede even the persona's vocation. As much as Whitman may have known the doubts, torments, and joys of such love, we must acknowledge that he deliberately developed the "Calamus" section for larger purposes linked to the thrust of the 1860 edition as a whole. These purposes he specifically revealed on several occasions (within and without the cluster), but perhaps most pointedly in *Democratic Vistas,* when he indicated one of the most important themes he felt should be taken up by the poets following him: "intense and loving comradeship, the personal and passionate attachment of man to man—which, hard to define, underlies the lessons and ideals of the profound saviours of every land and age, and which seems to promise, when thoroughly develop'd, cultivated and recognized in manners and literature, the most substantial hope and safety of the future of these States."[8] Statements similar to this abound in the 1860 edition, informing virtually all the "Calamus" poems in which the poetic "saviour" spouts the public significance of "manly affection."

> There shall from me be a new friendship—It shall be called
>   after my name,
> It shall circulate through The States, indifferent of
>   place,
> It shall twist and intertwist them through and around each
>   other—Compact shall they be, showing new signs,
> Affection shall solve every one of the problems of Freedom,
> Those who love each other shall be invincible,
> They shall finally make America completely victorious, in
>   my name.[9]

In Whitman's program individualistic tendencies to fragmentation would be held in check by the loving communality that had been part of his visions from the beginning but about which he became increasingly anxious as the States appeared on the verge of disunion. The temperament he celebrates and exemplifies in the sequence is part of an ethos to which he seeks to convert his audience. And in doing this he sees himself not simply as a political leader, but as a religious visionary.

In the process of conveying both an ethos and a world view—in fact, fusing these so that the ethical norms proposed will seem in harmony with the cosmos as it is supposed actually to exist—the religious prophet tries to shape the very temperament of his audience. To accomplish this he uses symbols with ideological, psychic, and cosmic resonances—as Whitman used the leaf of grass in "Song of Myself." "Calamus" poem number two (known today as "Scented Herbage of My Breast") is one piece that clearly exemplifies such a process. Here the calamus symbol becomes emblematic of a religious regime.

However, the religious force of a symbolic system can be fully conveyed only by way of ritual action, which frequently repeats the drama of the dominant symbol's origination, the process by which it first was "discovered." This is true, for example, with regard to the leaf of grass in "Song of Myself." To understand the ritualistic nature of the calamus symbol, we need only consider the poet's account of how he came upon it, recounted in "Calamus" number four (later "These I, Singing in Spring"). This poem, central to the entire cluster, defines a repetition. As the poet "sings" his calamus leaves, he repeats an experience by which his theme and symbol first were given to him. The poem narrates a quest in which the speaker withdraws to a liminal terrain and passes out of the "world" through the "gates" that link the profane to the sacred. In this landscape he encounters silent spirits of friends:

> Collecting, I traverse the garden, the world—but soon I
>   pass the gates,
>
> . . . .
>
> Far, far in the forest, before I think where I get,
> Solitary, smelling the earthy smell, stopping now and then
>   in the silence,
> Alone I had thought—yet soon a silent troop gathers around me,
> Some walk by my side, and some behind, and some embrace my
>   arms or neck,
> They, the spirits of friends, dead or alive—thicker they
>   come, a great crowd, and I in the middle,
> Collecting, dispensing, singing in spring, there I wander
>   with them.[10]

Ultimately, he discovers his chief token of comradely love, which he will carry back into the social world as a symbol.

> And here what I now draw from the water, wading in the
>   pond-side,
> (O here I last saw him that tenderly loves me—and returns
>   again, never to separate from me,
> And this, O this shall henceforth be the token of comrades—
>   this calamus-root shall,
> Interchange it, youths, with each other! Let none render
>   it back!)
>
> > (348.18–21)

The landscape is reminiscent of that in "Song of Myself" where the speaker, accompanied by animals, in a quasi-paradisal condition discovers "tokens" of himself:

> I do not know where they got those tokens,
> I must have passed that way untold times ago and negligently
>   dropt them,
> Myself moving forward then and now and forever,
> Gathering and showing more always and with velocity,
> Infinite and omnigenous and the like of these among them;

> Not too exclusive toward the reachers of my remembrancers,
> Picking out there one that shall be my amie,
> Choosing to go with him on brotherly terms.[11]

One perhaps needs to be reminded that the "amie" referred to turns out to be a stallion that carries the speaker toward the great vision of section thirty-three in "Song of Myself." Yet the passage might easily be mistaken for part of a "Calamus" poem. The landscape of "Calamus" number four reminds one as well of that in "A Word Out of the Sea" or that in "When Lilacs Last in the Dooryard Bloom'd," in which the poet, accompanied by the "thought of death" and "the sacred knowledge of death," enters the swamp to open communication with his demon / mate / brother bird. Located in a sort of "sacred wood," the pond seems an interface between spiritual realities and the world of "appearances" (as do bodies of water in a host of other Whitman poems, and in shamanism as well). When the speaker wades into the pond to draw his "token" from the water, he enters a sphere that momentarily annuls his entrapment in diachronic time and space—"(O here I last saw him that tenderly loves me—and returns again, never to separate from me)." He returns to a "sacred center," so to speak, in which not only does the lost lover return "for good," but the dominant symbol of a new ethical program offers itself to the poet's use.

"Realistically," the lover cannot possibly have returned to the poet at the pond-side (just as the wine and wafer "cannot" be the blood and flesh of Jesus in the Christian communion ceremony) and this fact helps emphasize the ritual nature of the experience. Moreover, the "thicker" the spirits come, the more they remind us of the spiritual companions who aid the poet's inspiration in a number of visionary episodes from 1855 through 1865, in each case functionally adapted to the particular occasion of the poem.

> These I, compassed around by a thick cloud of spirits,
> Wandering, point to, or touch as I pass, or throw them
>   loosely from me,
> Indicating to each one what he shall have—giving something
>   to each,
> But what I drew from the water by the pond-side, that I
>   reserve,
> I will give of it—but only to them that love, as I myself
>   am capable of loving.
>
> (348.24–28)

"Calamus" number four, incidentally, was apparently one of the first poems in which the symbolic possibilities of the calamus plant occurred to Whitman, "engulfing" the live-oak symbol and later unfolded further in additional poems.[12] (Interestingly, both the lilac and the moss pulled from a live-oak appear in the poem as tokens discovered by the pond-side.) "The whole poem, in its 1860 form," says Thomas, "can . . . be interpreted as a piece of white magic—the development of a fantasy ritual whose (unconscious) intention is to secure the perpetuation of love."[13] The calamus symbol fuses ethical, emotional, and political demands while, implicitly promised to the reader through an "illocutionary act," it enforces audience participation. In the many poems of the "Calamus" cluster, Whitman unfolds the various meanings of his symbol at all different levels of experience. We only dismember it by attempting to separate its "public" from its "private" significations and by ignoring the liminal context of its discovery. But when we view the calamus plant as a religious symbol, its multidimensional resonances are restored to us and synthesized.

So far I have not taken account of the intensely private, often tortured, confessional quality of certain "Calamus" pieces, as well as such related poems as "As I Ebb'd with the Ocean of Life" (the first poem of the cluster entitled "Leaves of Grass" in 1860). This confessional quality it is that draws scholars to hunt for the autobiographical impulse behind the persona's voice. Why, then, have we not considered more seriously the centrality of the poet's vocation to his life, and the overwhelming personal threat posed by historical developments? It seems to me no "accident" that the impulse to confession and self-doubt coincided in Whitman with the period when America was on the verge of Civil War; in 1859 Whitman's entire system of belief stood radically challenged. We can hardly measure today the depth of the despair that confronted him as his powerlessness before the processes of history overcame all hope. Confession, according to Paul Ricoeur, arises from a spiritual crisis—the threat of meaninglessness presented by the experience of radical evil.[14] By "radical evil" is meant the event through which one is confronted, in the depths of one's being, with the spectre of chaos. Bafflement before the "mystery of iniquity," the possibility of disorder in the cosmos, entails the threat of self-alienation insofar as our "truest" self seems bound to the sacred and thus becomes distanced from us as the sacred recedes. But the loss of the belief-grounded orientation to "reality" actually increases our sense of dependence upon the sacred, intensifies our dread of being "lost." As it slips away, the sacred seems ever more dear.

Let me suspend the consideration of "Calamus" a moment to discuss "As I Ebb'd with the Ocean of Life," the most poignant illustration of the confessional mode in the 1860 edition. The poem appeared first as "Bardic Symbols" in the *Atlantic Monthly* in 1860, and then as "Leaves of Grass" number one in Whitman's 1860 volume. Its composition apparently coincided roughly with that of "A Word Out of the Sea" and with the expansions of both "Calamus" and "Protoleaf." In the 1860 edition, the poem begins with a revealing plea: "Elemental drifts! / O I wish I could impress others as you and the waves have just been impressing me."[15] Acknowledging the poet's despair at being ignored by his potential audience, the apostrophe voices as well his desire to learn the secret of expression that the ocean so powerfully exemplifies as she "cries for her castaways." The bulk of the poem recounts an immediately preceding experience during which the poet went into a state of absorption, "seized by the spirit that trails in the lines underfoot," and moves toward a merging of that experience with the moment in which the poet speaks and, with the "spirit" of *his* lines, seizes the reader.

Melancholy and doubt dominate the body of the poem as the ocean "drifts" its debris up against the fatherland, speaking mysteriously, burdened with "the voices of men and women wrecked" but giving out no assurances of meaning in the wreckage. The apparent incoherence of nature, connected with the incoherence of history, afflicts the poet with doubt of his role in life and of the faith that sustains him:

> Oppressed with myself that I have dared to open my mouth,
> Aware now, that, amid all the blab whose echoes recoil upon
>   me, I have not once had the least idea who or what I am,
> But that before all my insolent poems the real ME still stands
>   untouched, untold, altogether unreached,
> Withdrawn far, mocking me with mock-congratulatory signs and
>   bows,
> With peals of distant ironical laughter at every word I have
>   written or shall write,
> Striking me with insults till I fall helpless upon the sand.
>   (196–97.5)

These lines confess precisely the form of self-alienation I discussed a moment ago—the sense of being "lost," the straining of the all-important relation between self and world brought about by bafflement and the recession of the sacred sphere. "O I perceive I have not understood anything—not a single object—and that no man ever can" (197.6). Nature, so central to Whitman's conception of the sacred since it is that part of the cosmos with which we daily traffic and in which we have our being—that to which transcendentalists looked as the model of order making visible the sacred order—becomes, in "Leaves of Grass" number one, a mocking and uncanny threat.

> I perceive Nature here, in sight of the sea, is taking advantage
>   of me, to dart upon me, and sting me,
> Because I was assuming so much,
> And because I have dared to open my mouth to sing at all.
>
> (197.7)

Incomprehension of nature and self-alienation necessarily coincide; they demand the poet's submission to an indeterminate fate, the loss of control over his personal history, and an adoption of total passivity before both "mother" and "father" in the ancestral landscape of Paumanok.

I do not want to press too hard upon the identity of the father in this poem, whom psychoanalytic and other critics have interpreted as a projection of Walter Whitman, Sr., but if we can catch the conflation of "father" with "founding father" in Whitman's "family romance," the poem gains a dimension that reveals its relationship to the historical "ground" of the 1860 volume. Whenever, in his poetry, Whitman considered heritage and place together, he thought less of his personal family history than of the national lineage and the land soaked in the blood of the Revolutionary soldiers, "charged" with the names of Indians, absorbing the torn flesh of the fathers and of the sacrificed sons. Consider the effect of such connotations upon a reading of stanzas 10 and 11 in "Leaves of Grass" number one:

> I too am but a trail of drift and debris,
> I too leave little wrecks upon you, you fish-shaped island,
>
> I throw myself upon your breast, my father,
> I cling to you so that you cannot unloose me,
> I hold you firm, till you answer me something.
>
> (198.10–11)

Read with relation to both the national crisis and the crisis of self-alienation that motivates the poem, the poet's craving for Father Paumanok's embrace resonates sympathetically with the iconic embrace of Lincoln by Washington in the photo Whitman kept from his later years in the capitol until his death. The meaning he seeks must have ancestral grounding and an aboriginal voice; but at first the father is mute, the mother mocking. Helplessly the son cries for an answer to his doubts, submits himself, and directs the father to embrace him:

> Kiss me, my father,
> Touch me with your lips, as I touch those I love,
> Breathe to me, while I hold you close, the secret of the
>   wondrous murmuring I envy,
> For I fear I shall become crazed, if I cannot emulate it, and
>   utter myself as well as it.
>
> (198.12)

The father, closest to the ocean, knows the secret the son craves. The demand for an embrace also contains a desire to replace the father, to be "bequeathed" the secret in order to come into full self-possession and possession of the ocean/mother's (and cosmic Democracy's?) murmuring.

It is not the father alone who finally answers the speaker, however. The poet also addresses the mother, begs her not to reject him but to let him "gather" from her the "types" he has been seeking for his eternal spirit and himself. Ultimately the poet seems to learn the secret of the "wondrous murmuring"—he kisses the father, nestles close to the mother (as does Lincoln in "When Lilacs Last in the Dooryard Bloom'd"); but this ecstasy is death itself. In the final movement of the poem, the speaker dramatizes his own end and becomes one more addition to the "debris" washed by the ocean against the land (yet another resonance with "Lilacs," in which the poet sees "the debris and debris of all the slain soldiers of the war"). His verses join the ancestral "lines" underfoot—"Up just as much out of fathomless workings fermented and thrown" (199.16)—that is, under *our* feet. "We, capricious, brought hither, we know not whence, spread out before You, up there, walking or sitting, / Whoever you are—we too lie in drifts at your feet" (199.16). Whitman has again used the device of putting the reader, at the conclusion of a poem, into the position in which he himself began his meditation. These final lines, then, convey a less bleak tone than some scholars have found in the poem. Indeterminacy reins, but not the despair through which the poem has moved. As the opening lines indicated, the father and mother have, in some sense, answered the poet's demand for their secret; he "gathers" the washed debris for himself and his "phantom" and finally utters his knowledge to us in a way precisely repeating that by which the debris first spoke to him out of the "rolling" froth: "(See! from my dead lips the ooze exuding at last! / See—the prismatic colors, glistening and rolling!)" (199.16). The tone is one of achievement rather than terror, and of relief in the achievement that was once doubted. It is difficult to call the poem tragic, or even pathetic, in the end. The final stanza lifts itself toward a precarious balance between comedy and tragedy, leaving us with a greater sense of indeterminacy than we felt, for example, in the final stanzas of "Song of Myself." And if this is so, we can assume that the poet facing the debris in 1860 is not so sure as he once was of where he is drifting from or to.

Another of Whitman's better confessional poems is "Calamus" number seven ("Of the Terrible Doubt of Appearances"), which expresses precisely the sort of dread conveyed by "Leaves of Grass" number one. Nothing in the poem indicates the impetus of the speaker's doubt, but the form of that doubt is unquestionably related to his religious stance as an uprooting of the *axis mundi* and a consequent distancing of the sacred that brings fear of permanent alienation.

> Of the terrible question of appearances,
> Of the doubts, the uncertainties after all,
> That may-be reliance and hope are but speculations after all,
> That may-be identity beyond the grave is a beautiful fable only,
> May-be the things I perceive—the animals, plants, men, hills,
>   shining and flowing waters,
> The skies of day and night—colors, densities, forms—May-be
>   these are, (as doubtless they are,) only apparitions, and the
>   real something has yet to be known.[16]

The diction of the poem is at times perilously close to that of "Leaves of Grass" number one when describing the terror of spectral appearances: "(How often they dart out of themselves, as if to confound me and mock me! / How often I think neither I know, nor any man knows, aught of them;)" (353, 11.7–8). Nature again exerts its power of mockery, "darting" out to "sting" the poet, to upset every stay against confusion but one: the adhesive love that is described in terms consistent with (though less fervent than) the ecstatic passages of "Song of Myself."

> To me, these, and the like of these, are curiously answered by
> my lovers, my dear friends;
> When he whom I love travels with me, or sits a long while
> holding me by the hand,
> When the subtle air, the impalpable, the sense that words and
> reason hold not, surround us and pervade us,
> Then I am charged with untold and untellable wisdom—I am
> silent—I require nothing further.
>
> (353, 11. 10–13)

The poem, like "Leaves of Grass" number one, concludes with a rather precarious equilibrium, revealing the poet's sense of his compromised position *vis-a-vis* historical "appearances." He has made a strategic retreat, however, for if he does not claim positive assurance of the meaning of the external forms, his stay against confusion, the love of a "comrade," precisely expresses the ethos upon which fulfillment of the democratic world-view depends.

"Calamus" number seven and "Leaves of Grass" number one express most directly Whitman's anxiety at the threshold of self-alienation, coincident with the experience of radical evil and mobilizing the confessional response. The dread that surfaces in these poems and at the critical moment of "A Word Out of the Sea" encompasses private emotion, political ideology, and moral conviction. Hence, Whitman's quest for intimacy (with his reader, in particular) through confession is part of the response to a religious crisis, precipitated by national events that threatened his entire world-view and vocation. The political crisis did not have simply political ramifications. It called out all his private demons.

Those demons make themselves known in "Calamus" and throughout the third edition of *Leaves of Grass,* and they are intimately linked to the poet's sexual nature. There can be little question that Whitman largely sublimated his sexual instincts. (Indeed, virtually all the evidence of his homosexuality indicates a high degree of sublimation.) Part of the pathos and intensity of "Calamus" is owing to such sublimation and the great longing that therefore tormented him, as well as his tremendous responsiveness to touching—the physical intimacy he did not get enough of in life.[17] Spiritual crisis for Whitman— the "terrible doubt of appearances"—always called out his repressed yearning for sensual fulfillment, a yearning to which he attested in a revealing way in "The Two Vaults," a fragment of 1861–62, apparently based upon the poet's feelings while in Pfaff's observing the pedestrians passing on the sidewalk: "(You phantoms! oft I pause, yearning, to arrest some one of you! / Oft I doubt your reality—whether you are real—I suspect all is but a pageant.)"[18] Whitman's usage of "phantoms" here seems inspired by a usage of Carlyle—people who do not realize themselves are referred to as "phantoms" in *Sartor Resartus.* However, the "unreality" of the pedestrians also seems attributable to a crisis in the observer's own psyche which must be overcome by personal relationship. "Calamus" number forty (later "That Shadow My Likeness") describes a similar crisis of alienation, but in this case it is the poet's own "shadow" rather than the "phantoms" of others that becomes the focus of interest:

That shadow, my likeness, that goes to and fro, seeking
  a livelihood, chattering, chaffering,
How often I find myself standing and looking at it where it
  flits,
How often I question and doubt whether that is really me;
But in these, and among my lovers, and carolling my songs,
O I never doubt whether that is really me.[19]

Notice the connection here with the function of the "Calamus" symbol in "These I, Singing in Spring": there the poet implicitly insists that we not fail him, not return the token of his love and thus ignore his "song." As he reserves his emblem for "some one" of us (to steal a phrase from "The Two Vaults"), he seeks to draw us into response—and more than this, into the "responsibility" of love.

The usage of "phantoms" I have noted in "The Two Vaults" applies as well to a passage in "A Word Out of the Sea," the 1860 version of "Out of the Cradle Endlessly Rocking," coming at the moment of crisis that precedes the sea's response to the boy:

O a word! O what is my destination?
O I fear it is henceforth chaos!
O how joys, dreads, convolutions, human shapes, and all
  shapes, spring as from graves around me!
O phantoms! You cover all the land, and all the sea!
O I cannot see in the dimness whether you smile or frown
  upon me;

O vapor, a look, a word! O well-beloved!
O you dear women's and men's phantoms![20]

As I shall point out later in a discussion of this passage, the "phantoms" are undoubtedly the poet's democratic subject/audience, deaf to the calls of 1855 and 1856. In both these lines and those cited from the fragment "The Two Vaults," we find a crisis similar to that described in several of the "Calamus" poems (particularly "Of the Terrible Doubt of Appearances") and answered by sensual intimacy. In "A Word Out of the Sea," that intimacy comes from the ocean in a transformative spiritual awakening and reassurance: ecstasy erotically answers "the craving and glut of the soul." This was also true, we must remember, in "Song of Myself" and "The Sleepers."

Roger Asselineau has emphasized in Whitman "a hyperesthesia of all the senses, particularly that of touch, which explains the chronic nature of his mysticism and which is perhaps connected with the repression of his sexual instincts."[21] Similarly, the intense need for contact created by the shaman's isolation and sexual repression (particularly if he is "homoerotic" or bisexual) is in part answered by the erotic relation with the spiritual helper. Intimacy with a patient or an audience further answers the need for human contact, their "faithfulness" to the shaman energizing and sustaining the psychic intensity of the performance. The contact Whitman seeks with his reader at certain moments of "Calamus" serves a function comparable to the spiritual coitus he so often dramatizes; in some cases the two forms of erotic fulfillment are fused, as in the concluding stanzas of *"So long!"*—in which the poet, as spiritual lover, consummates an erotic relation with his ideal reader. Thus we can learn much about Whitman's poetic process from the fact that the shaman's needs for love and acceptance (erotically charged) are hypnotically projected into his relations with the spirits that aid him, his audience, and in some cases his patients themselves. These relations, moreover, intensify during the moments of spiritual crisis that form the heart of the ritual performance, the confrontation with radical evil or cosmic disorder, which demands self-sacrifice and symbolic death. Personal frustrations, erotic urges, the need for love and omnipotence, are sublimated in artistic creativity of a religious nature and given a public significance that purges threats to the self. The artist transforms personal anxieties into agencies that promote physical health or revitalization of the "body politic." The private aspects of "Calamus" are similarly enfolded by Whitman's prophetic role-playing, particularly in the intensely political and nationalistic 1860 edition. Hence, there is no contradiction or conscious evasion involved in Whitman's statement that the "Calamus" poems were chiefly of political significance, nor in his statement that one of his deepest purposes in *Leaves of Grass* as a whole—through its many editions—was to draw affection from the multitudes toward himself.[22] The "Calamus" poems did not arise from the loss of a lover—nor from a homosexual "conversion"—but from the dread of being "lost," an existential anxiety that threatened the poet's vocation. In view of the complete lack of evidence for an actual lover or loss of one in the late 1850s, the ecstatic revitalization model provides a compelling framework for explaining the impetus and nature of the 1860 edition; it helps us recognize how political developments precipitated the crisis of 1856–60, and how "Calamus" is related to Whitman's religious "calling." The introductory and closing poems of the 1860 edition, embracing the volume as a whole, illuminate more comprehensively the nature of that calling and the aesthetic that empowers it.

"Proto-leaf"

"Proto-leaf" has long been recognized as a "program poem," announcing the themes and intentions of the new *Leaves of Grass*. Furthermore, it preserves and integrates through its ecstatic structure the actual revision process that transformed the poet's original intentions for a one-hundred-poem edition of 1857 into the fuller and more tightly organized, "clustered" edition scholars now recognize as one of Whitman's most important.[23] Critics have generally emphasized either the new treatment of "comradeship" or the correspondences of certain lines with particular poems and clusters of Whitman's book. However, the revisions of 1859–60 are also important in that they caused the earlier "Premonition" to acquire a structure roughly like that of "Song of Myself."[24] Recognition of this development is critical both for appreciating the new "Proto-leaf" and for understanding how Whitman's ecstatic process integrated new themes of his verse. Caught up in the quandary of how the "Calamus" theme relates to Whitman's personal life, students have tended to ignore what the ecstatic structure has to tell us, thus avoiding a discussion of the literary merits of the poem. Nonetheless, whereas the poem lies before us—and as more than the introduction of a program— we still know virtually nothing about its author's personal life at the time of composition, despite persistent digging and speculation.

We do know that Whitman was working on the opening lines of the poem (in early mss. called "Premonition") as early as October 1856; it was thus one of the first poems of the 1860 edition that the poet had in mind.[25] This initial version of the poem was a flat announcement of themes and displayed little that was new and original. Fredson Bowers implies that the late additions were primarily concerned with the themes of "Calamus," but a survey of the stanzas Bowers himself lists among those additions shows that much more went into the poem at this stage than he and others have suggested.[26] Stanzas 6–12, for instance, correspond primarily to "Chants Democratic" rather than "Calamus." They harp upon the idea of the masses and the broad lands of the people:

> Americanos! Masters!
> Marches humanitarian! Foremost!
> Century marches! Libertad! Masses!
> For you a programme of chants.[27]

Here, as in the first cluster of verse in the 1860 edition, the main motif is that of "Chants of the Many In One" (8.10). Other important additions to the poem do indeed bring in the theme of "Calamus," but they also allude to "A Word Out of the Sea" and especially to religion.

In fact, it looks as if Whitman added the "en-masse" democratic message and the "love" theme of "Calamus" (and, less importantly, of "Enfans d'Adam") as opposing elements that were then fused in the ecstatic episode of stanzas 34 through 37 (also added in 1859 or 1860). In the ecstasy religion rises as the "inclusive and more resplendent" answer to "Love" and "Democracy" that the poet shares with his new comrade-reader. As if to reinforce the revitalizing end of this sequence the poet has then added a summary of the crucial initiatory experience recorded in "A Word Out of the Sea"—though a "happier" version, to be sure—which leads to an apostrophe to his great object:

Democracy!
Near at hand to you a throat is now inflating itself and
   joyfully singing.

Ma femme!
For the brood beyond us and of us,
For those who belong here, and those to come,
I, exultant, to be ready for them, will now shake out
   carols stronger and haughtier than have ever yet
   been heard upon the earth.

                                 (14–15.41–42)

It should be evident from this brief synopsis that without the additions of 1859–60 the poem would be insubstantial—a scattering of bones pillaged from the inspiration of 1855. But if the new form of the poem shows an extension of old ideas and the development of new emphases, it also exemplifies a new employment of the ecstatic process that gave life to the first edition of *Leaves of Grass*.

"Proto-leaf" begins with a characterization of the poet as the "Friendly and flowing savage" of "Song of Myself"—that is, the generic and mythical savage of every part of America, identified with the people, plants, and animals of the continent, and withdrawn, for the purposes of his chants, to a liminal terrain. The persona of the savage expresses imperviousness to social boundaries and a superhuman ability to communicate with all beings, since the structures confining humans within a single consciousness and alienating them from nature are here nullified. Significantly, the final lines of the first stanza echo the motif of "A Word Out of the Sea," the poem Whitman released to the *Saturday Press* in 1859, apparently to announce his return to creativity:[28] "Aware of the mocking-bird of the wilds at daybreak, / Solitary, singing in the west, I strike up for a new world" (6.1). Though "striking up" alone, the poet hopes to awaken someone as the mocking-bird of "A Word Out of the Sea" has awakened him. Moreover, it is the "new world"—not only love or death-consciousness or gay liberation—that is the end of this awakening. Love, comradeship, and death-consciousness are ethical components of the religious and cultural revitalization that is the ultimate end of *Leaves of Grass*.

Basic clues to the poet's religious temperament in stanzas 2 through 4 lead to the visionary motif introduced in stanza 5, which opposes the western to the eastern hemisphere, the "new" world to the "old." Projecting the future from this opposition in space and time and identifying his intended audience, the poet then announces the themes of "Chants Democratic and Native American," calling attention to the "Many In One" who are henceforth descendants of the poet-prophet:

> Successions of men, Americanos, a hundred millions,
> One generation playing its part and passing on,
> And another generation playing its part and passing on in
>   its turn,
> With faces turned sideways or backward toward me to listen,
> With eyes retrospective toward me.

(7.8)

Although the 1855 edition also included this theme and this mode of projection, the stanzas in which they appear were added at the time Whitman was developing the cluster organization of his 1860 volume; thus they are clearly intended to call attention to the first "programme of chants" in the book. As if to prove that these are indeed "native American" chants, the speaker asserts his American ancestry; and to show himself truly autochthonous he insists upon the freedom from "creeds and schools" by virtue of which he permits "Nature" to "speak"—"without check, with original energy" (8.12).

Since the primitivism of this claim might seem to conflict with his supposed "modernity," the poet claims that the creeds and schools are merely in "abeyance" and, in stanzas 14 through 16, that he has indeed "perused" the "antique." He even includes the dead among his audience, hoping they might, "if eligible," return and study him. In the diction of these stanzas Whitman carefully avoids any implication that he has imitated others (including the ancient oracles and gods), implying instead that he has remained aloof from particular teachings in order to glean from all of them the hints he can merge into a new utterance for his lands and time: "I regard it all intently a long while, / Then take my place for good with my own day and race here" (9.16).

The poet must return, after serving apprenticeship, to the beginning of all creeds to allow inspiration to well up out of the materials of his own, new world. Insofar as his nation has surpassed those preceding it, so will the message of the poet. When inspiration comes it is indeed of an ancient mode, the "flame of materials," the hidden property of life that arrives as an ecstatic partner:

Here Spirituality, the translatress, the openly-avowed,
The ever-tending, the finale of visible forms,
The satisfier, after due long-waiting, now advancing,
Yes, here comes the mistress, the Soul.

(9.17)

The primitivism of Whitman's message is fully wedded to its modernity and Americanism, since eternal qualities underlie appearance; the belief that "the poems of materials . . . are to be the most spiritual poems" (9.19) derives from his study of the antique, but his inspiration is not imitative, for it springs from the same sources as that of "primitive" man; it *is* "original"—and thus aboriginal as well. It rises out of the tension of American conditions to transfigure them.

As stanzas 6 through 13 describe primarily whom Whitman's poems are *for,* stanzas 17 through 32 have to do with what they are *about.* The transition occurs through the acknowledgment of the antique (which the speaker regards as part of his audience), the announcement that the poet takes on a role in his own time and place (i.e., he has adopted a "mask"), and then the invitation of the soul, the encloser of all—the possession of which opens all subjects to exploration. The announcement of subject matter then moves from spirituality through materials and the body to current political conditions, enforcing a classic ritual complex, the axis around which social life revolves—or, from another point of view, a "gyre" of human consciousness.

Stanza 20 specifies the chief political themes of the 1860 edition and, implicitly, certain paradoxes of democracy that *Leaves of Grass* must resolve; historically, these paradoxes (broached in a more oblique and general manner in 1855) have come to catalyze around the problem of states' rights and national unity—a subcategory of the unity and diversity problem underlying all being.

I will make a song for These States, that no one State
   may under any circumstances be subjected to another
   State,
And I will make a song that there shall be comity by
   day and by night between all The States, and between
   any two of them,
And I will make a song of the organic bargains of These
   States—And a shrill song of curses on him who would
   dissever the Union;

And I will make a song for the ears of the President, full
of weapons with menacing points,
And behind the weapons countless dissatisfied faces.

(10.20)

Such songs are prominent throughout the 1860 edition. They have clashed with literary critics' insistence upon "universality" in literature and our general discomfort with outright propaganda in poetry, but if we are to comprehend the Whitman canon at all we must take full account of them. The poet always kept himself grounded in his own time and place, finding in contemporary history the conditions prerequisite to cosmic discovery.

The presentation of subject matter spirals toward the theme of faith by way of geography, employments, sexual organs and acts, and adhesiveness (stanzas 21–24). Since Whitman considered the "adhesive" love between men more "ethereal" and complete than love between man and woman, this progression registers a process of consciousness that was natural to the poet. From the mention of "unrestricted faith" the poet moves to the inclusion of evil in his message—an element we recognize as essential to Whitman's role and religious sensibility. Its appearance at this point of the role-process enacted in the poem is typical of his mode of inspiration. As if to reinforce the importance of embracing evil (as well as its *position* in the spiritual process, which is a response to the existential crisis engendered by the threat of disorder, the "mystery of iniquity"), the speaker announces only now that he "inaugurates" a "Religion" (11.25).

Should there be any question in our minds about the most important thrust of the 1860 edition of *Leaves of Grass,* we should take note of the fact that Whitman devotes a full thirteen stanzas—the heart and soul of "Proto-leaf"—to exposing the centrality of "religion" to his program. This centrality is further emphasized by the ecstatic context in which "religion" as a theme comes forth.

If the stanza near the beginning of Whitman's list of subject matter was devoted to the political problems of the nation, the climax of this list indicates the foundation of the answer to those problems: "I specifically announce that the real and permanent grandeur of These States must be their Religion, / Otherwise there is no real and permanent grandeur" (12.28). In the stanzas that follow this announcement, the poet asserts the importance of religion negatively by telling us what it transcends—including, specifically, love for man or woman, the themes of "Calamus" and "Enfans d'Adam":

> What do you seek, so pensive and silent?
> What do you need, comrade?
> Mon cher! do you think it is love?
>
> Proceed, comrade,
> It is a painful thing to love a man or woman to excess—
>   yet it satisfies—it is great,
> But there is something else very great—it makes the
>   whole coincide,
> It, magnificent, beyond materials, with continuous hands,
>   sweeps and provides for all.
>
> O I see the following poems are indeed to drop in the
>   earth the germs of a greater Religion.
>   (12–13.31–33)

We know from "Song of Myself" that when Whitman drops "germs" in the earth he frequently alludes to the ecstatic origins of his poetry, and the description of such ecstasy begins in the statement that the fusion of "Love" and "Democracy" gives rise to the "more resplendent" "Religion" (13.34). Spiritual beings residing behind appearances help induce the visionary's ecstasy:

> Melange mine!
> Mysterious ocean where the streams empty,
> Prophetic spirit of materials shifting and flickering
>   around me,
> Wondrous interplay between the seen and unseen,
> Living beings, identities, now doubtless near us, in
>   the air, that we know not of,
> Extasy everywhere touching and thrilling me,
> Contact daily and hourly that will not release me,
> These selecting—These, in hints, demanded of me.
>   (13.35)

Even the ennobling relations with his male lovers are less significant to Whitman's vocation than his spiritual relations:

> Not he, adhesive, kissing me so long with his daily kiss,
> Has winded and twisted around me that which holds me to him,

Any more than I am held to the heavens, to the spiritual
   world,
And to the identities of the Gods, my unknown lovers,
After what they have done to me, suggesting such themes.

(13.36)

These verses state as explicitly as possible the primacy of the shamanistic ecstasy, as compared to the homosexual relationship, in determining Whitman's vocation and personal triumph. Moreover, they differentiate between the shamanistic love affair and the earthly one with a companion either male or female.[29]

In stanzas 38 to 40 the poet presents a version of the shamanistic initiatory experience enacted in "A Word Out of the Sea" and then, maintaining the metaphor of the boy-become-bird, specifies that his resultant carols are celebrations of "Democracy"—"ma femme"—for camerados of the present and the future.

Stanzas 43 to 46 characterize the subject matter of Whitman's songs and his assurance of cosmic perfection much as stanzas 19 to 24, preceding the ecstasy, had to do with subject matter. In fact, following the ecstasy at the center of the poem, Whitman presents virtually a mirror-image of the stanzas preceding the ecstasy, progressing from an account of the subjects of his poetry (stanzas 43–47, an approximate inversion of stanzas 19–24) to a discussion of the soul as inhabitant of matter. Stanza 46, for example, refers to the problem of unity and individuality that underlies the political message of stanza 20. More striking is the correspondence of stanzas 47–48 with stanza 19:

Was somebody asking to see the Soul?
See! your own shape and countenance—persons,
   substances, beasts, the trees, the running rivers,
   the rocks and sands.

All hold spiritual joys, and afterward loosen them,
How can the real body ever die, and be buried?

(16.47–48)

I will make the poems of materials, for I think they
   are to be the most spiritual poems,
And I will make the poems of my body and of mortality,

For I think I shall then supply myself with the poems of
my Soul and of immortality.

(9–10.19)

As the discussion of the soul helped, in the first half of the poem, to accomplish the transition from audience to subject matter, in the second half it facilitates the transition from subject matter to audience:

Behold! the body includes and is the meaning, the
main concern—and includes and is the Soul;
Whoever you are! how superb and how divine is your body,
or any part of it.

Whoever you are! to you endless announcements.

Daughter of the lands, did you wait for your poet?
Did you wait for one with a flowing mouth and
indicative hand?

(17.51–53)

This structural technique is made possible by Whitman's view of the soul as both matter and spirit—a janus mask through which he can pass back and forth between the dual realms of his poems. Furthermore, the soul is the medium that, by virtue of its contribution to "ecstasy," allows the subjects and the audience of his poems virtually to be "transpositions" of each other.

The inverted pattern continues as the poet addresses the "daughter of the lands," the "male" and "female" of the states, as well as the president, the Congress, the governors and judiciary of his own time; he then turns to address the continent itself with praises—"Live words—words to the lands" (17.54). These verses correspond to those at the end of stanza 16 and the beginning of stanza 17 in which the poet asserts that he takes his place with his own day and race and then announces, "Here lands female and male, / Here the heirship and heiress-ship of the world" (9.17). (Note the transposition, however: in the earlier instance they were treated as subject matter; in stanzas 54–55 they are addressed as part of the audience.) Stanza 55 is a celebratory apostrophe to the lands of the continent that gradually becomes also an identification with all of its people.

In stanzas 56 to 58, as in certain passages of "Song of

Myself," the poet halts a moment to encourage the audience before holding in abeyance the present and future and pronouncing "what the air holds of the red aborigines" (20.59). This movement parallels that of stanzas 13 to 15, in which the poet would have "precedents" "connect lovingly" with his leaves as he pronounces that the States are "the children of the antique" (pp. 8–9). In the present case, however, he refers exclusively to the aboriginal antique. If the current inhabitants of the continent have already been identified with the "lands," at this point, as the lands are "charged" with the names of the "red aborigines," the poet implies that Americans have also become inheritors of an indigenous status—the passage is Whitman's version of an old Leatherstocking concern.

At this point subject and audience have begun to merge, as have past, present, and future. Such interfaces frequently precipitate visionary episodes in Whitman's poems, and in stanza 61 a version of the primordial/prospective breaks forth out of the leavings of the first Americans:

O expanding and swift! O henceforth,
Elements, breeds, adjustments, turbulent, quick, and
    audacious,
A world primal again—Vistas of glory, incessant and
    branching,
A new race, dominating previous ones, and grander far,
New politics—New literatures and religions—New inventions
    and arts.
                         (20.61)

We have seen before, in both "The Sleepers" and "Song of Myself," how prophecy comes to Whitman through contact with the underworld or a paradisal condition; an American millennium surfaces in the visions of stanza 63 as the poet awakens amid the surging of an inner flood. Stanzas 5 through 7 exhibit in feebler form the same promise, one yet unrealized, and are punctuated (like each line of stanza 63) with the imperative, "See."

After his prophetic vision, in the final two stanzas, the speaker calls upon his reader/comrade like a spiritual lover, promising power, liberty, eternity, and democracy. Whereas the introductory verses portrayed the poet "solitary, singing in the west," in the course of the poem he has emerged to claim his relationship to us and thus to claim also our ecstatic participation in the triumph of democracy that *Leaves of Grass* announces. The process of the poem is itself a means of realizing its own vision, of melding subject and audience ("objective" and "subjective" referents, from the audience's point of view) and therefore not only envisioning, but also creating the future.

To recapitulate, the model on page 121 should help clarify the structure of the poem according to the foregoing discussion. The right side of the diagram is inverted to accord with the nature of the poem and to show the reversed correspondences between its sections. Such correspondences are not in all instances exact. The subject of "adhesiveness" that appears in stanza 22 is notably absent from the second half of the poem until the last two stanzas, where it appropriately appears as the connector between ourselves and the prophet. Whitman did not trouble himself with uniform structural correspondences; yet the relationships between certain crucial sections of the poem are unmistakable. Moreover, they were the results of his careful revisions of 1859–60. The poem thus came to resemble "Song of Myself" and "The Sleepers," the structures of which also display a "progressive" symmetry (that is, a symmetry the second side of which shows realization of the first side's promise) centering in the critical ecstasy near the middle of each poem. The first part of each poem represents a concentration of forces and induction of ecstasy, the second an application or fruition of the power thus acquired.

It is necessary to ask what significance this structure of "Proto-leaf" has, and to answer the question we must return to a consideration of Whitman's claim to "inaugurate" a religion. What can this mean? The anthropologist Clifford Geertz provides a definition of religion that seems well-suited to analysis of *Leaves of Grass;* according to Geertz a religion is

(1) *a system of symbols which acts to*
(2) *establish powerful, pervasive, and long-lasting moods and motivations in men by*
(3) *formulating conceptions of a general order of existence and*
(4) *clothing these conceptions with such an aura of factuality that*
(5) *the moods and motivations seem uniquely realistic.*[30]

The systems of symbols that inform a culture are models of and for "reality"; they make the world intelligible ("interpret" it) but also shape reality to themselves. The religious complex tries to induce certain moods and motivations and to place

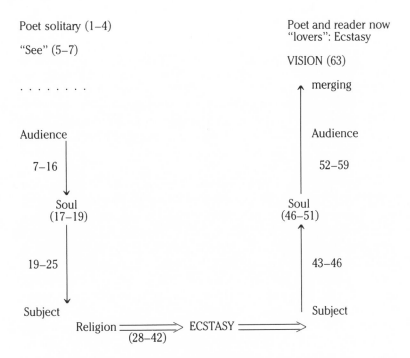

Poet solitary (1–4)

"See" (5–7)

Poet and reader now
"lovers": Ecstasy

VISION (63)

. . . .   ↑ merging

Audience   Audience

7–16   52–59

Soul   Soul
(17–19)   (46–51)

19–25   43–46

Subject   Subject

Religion ======> ECSTASY ======>
(28–42)

these ethical models in a cosmic framework so that the pre-
scribed dispositions seem fitted to reality itself. It is for this
reason that when the experience of the actual world falls out of
phase with the ethical prescriptions one feels bafflement and
dread, entering a soul-threatening crisis. The prophet (or religious complex) responds to such bafflement, such a suspicion of chaos, by formulating "by means of symbols, . . . an
image of such a genuine order of the world which will account
for, and even celebrate, the perceived ambiguities, puzzles,
and paradoxes in human experience."[31]

Belief in the religious concept depends, however, upon
the "aura of factuality" that makes it convincing, and here
ritual plays its most significant role. A self-referential phenomenon, the ritual gives authority to the symbolic complex by
fusing "the world as lived" and "the world as imagined" ("objective" and "subjective" referents), inducing the desired
moods and motivations while affirming the order of existence
posited by the ideology of the religious complex. In other
words it allows participants to experience the order of the
cosmos that it also defines. In the rite, "men attain their faith as

they portray it." "The acceptance of authority that underlies the religious perspective that the ritual embodies thus flows from the enactment of the ritual itself. By inducing a set of moods and motivations—an ethos—and defining an image of cosmic order—a world view—by means of a single set of symbols, the performance makes the model *for* and model *of* aspects of religious belief mere transpositions of one another."[32] Thus "ethos" and "world" are made to coincide. When one acts ethically—to the dictates of the "soul"—one acts in accord with the cosmic order.

Interestingly, in the Balinese ritual studied by Geertz, the "moods and motivations" as well as the perception of reality are enforced by the induction of trance, physically involving the people in the ritual performance and thereby overcoming the usual theatrical separation from the "actors" or priestly functionaries, allowing the people fully to enter the sacred relation. The audience-participants return from the experience of the ritual changed, bearing a new (or "revitalized") perception of everyday reality and of its participation in the cosmic scheme of things.[33] Thus the individual life is infused with meaning and joined to the larger project of communal religious integration. Such integration Whitman hopes to induce in his community not only in "Starting from Paumanok" (or *"So long!"* or "Song of Myself") but in the 1860 edition of *Leaves of Grass* as a whole, which attempts, beyond "representing" reality, to shape reality to itself at the same time that—paradoxically—it "reveals" the order of the cosmos. Like "Song of Myself," "Proto-leaf" is not an epic narrative but an effort in writing to enact a participatory rite. And this rite is deeply related to (is, in many respects, a repetition of) an initiatory role drama such as that created in "A Word Out of the Sea."

"A Word Out of the Sea"

As the best new poem in the 1860 edition of *Leaves of Grass*, "A Word Out of the Sea" (later "Out of the Cradle Endlessly Rocking") demands attention in every broad reinterpretation of Whitman's poetry. It beckons from practically the center of the book, between the "Leaves of Grass" and

"Enfans d'Adam" clusters. Whitman has already told us in "Proto-leaf" that the awakening recorded in this poem (though a lighter version of it) had led to his determination to sing for democracy and her "brood." Moreover, in a self-review of the version printed in the *Saturday Press* in 1859, he had indicated the importance he attached to the poem:

> We feel authorized to announce, for certain, that the Mocking-Bird, having come to his throat again, his cantabile, is not going to give cause to his admirers for complaining that he idles, mute, any more, up and down the world. His songs, in one and another direction, will, he promises us, after this date, profusely appear.
>
> We are able to declare that there will also soon crop out the true "Leaves of Grass," the fuller-grown work of which the former two issues were the inchoates—this forthcoming one, far, very far ahead of them in quality, quantity, and in supple lyric exuberance.[34]

The diction of the review is that of a village peddler hawking his latest snake oil, and Whitman, indeed, felt very confident in what he had to sell.

He was a confirmed addict of the "lyric exuberance" by which the child in the poem had transcended the despair of loss. For despair threatened Whitman periodically throughout his life—not only in the years 1856–60, which scholars often have singled out as his darkest—and his answer to despair was always artistic productivity in an ecstatic mode. It is thus significant that "A Word Out of the Sea" was written apparently just before "Proto-leaf" acquired its 1860 ecstatic pattern. Biographically speaking, the ecstasies of "Proto-leaf" and "A Word Out of the Sea" are coextensive, which accounts for Whitman's references to the boy-poet's awakening at two critical junctures in the poem that opens the 1860 edition.

The question of how "A Word Out of the Sea" relates to Whitman's career has long attracted critical investigation, since the poem seems closely linked to the motivation of the 1860 edition even while it poses as a reminiscence of the poet's first awakening. The structure and aesthetic qualities of this much-explicated poem are far clearer than are those of "Proto-leaf"; the main issues to be faced in interpreting it at this point have to do with understanding the change of status that it records and the relationship of the "initiation" to Whitman's poetic status in 1860.

According to Gay Wilson Allen, the poem was probably written in 1858, the year Whitman read it to the Price family, telling them it was "'founded on a real incident.'"[35] Many scholars have in fact read a real personal experience into the poem, though there is no external evidence to support such readings.[36] Personal anguish probably contributed to a crisis and consequent ecstatic reintegration, but scholars need to be more cautious in this area than they have been, because Whitman did not awaken to death for the first time in 1858; nor do we have any trustworthy evidence of a broken love affair, except for inferences from poems.

The theme of unsatisfied love—more specifically, the loss of a lover—had stirred Whitman profoundly long before the reawakening of 1858. As a matter of fact, if Whitman was remembering a personal experience as he wrote this poem, it was probably that of hearing, in 1851, Allesandro Bettini singing the sorrowful aria at the end of *La Favorita*—"one of the poet's favorite scenes in all opera," according to Robert D. Faner.[37] Faner missed the connection between the opera and the poem because of a misapplication of Whitman's statement to Mrs. Fanny Ritter that in writing of a mocking-bird or any other bird he could not forget the emotion that had stirred him in listening to Marietta Alboni.[38] On the basis of this evidence, Faner assumes that the he-bird's voice is based on Alboni's; but the bird is a male tenor. Whitman heard both Alboni *and* Bettini—the male tenor—in *La Favorita,* which he swooned over in a "Letter from Paumanok" of 1851. Alboni played the part of the female lover in this opera and Bettini the male.[39] Furthermore, Whitman mentioned Alboni and Bettini together when, in later life, he wished to acknowledge the influence of singers, composers, and dramatists on his career.[40] In the 1851 "Letter from Paumanok," Whitman writes that Bettini's voice in this opera moved him to tears and describes in detail the tragic aria of the young man who has lost his love. Fernando's breast is

> filled with a devouring anguish, his eyes showing the death that has fallen upon his soul. *The strains of death, too, come plaintively from his lips. Never before did you hear such wonderful gushing sorrow, poured forth like ebbing blood, from a murdered heart.* Is it for peace he prays with that appealing passion? Is it the story of his own sad wreck he utters?
>
> Listen. Pure and vast, that voice now rises, as on clouds, to the heaven where it claims audience. *Now, firm and unbroken, it*

spreads like an ocean around us. Ah, welcome that I know not the mere language of the earthly words in which the melody is embodied; as all words are mean before the language of true music.

Thanks, great artist. For one, at least, it is no extravagance to say, you have justified his ideal of the loftiest of the arts. Thanks, limner of the spirit of life, and hope and peace; of the red fire of passion, the cavernous vacancy of despair, and the black pall of the grave.[41]

Not only the emotion, but at times the very diction and imagery of this description anticipate "A Word Out of the Sea," and the date of the review coincides with the period of Whitman's struggle toward ecstatic poetry. Other important passages from this newspaper piece mark the author's adoption of the familiar address to the reader he would use in *Leaves of Grass* and the beginning of his ability, through ecstasy, to withstand and finally match nature's power (see chapter 2). Bearing these facts in mind, we should also recognize that Whitman was nearly as gloomy and despairing in the late 1840s—before his "conversion" and novitiate—as he would ever be, perhaps for much the same reason he felt discouraged prior to the reawakening of 1859. The ecstatic capability and artistic productivity were what pulled him out of his gloom; "A Word Out of the Sea" accurately reflects his original awakening.[42]

This interpretation gains support from a retrospective poem Whitman published in 1884, "The Dead Tenor," ostensibly eulogizing Signor Pasquale Brignole. The reference to "Fernando" of *La Favorita* indicates that Whitman was thinking not so much of Brignole himself as of the general influence of opera upon the poet's movement toward ecstatic verse. Brignole's death reminded Whitman of his early opera-going and the period of his transformation into a poet:

> Back from the fading lessons of the past, I'd call,
>   I'd tell and own,
> How much from thee! the revelation of the singing voice
>   from thee!
> (So firm—so liquid-soft—again that tremulous, manly timbre!
> The perfect singing voice—deepest of all to me the lesson—
>   trial and test of all:)
> How through those strains distill'd—how the rapt
>   ears, the soul of me, absorbing
> *Fernando's* heart, *Manrico's* passionate call, *Ernani's*,
>   sweet *Gennaro's*,

I fold thenceforth, or seek to fold, within my chants
  transmuting,
Freedom's and Love's and Faith's unloos'd cantabile.[43]

Note the use of "cantabile," which appears also in the self-review of 1859 for the *Saturday Press;* the "tremulous" timbre, "liquid-soft," which the soul of the poet "absorbs" through "rapt ears"; and the "revelation of the singing voice" presented, as in "A Word Out of the Sea," as a reminiscence of initiation into the sorrows of the heart and their transmutation into songs of freedom, love, and faith (a revealing trio of terms).

I would not suggest, as Faner has, that opera was the cause of Whitman's awakening as a poet; but I would suggest that Whitman felt a powerful association between his opera experience and his novitiate, which stirred him to remember *La Favorita* in creating an ideal initiatory experience in "A Word Out of the Sea." Death was always at the heart of Whitman's ecstasies; even in his youth he connected extreme death-consciousness with the power of the seer.[44] In the first flush of his ecstatic discovery, the paradisal visions, results of shamanistic self-cure, tended to be more prominent than the darker vortices of his adventures, but "A Word Out of the Sea" has a different preoccupation than the 1855 poems chiefly because the poet was accurately remembering the prelude to his role change (as opposed to its results, which are only indicated in the poem) and because he wanted to exhibit the religious confrontation and transcendence of an ultimate existential despair.[45] As the nation hovered around disintegration, the poet once again felt driven to such ultimates in voicing his retort from the ground of the sacred. In shamanism, significantly, each seance reenacts, in a new form and for a specific purpose, the crisis of the initiatory possession.

The poem dramatizes an achievement of control over threatening powers through a form of acceptance of them and a surrender of the self—represented in the bird's "possession" of the child and then an opening of ego-boundaries to the sea—which miraculously ends in self-possession and a stable relationship with the powers. The progression embodies a specific form of role-process by which the ground of affliction is mastered, its closest relative being the shamanic "call." As a few scholars have noted, this piece presents Whitman's "poetic epistemology," and its ecstatic structure can be related to the poems I have already discussed if we consider that the initiatory experience is a model for recurrent ecstatic episodes in shamanic practice.[46] Through a hypnotic relation with mediating actors which at first torment the child, a process of role transformation begins and a fusion of symbolic elements forms in the child's own "song," which represents a form of control over the spiritual realm. Such achievement assures the novice of a recurrent capability for handling disharmony and affliction. As I. M. Lewis says of the shaman's initiatory experience, man's ability to control his "spiritual environment" is asserted in the process of the self-cure; "And this hard-won control over the grounds of affliction is re-enacted in every shamanistic seance."[47] Such control is specifically a mode of sacred artistry, according to Andreas Lommel: "The essential factor in [the shaman's] experience of being called is the demand made upon him to become artistically creative."[48]

In "A Word Out of the Sea," the first step in the process of transformation is, of course, the gradual understanding of the mocking-bird's song, followed by a role-change through which the boy replaces the lost mate. The bird's call is hypnotic in effect, gradually accomplishing the substitution of boy for mate:

> *But soft!*
> *Sink low—soft!*
> *Soft! Let me just murmur,*
> *And do you wait a moment, you husky-noised sea,*
> *For somewhere I believe I heard my mate responding to me,*
> *So faint—I must be still to listen,*
> *But not altogether still, for then she might not come*
>   *immediately to me.*[49]

Beneath the patient pressure of these lines we sense the child's apprehension, his hesitation to accept the call even as he begins to answer it.[50] The boy's substitution for the she-bird is marked by these lines, a transformation whose end is spiritual union and resulting equivalence of the spirit "brother," mate, or demon and the initiate, until a more encompassing voice allows the boy to pass on to a yet more masterful identity.

Thus the initial "possession" of the boy by the demon's message gives way to a new relationship between them expressed as brotherhood, following a typical shamanic pattern: "The attainment of the shaman's calling is normally the climax of a series of traumatic experience and 'cures' in the course of which the extent of his control of trance progressively increases. Ultimately he achieves a stable relationship with a spirit which is formulated either in terms of marriage, or of direct kinship."[51] It is interesting that Whitman should drama-tize his spiritual brother/demon/mate as a bird. Leo Spitzer has seen in this poem an echo of bird-poetry with a long tradition in western literature, though he is cautious not to posit specific "sources." However, the role of the bird in this poem bears relation not only to western tradition; it has universal corre-spondences, birds having archaic connections with religious awakening and with the concept of the soul. They frequently serve as spiritual guides in initiatory experiences (including shamanistic ones)—a fact suggesting archetypal as well as "traditional" roots.[52]

Spitzer's well-known identification of "Out of the Cradle" as an Americanized ode is weak specifically at those points that differentiate the ode from shamanic phenomena. Like the ode, the poem is long and solemn in tone with a "lyric-epic" structure. It depends upon a "divine enthusiasm" occasionally reflected in "stylistic variation" and unexpected changes in rhythm and tone coincident with the "fragmentary nature of the inspiration of the poet."[53] However, as Spitzer also points out, the poem is antithetical to the aristocratic qualities of the ode: the erudite mythological allusions associated with a system-atized pantheon, the difficult language, and the association of a heroic subject with deific ancestry. Bearing in mind Whit-man's self-education in what he considered the origins of re-ligion (and particularly the "architypes" mentioned by Volney), we can meet another of Spitzer's compromises with Greek tradition: "Theoretically, [Whitman] could have borrowed ex-pressions of his pantheistic beliefs from the mythology of the Greeks, but in reality, he did away with *all* mythology, pagan as well as Christian. He replaces the pagan Pantheon by the de-ified eternal forces of nature to which any American of today may feel close."[54] Recognizing the value of Spitzer's reading, I suggest that rather than "democratizing" the ode, Whitman probed the functionally different sort of expression that may in its primary form have contributed to the development of the Greek subgenre. Rather than celebrating an "athlete born of Gods," Whitman's poem dramatizes the birth of what Spitzer himself aptly calls "the American national poet, the democrat-ic and priestly *vates Americanus.*"[55]

Considering the fact that Whitman's calls to the nation of 1855 and 1856 had been fruitless and that America was poised for disunion, the theory that "A Word Out of the Sea" is connected with a second vocational crisis in the late 1850s seems plausible. The review of the poem in the *Saturday Press* indicates a renewed devotion to poetry and a desire to awaken the nation; and the position of the mocking-bird episode in "Proto-leaf" further connects the crisis the poet had gone through with his commitment to democracy; there, after mentioning how he was awakened by the bird, the poet continues:

> it came to me that what he really sang for
>   was not there only,
> Nor for his mate nor himself only, nor all sent back by the
>   echoes,
> But subtle, clandestine, away beyond,
> A charge transmitted, and gift occult, for those being born.
>   ("Proto-leaf," 14.40)

"Inflating" his throat and "joyfully singing" like the he-bird mentioned a stanza earlier, the poet next addresses "Democracy!" "Ma femme!"; as he replaces the he-bird, democracy—rather than death—replaces the lost mate as mother of a new brood. Like the ancestral spirit of 1855, the mockingbird of 1860 would awaken his countrymen with his plaintive cries, reassure them with his triumph. Through the possession sequence—arising from fear and rage, a response to existential oppression—the religious answer to human crisis surfaces in the form of omnipotence. One is equal to all the vagaries of fate.

One intriguing implication of such an interpretation of "A Word Out of the Sea" has to do with the fact that death for Whitman was a potent metaphor for democracy.[56] In 1860 he refers to them both as "Mother," a fact that should be highly suggestive to psychoanalytic critics, as it implies the connection of Whitman's oedipal conflicts with national identity. (This is not to rule out the possibility that other, more personal problems intersected with Whitman's anxieties for the nation, as had always been true for him. Whatever problems of the more private sort he might have had, however, were subsumed by his more all-encompassing vocational role-drama.) Considering the deep ambivalence toward the savage "mother" sea expressed prior to the ecstatic climax of the poem, we can infer a profound fear both *of* and *for* the democracy the poet loved, a fear dramatically awakened in the period of "The

States'" intransigence and in apprehension of America's self-immolation.[57] But does the text itself support such an inference? In the 1860 version it does. Near the climax of the poem, after the boy despairingly asks for "some clew," he expresses in greater detail than in the post-1881 version the form of the chaos that threatens him and the promise "Death" will restore:

> O a word! O what is my destination?
> O I fear it is henceforth chaos!
> O how joys, dreads, convolutions, human shapes, and all
>   shapes, spring as from graves around me!
> O phantoms! you cover all the land, and all the sea!
> O I cannot see in the dimness whether you smile or frown upon
>   me;
> O vapor, a look, a word! O well-beloved!
> O you dear women's and men's phantoms!
>
>   (276.31)

The "phantoms" referred to here—with, as I mentioned earlier, a metaphor that Carlyle had used for the unawakened—can be none other than the democratic subject and audience Whitman craved (and addressed in both "Calamus" and "Enfans d'Adam"); the sense of his messages of 1855 and 1856 falling on deaf ears—and subsequent questioning of his faith itself—finds its parallel in the desperation of the mockingbird. The passage is very shamanistic, but Whitman deleted it when he wished to "clean up" the poem later on, for the intrusion of the "phantoms" breaks the poem's central fiction; the author's own torment intrudes upon the child's. On the other hand, the deletion also robbed the poem of its most direct confrontation with chaos, which immediately precedes the answer from the sea. Curiously, the effect of the deletion is similar—structurally, aesthetically, morally, and historically—to that of Whitman's revision of "The Sleepers," the excision of Lucifer's heir and of the whale whose tap was death.

"So long!"

One of the best poems of the 1860 edition, "So long!" has attracted remarkably little attention in the critical literature, though it stands in an important position—the closing one—in every edition of *Leaves of Grass* from 1860 on.[58] Here Whitman employs once more the ecstatic technique of implanting himself in the life of the reader—to enjoin us to transformation through our relationship with the poet. Here his rhythmic control is nearly at its finest and contributes to a rising expectation, a gradual "entrainment" of the audience in the visionary process that sustains his poems and his faith in democracy. The prophetic setting of *"So long!"* is so integral to Whitman that we can easily believe the defeat of Union democracy (as Whitman understood it) could have made him question his religious faith and made further expression useless. The poet crouches at the gates of the millennium, intent upon converting us in one final ecstasy: "What is there more, that I lag and pause, and crouch extended with unshut mouth? / Is there a single final farewell?"[59] A send-off to the reader, the poem emphasizes the motif closing "Song of Myself"—that of the reader, converted through participation in the poet's rite, picking up where Whitman leaves off. But in this poem the reader is actually the lover whom the poet embraces as his mate; Whitman has become the spiritual spouse. This fiction is the chief difference between the poet-reader relation of 1855 and that of 1860. It also informs the final lines of "Proto-leaf," which are symmetrical with those of *"So long!"*—the first poem ending with the poet about to "haste on" with the new lover and the latter ending with the poet's departure after a sexual union with the surviving mate.

The triadic dramatic situation is again important in this poem, its intended effect religious as well as nationalistic. Central to Whitman's religion is faith in the glad tidings of death, which in 1876 he would call "the last inclosing sublimation of race or poem": "As, from the eligibility to this thought, and the cheerful conquest of this fact, flash forth the first distinctive proofs of the Soul, so to me . . . the ultimate Democratic purports, the ethereal and spiritual ones, are to concentrate here, and as fixed stars, radiate hence."[60] If "A Word Out of the Sea" dramatized the poet's first awakening to the "proofs of the soul," *"So long!"* includes the reader in a drama that assures us all of immortality to help realize "the ultimate Democratic purports."

As Whitman believed the nation lacked leaders with true democratic faith, he believed it also lacked people with faith in death; a conversion in the one sphere would go hand-in-hand with a conversion in the other. The connection between death and democratic awakening is a ritual necessity, since one's change of status is marked by a symbolic death and rebirth. Whoever is not willing to die into the new world can be no democrat. *"So long!"* is an exemplification of the sort of faith Whitman would have us all die into, and from the poet's point of view, America's answer to him was to be the Civil War. Since the religious message is integral with a national purpose, Whitman does not shrink from including specific political messages amid his messianic pronouncements:

> I announce that the identity of These States is a single
>   identity only,
> I announce the Union more and more compact,
> I announce splendors and majesties to make all the
>   previous politics of the earth insignificant.

(453.11)

It is necessary to recognize the dubious future of these "announcements" at the time the poem was written if we are to appreciate fully the sensibility they reflect—one that waxes prophetic precisely at the points of tension in the national life.

Significantly, the trance-inducing "announcements" in the first fourteen stanzas of *"So long!"*—like the "chants" of the 1860 *Leaves of Grass* itself—move from the plural to the singular, the general to the specific, with the reader at the ultimate point of contact. The progression parallels that of the first half of "Proto-leaf." From an emphasis upon the democratic masses, the poet moves toward the theme of "adhesiveness," which in turn gives way to the life of the individual reader immediately before the ecstasy:

> *So long!*
> I announce a man or woman coming—perhaps you are the one,
> I announce a great individual, fluid as Nature, chaste,
>   affectionate, compassionate, fully armed.
>
> *So long!*
> I announce a life that shall be copious,
>   vehement, spiritual, bold,
> And I announce an old age that shall lightly and joyfully
>   meet its translation.

(454.13–14)

The announcements that thus converge upon the reader also help induce the poet's altered state of consciousness, which is marked by spiritual visitation, foresight, and symbolic death:

> O thicker and faster!
> O crowding too close upon me!
> I foresee too much—it means more than I thought,
> It appears to me I am dying.
>
> (454.15)

The rhythmic technique up to this point has contributed to the transformation of consciousness, the refrain, *"So long,"* coming in gradually decreasing intervals and with increasing urgency as the rhythm of the announcements builds, like a drum beating from a low suggestion into a furious tantrum.

As the sensation of death gives in to the orgasm of stanza 17, the voice becomes that of a possessed ecstatic:

> Screaming electric, the atmosphere using,
> At random glancing, each as I notice absorbing,
> Swiftly on, but a little while alighting,
> Curious enveloped messages delivering,
> Sparkles hot, seed ethereal, down in the dirt dropping,
> Myself unknowing, my commission obeying, to question it never
>   daring.
>
> (454.17)

The "seed ethereal" consummates a promise voiced in "Proto-leaf": "O I see the following poems are indeed to drop in the earth the germs of a greater Religion" ("Proto-leaf," 13.33). In this final poem, as in many of the others, the poet envisions the results of his sowing: "To ages, and ages yet, the growth of the seed leaving, / To troops out of me rising—they the tasks I have set promulging" (454–55.17). The poet thus sacrifices himself to the fertility of the nation. Given Whitman's view of death and his longing to be an American martyr, no tragic consciousness should be attached to these lines.[61] The whole of *"So long!"* is fundamentally comic; such expression is possible only after the tragic consciousness has surrendered to an intuition of triumph that has no reasonable foundations but apparently supports further life.

The further life we undeniably find in *"So long!"* A movement into the future, paralleling the death and subsequent "invisibility" of the poet, opens his attempt to make of himself a spiritual presence—"The best of me then when no longer visible—for toward that I have been incessantly preparing" (455.17). The progress to invisibility gives the poet the opening for a new ecstasy as spiritual partner to the reader of a later date:

> This is no book,
> Who touches this, touches a man,
> (Is it night? Are we here alone?)
> It is I you hold, and who holds you,
> I spring from the pages into your arms—decease calls me
>   forth.
>
> (455.20)

The poet is a shaman become comrade-deity and a resource for the nation's further realization. This transfiguration Whitman had striven for repeatedly since the early 1850s, though his relation to the reader reaches its most extreme concentration only in 1860. Hence the final orgasm of *Leaves of Grass* assumes our participation as it asserts the poet's success; the dead prophet is our mate:

> O how your fingers drowse me!
> Your breath falls around me like dew—your pulse lulls
>   the tympans of my ears,
> I feel immerged from head to foot,
> Delicious—enough.
>
> Enough, O deed impromptu and secret!
> Enough, O gliding present! Enough, O summed-up past!
>
> (455–56.21–22)

In the closing stanzas of *"So long!"* Whitman imagines a death modeled upon the shamanic ecstasy. One effect of this strategy is to assert the reality of the world envisioned through the ecstatic experience by actually communicating from the condition of being dead.

> The unknown sphere, more real than I dreamed, more direct,
>   darts awakening rays about me—*So long!*
> Remember my words—I love you—I depart from materials,
> I am as one disembodied, triumphant, dead.
>
> (456.23)

"So long!" was to remain Whitman's ultimate assertion of the connection between the unseen and the seen, the connection that undergirded his incorrigible faith in democracy.

As *"So long!"* uses the poet-reader relationship to enforce the democratic conversion central to the purpose of *Leaves of Grass* in 1860, it can also be seen as a good-bye to a young America. The nation was about to awaken to its "sweet hell within"—a hell Whitman would strive to inhabit as guide, nurse, and motherly friend. It is commonplace to say that the poet would see the war as America's necessary confrontation with herself, a national *rite de passage* in which instances of the faithful meeting with death would be proofs of democracy's success. Then how can we fail to apply the insight that the very principles undergirding social order also ultimately threaten it and that the central moment of the rite allows the forces of destruction within a culture's foundations to surface as a spectre of chaos? This was a vision Whitman had known from the beginning and which became only more urgent in 1860. After that, he could only guide his people through the perilous moment and interpret its meaning in the sacred landscape. All of Whitman's faith would depend upon the outcome of the Civil War.

CHAPTER FIVE

The Ritual
of War

*I*F WE WOULD interpret the Civil War as Whitman did, we must interpret it ritualistically, as a sacred event of which each episode, each character in its unfolding harbored symbolic value. Whereas before the war Whitman attempted to invent a rite, during it he tried to inhabit one; his perception of the war and of his hospital experience bears strong resemblance to our perception of his visionary poems. And if the war brought to the surface contradictions at the foundations of American culture, the restoration of national identity marked the successful completion of a rite:

> I have myself, in my thought, deliberately come to unite the whole conflict, both sides, the South and North, really into One, and to view it as a struggle going on within One Identity. Like any of Nature's great convulsions, wars going on within herself—not from separated sets of laws and influences, but the same—really, efforts, conflicts, most violent ones, for deeper harmony, freer and larger scope, completer homogeneousness and power.[1]

In referring to natural process (which ritual often mimes) and noting the engagement in necessary conflict—a descent into chaos that leads to reformation and aggrandizement of identity—the poet clearly betrays his sense of the war as a ritual initiation. In fact, Whitman likened the result of the war to a rebirth: "that parturition and delivery of our at last really free Republic, henceforth to commence its career of genuine homogeneous Union, compact, born again, consistent with itself."[2] The parallelism between war as a ritual process and Whitman's great visionary poems, which has yet to be consistently explored, brings light to his puzzling and often disparaged claim that *Leaves of Grass* "revolves around that Four Years' War, which, as I was in the midst of it, becomes, in *Drum-Taps*, pivotal to the rest entire."[3] Just as the war became the crisis of national identification Whitman's visionary poems had consistently sought to establish, his involvement in it paralleled, in the most important respects, his shamanistic role as a poet.[4] This parallelism appears strikingly not only in his actions during the war, but also in the quality of his recorded perceptions and in his meditative process.

America, "brought to hospital in her fair youth"

Whitman prepared himself for war's challenge in a manner typical of virtually all ritual preparation—by purifying himself in body and in soul: "I have this day, this hour, resolved to inaugurate for myself a pure, perfect, sweet, clean-blooded robust body, by ignoring all drinks but water and pure milk, and all fat meats, late suppers—a great body, a purged, cleansed, spiritualized, invigorated body."[5] The impulse to such purgation bespeaks both athletic preparation and a thoroughly ritualized stance toward experience. Whitman was not simply repudiating "unclean" habits of his "Bohemian" phase; specifically, the outbreak of war represented an important test of his visionary profession.

The calling Whitman adopted during this time illustrates forcefully his shamanistic disposition. As Asselineau has pointed out, Whitman became the sort of "mystical healer" he had hoped to be since 1855.[6] He did not operate in a state of trance, of course, but it was the psychosomatic effect of his hypnotic presence that he recognized as his greatest gift: "I should say that I believe my profoundest help to these sick & dying men is probably the soothing invigoration I steadily bear in mind, to infuse in them through affection, cheering love, & the like, between them & me. It has saved more than one life."[7] In a letter to Margaret Curtis, he says he finds himself particularly useful to patients

who are . . . trembling in the balance, the crisis of the wound, recovery uncertain, yet death also uncertain. I will confess to you, madam, that I think I have an instinct & faculty for these cases. Poor young men, how many have I seen, & known—how pitiful it is to see them—one must be calm & cheerful, & not let on how their case really is, must stop much with them, find out their idiosyncrasies—do any thing for them—nourish them, judiciously give the right things to drink—bring in the affections, soothe them, brace them up, kiss them, discard all ceremony, & fight for them, as it were, with all weapons.[8]

And again in a letter to Hugo Fritsch he characterizes his suit-
ability for his work in terms matching the elements that distinguish the shaman from the physician: "I will confess to you,
dear Hugo, that in some respects I find myself in my element
amid these scenes—shall I not say to you that I find I supply
often to some of these dear suffering boys in my presence &
magnetism that which nor doctors nor medicines nor skill nor
any routine assistance can give?"[9] As scholars now commonly
recognize, the reciprocal emotional dependence that we find
in Whitman's hospital experience fulfilled needs and ambitions that had informed his initial role-transformation in the
early 1850s and had contributed to the "adhesive" intensity of
the 1860 edition.

Whitman considered the heart of the national crisis to be
concentrated in the hospitals; his own role there was vitally
connected, in his own mind, with his ministrations to the
Union: "These days, the state our country is in, and especially
filled as I am from top to toe, of late with scenes and thoughts
of *the hospitals*, (America seems to me now, though only in
her youth, but brought *already here* feeble, bandaged and
bloody *in hospital*)."[10] Furthermore, he viewed the war as a
drama in which he plumbed the spiritual reservoirs of the
nation as he ministered to the wounded and dying amid a
hellish landscape, "the marrow of the tragedy" of the war:
"Future years will never know the seething hell and the black
infernal background of countless minor scenes and inte-
riors . . . of the Secession War; and it is best they should not"
(*Memoranda*, p. 5). The metaphor is telling: Whitman kept a
copy of the *Inferno* with him during his hospital-visiting years,
took notes from it, and, in his letters and memoranda, often
compared Dante's hell to war scenes or the hospitals he fre-
quented. The graphic descriptions of the suffering in "The
Wound-Dresser," for example, may owe much to the impact of
Dante's descriptions of infernal suffering—a connection supported by the motif of descent introducing the poet's journey
(accompanied by the reader) into the hospitals of the past:
"With hinged knees returning I enter the doors, (while for you
up there, / Whoever you are, follow without noise and be of
strong heart.)."[11] The association of a curative landscape with
an infernal one may seem peculiar against the background of
earlier American literature and European tradition; but it is an
association we find at the center of "The Sleepers" and directly

connected with Whitman's methods of purging or retrieving the soul to restore spiritual equilibrium to his community.

Other motifs derived from Whitman's shamanistic stance include the framing of war episodes within dreams or visions (as in "The Artilleryman's Vision," "The Wound-Dresser," and "The Centenarian's Story") and the imagery of soul-flight, most notably in "From Paumanok Starting I Fly Like A Bird." Even more interesting technically is the poet's adaptation of the visionary dramatic structure in "Song of the Banner at Daybreak" and "The Centenarian's Story," two rhetorically crucial poems near the beginning of *Drum-Taps*. "Song of the Banner" dramatizes the poet's awakening as bard of the war, prompted by the awakening of a child-soldier; "A Centenarian's Story" marks the transition in *Drum-Taps* from naive bellicosity to the tragic awareness informing a more truly heroic determination.

Though not one of Whitman's more successful poems, "Song of the Banner" is interesting both for its generic relationship with "Out of the Cradle" and "When Lilacs Last in the Dooryard Bloom'd" and as an example of how Whitman applied the "possession" motif to the war. As M. Wynn Thomas has explained, the poem shows Whitman facing the problem of reconciling democracy and war;[12] but the process of this reconciliation is intriguing in its own right, representing an improvisation upon the ecstatic structure fundamental to Whitman's visionary poetry. The central figure of the poem is a child-initiate whom the banner's song wins away from the father's attachment to material wealth and security in an oedipal drama—the banner representing the mother (American democracy, identified in one of Whitman's worst lines: "O father it is alive—it is full of people—it has children") and the pennant a phallus ("like a snake hissing," "sword-shaped pennant for war"). The process of the poem dramatizes the gradual "possession" of the child by the message of banner and pennant, paralleled by the poet's own awakening to the call of battle. At one point, inspired by beating drums and blowing trumpets, the poet flies on a vision-journey over the continent: "I myself move abroad swift-rising flying then, / I use the wings of the land-bird and use the wings of the sea-bird, and look down as from a height" (287.65–66). Ultimately, banner and pennant overcome the father's appeals for a secure passivism while the poet, possessed like the child by banner and pen-

nant's song, achieves a realization expressed in terms close to
those of the awakening of "Out of the Cradle":

> My limbs, my veins dilate, my theme is clear at last,
> Banner so broad advancing out of the night, I sing you
>   haughty and resolute,
> I burst through where I waited long, too long, deafen'd
>   and blinded,
> My hearing and tongue are come to me, (a little child
>   taught me,)

(290.121–24)

The end of the poem shows the sacrifice of safety and pros-
perity for the spirit of war, by which alone the nation can be
purged of its corruption. The oedipal conflict dramatized here
is connected to the psychological tension Whitman had developed in youth, the attachment to a mother both personal and
public, and the corresponding difficulty in relationship to the
"father," whom in this poem and throughout the Civil War
experience he unconsciously replaces. The war was to be, for
Whitman, a resolution of oedipal tension both public and private. Thus we have interpreted a psychological symbolism in
the "Washington photo" he kept after Lincoln's death, which
showed Whitman's spiritual twin and the founding "father"
embracing in heaven. In his "Death of Lincoln" address, the
poet intimated that his cohort's "idiosyncracy [sic], in its sudden appearance and disappearance, stamps this Republic
with a stamp more mark'd and enduring than any yet given by
any one man—(more even than Washington's;)" (*Memoranda,* p. 11).

"The Centenarian's Story," another dramatic poem, does
not make prominent use of the hypnotic process represented
in "Song of the Banner," but it is organized as a "frame tale" in
which the narrative of the "Centenarian" operates with ritualistic and rhetorical intentions similar to those of the Revolutionary War episodes in "The Sleepers" and "Song of Myself."
The framed narrative of the veteran's vision/remembrance replaces the possession motif of the 1855 poems. Many elements of visionary experience recur here as the old warrior
sees the Brooklyn training ground "repeopled from graves"
and his "blind eyes" conjure up a battle of the past—the same
battle, in fact, that Whitman had recounted in "The Sleepers."
The slaughter of the southern youths defending Brooklyn is

identified, implicitly, with the Union defeat at the first battle of Bull Run, and the centenarian's final words, concerning the look on Washington's face as he retreated after his first battle—

> Every one else seem'd fill'd with gloom,
> Many no doubt thought of capitulation.
> But when my General pass'd me,
> As he stood in his boat and look'd toward the coming sun,
> I saw something different from capitulation.
>
> (298–99.89–93)

—are best read in connection with Whitman's statement about Lincoln's determination following the Union's stunning loss in the first test of northern troops:

> The President, recovering himself, begins that very night—sternly, rapidly sets about the work of reorganizing his forces, and placing himself in positions for future and greater work. If there were nothing else of Abraham Lincoln for history to stamp him with, it is enough to send him *with his wreath* to the memory of all future time, that he endured that hour, that day, bitterer than gall—indeed a crucifixion day—that it did not conquer him—that he unflinchingly stemm'd it, and resolv'd to lift himself and the Union out of it. (*Memoranda*, p. 62n., my emphasis)

Interestingly, in Whitman's "Washington-Lincoln photo" Lincoln received his "wreath" *from the father* as he was welcomed into the heavenly pantheon. The ironic reversal of northern and southern roles in "The Centenarian's Story" argues for the deeper blood-brotherhood of North and South (and perhaps oedipal replacement of the southern founder); it also exemplifies Whitman's ritualized, "synchronic" perspective upon historical events, essentially typological in effect. This quality is especially marked in the poem's *"Terminus"*: "The two, the past and present, have interchanged, / I myself as connecter, as chansonnier of a great future, am now speaking" (299.95–96).

If Whitman found in the opening of the secession conflict reason for beating the drum and comparing contemporary history with the heroic past, "A Centenarian's Story" also records the first glimmering in the North of what war might bring in loss and sorrow. The poem thus marks an important transition in *Drum-Taps* as the cluster is traditionally perceived.[13] Just as important as the newly tragic tone, however, is the fact that after the initial burst of bellicosity and his entry into the hospitals, Whitman began to find in life a reality as "spiritual" as his previous imaginative experience. Consider, for instance, his statement in a letter to Emerson of 17 January 1863, that in the hospitals he had discovered "a medium world, advanced between our well-known practised one of body and of mind, and one there may-be somewhere on beyond, we dream of, of the soul."[14] Our interpretation of this statement gains immensely in depth when we acknowledge the ritualistic nature of Whitman's perception. The "medium world" is no longer a landscape of the poet's imagination, but a world historically evident—the matter of sacred history, a fulfillment of prophecy and antitype of an earlier sacred moment of creation. Hence, what might have appeared earlier in the Whitman canon as a Revolutionary War scene in a possession sequence within an ecstatic poem appears now as immediate experience; life radiates with the aura of the ecstasy, and the poem, when true to the experience that delivers it, will be only a scene clipped from the unfolding life.[15] Passages of the *Memoranda* and letters reveal the poet's instinctive tendency to mime episodes of his earlier poems as he identifies with the wounded and dying:

> these thousands, and tens and twenties of thousands of American young men, badly wounded, all sorts of wounds, operated on, pallid with diarrhea, languishing, dying with fever, pneumonia, &c. open a new world somehow to me, giving closer insights, new things, exploring deeper mines than any yet, showing our humanity, (I sometimes put myself in fancy in the cot, with typhoid, or under the knife,) tried by terrible, fearfulest tests, probed deepest, the living soul's, the body's tragedies, bursting the petty bonds of art.[16]

One cannot help thinking of the surgical scene following the fight of the *Bonhomme Richard* in "Song of Myself" and the poet's testimonial, "I am the man, I suffered, I was there." Consider the pattern of his further meditations in a letter to Nathaniel Bloom and John Gray, the crest of omnipotence rising over the shoals of death:

> To these, what are your dramas and poems, even the oldest and the tearfulest? Not old Greek mighty ones, where man contends with fate, (and always yields)—not Virgil showing Dante on and on

among the agonized & damned, approach what here I see and take
a part in. For here I see, not at intervals, but quite always, how
certain, man, our American man—how he holds himself cool and
unquestioned master above all pains and bloody mutilations. . . .
This then, what frightened us all so long! Why it is put to flight with
ignominy, a mere stuffed scarecrow of the fields.[17]

In thus comparing the "medium world" he had mentioned to
Emerson with Dante's underworld and describing the response of the soldiers in terms reminiscent of the discoveries
of both "Song of Myself" and "Out of the Cradle" regarding
death, Whitman reveals the natural arc of his meditative process as he mused amid the hospital beds of Washington. In
this sense Chase's charge that "Whitman's career of hospital
visiting became a substitute for poetry" is correct; but it does
not follow that the career failed to inspire poetry.[18] On the
contrary it gave rise to a new type of poem, the snapshot of a
sacred event—such poems as "By the Bivouac's Fitful Flame,"
which frequently have been considered precursors of American literary realism.

Most of these justly admired "realistic" poems—the best
of *Drum-Taps*—take place in a kind of netherworld. Whitman's "visionary grasp of things" was not weakening, but the
visionary stance was transposed as the poet witnessed the
unfolding of sacred history.[19] Thus, although certain poems at
the center of *Drum-Taps* anticipate realistic perception in
America, their motive is profoundly different from that of realism in the mode of Clemens or Howells. The world the poet
records is filled with sanctity. Furthermore, Whitman's intu-
itive habit was to think of the events he lived through in these
years as dream episodes. In the letters of 1863–64, we see him
emerging from the hospitals into the bright light of the Capitol
and blinking in the change of atmosphere, the shutters of his
mind almost jammed by the juxtaposition of two such different
modes of reality. This juxtaposition carries over into the Civil
War poems in which plenty, wealth, fertility, and the light of
day stand up against dimness, suffering, dream, and death. To
enter the dim, visionary, sacred landscape becomes the challenge posed by history. This mode of perceiving historical
events is evidence of a sanctified state of mind.

When we consider Whitman's memory of the war scenes,
the dream-like atmosphere he often cast about them, we are
struck by the entranced, dissociated sensibility informing his
point of view:

It was a curious sight to see those shadowy columns moving
through the night. I stood unobserv'd in the darkness and watch'd
them long. . . . Along and along they filed by me, with often a laugh,
a song, a cheerful word, but never once a murmur. It may have been
odd, but I never before so realized the majesty and reality of the
American common people proper. It fell upon me like a great awe.
(*Memoranda*, p. 29)

To show how this point of view carried over into *Drum-Taps,*
we can refer to the finest poems of the group, and the most
"realistic" ones. "By the Bivouac's Fitful Flame" seems drawn
from an experience like that recorded above:

By the bivouac's fitful flame,
A procession winding around me, solemn and sweet and slow—
  but first I note,
The tents of the sleeping army, the fields' and woods' dim
  outline,
The darkness lit by spots of kindled fire, the silence,
Like a phantom far or near an occasional figure moving,
The shrubs and trees, (as I lift my eyes they seem to be
  stealthily watching me,)
While wind in procession thoughts, O tender and wondrous
  thoughts,
Of life and death, of home and the past and loved, and of
  those that are far away;
A solemn and slow procession there as I sit on the ground,
By the bivouac's fitful flame.

(301)

The tone is one of awe, the point of view that of a man partly
dissociated from his own experience, which appears as a
dream in which the figures are "phantoms" and the procession
a liminal force of inspiration.

Another poem that exploits the processional motif and
emerges from the liminal condition is "A March in the Ranks
Hard-Prest, and the Road Unknown." Here the image of the
procession achieves the most compelling form Whitman
would ever give it as the parallelism between the night-march
and the human journey through life and death emerges forcefully after the officer's call, *"Fall in, my men, fall in"*:

But first I bend to the dying lad, his eyes open, a half-
  smile gives he me,
Then the eyes close, calmly close, and I speed forth to the
  darkness,

Resuming, marching, ever in darkness marching, on in the
  ranks,
The unknown road still marching.

(306.21–25)

In the anonymous ranks of the marching army, humanity melts
into one identity, transcending time and individual death.
Moreover, the association of the hospital with the poet's ritual
landscape is made explicit by the fact that the scene at the
center of the poem—the stage through which, in a sense, the
procession passes—is "a large old church at the crossing
roads, now an impromptu hospital" (305.6). Whitman's description of the scene draws upon infernal imagery made
dream-like with a flickering indeterminacy:

Shadows of deepest, deepest black, just lit by moving
  candles and lamps,
And by one great pitchy torch stationary with wild red
  flame and clouds of smoke,
By these, crowds, groups of forms vaguely I see on the
  floor, some in the pews laid down,
At my feet more distinctly a soldier, a mere lad, in
  danger of bleeding to death, (he is shot in the
  abdomen).

(305.8–11)

The technique of moving from a description of the infernal
landscape to that of indistinct crowds of sufferers, thence to
particular notice of an individual, no doubt owes much to
Dante; yet here the hell is also hospital and place of worship
(indicating a theatre of shamanistic descent), and the youth's
death bears the aura of a benediction. Moreover, the procession that leads the poet through the church-hospital expresses
intense communality and bears onward the liminal quality that
emerges, indirectly, from the drenched sacral atmosphere of
the poem.

Many of the "realistic" *Drum-Taps* poems seem written by
a man immersed. Graceful, undulating rhythms permeate his
visions of even the most unlikely scenes—that of "An Army
Corps on the March," for instance:

With its cloud of skirmishers in advance,
With now the sound of a single shot snapping like a whip,
  and now an irregular volley,
The swarming ranks press on and on, the dense brigades
  press on,

Glittering dimly, toiling under the sun—the dust-cover'd
men,
In columns rise and fall to the undulations of the ground,
With artillery interspers'd—the wheels rumble, the horses
sweat,
As the army corps advances.

(301)

At first reading this piece might seem the least likely of Whitman's poems to be connected with his visionary sensibility, yet the entire atmosphere of the poem is really tidal, the cacophany suggested by the second line swallowed up in Whitman's characteristically wave-like rhythm and images of ranks pressing on, of columns rising and falling, part of a vision framed effectively by the short, echoing first and last lines. In *Specimen Days* Whitman would use similar imagery in commenting on Lincoln's death: "The soldier drops, sinks like a wave—but the ranks of the ocean eternally press on. Death does its work . . . but the Nation is immortal."[20]

The sense of immersion, which appears in "The Sleepers," "Song of Myself," and "When Lilacs Last in the Dooryard Bloom'd" as a reflection of the state of trance and underworld descent, informed Whitman's general experience of the war:

> More and more, in my recollections of that period, and through its varied, multitudinous oceans and murky whirls, appear the central resolution and sternness of the bulk of the average American People, animated in Soul by a definite purpose, though sweeping and fluid as some great storm—the Common People, emblemised in thousands of specimens of first-class Heroism, steadily accumulating, (no regiment, no company, hardly a file of men, North or South, the last three years, without such first-class specimens.) (*Memoranda*, p. 4)

The imagery of a fluid environment and of whirling forces—universally associated with dream, trance, or underworld experience—lends its effect also to the brief poem "Quicksand Years," in which the one firm reality is "the great and strong-possess'd soul," faithful to the poet while the years "whirl" him toward unknown destinations. These destinations finally became clear as the war drew to a close. And again the distinctly "ecstatic" nature of Whitman's response to the war (even as it ended) begs comparison with central episodes in his earliest visionary poems. As we know, those poems generally lead to an emergence into "light and air" and a perception of cosmic equilibrium coincident with cure. Such was Whitman's sense also at the close of the war, as he testified in the *Memoranda:* "Out of all the affairs of this world of woe and passion, of failure and disorder and dismay, was there really come the confirm'd, unerring sign of plan, like a shaft of pure light—of rightful rule—of God?" (*Memoranda,* p. 46).

Glad for an end of the suffering and for the nation's re-unification, the poet yet retained his reverence for the demonic spirit of war that he had sensed as a possessing force. That spirit he could not dismiss without propitiation in such poems as "Spirit Whose Work Is Done," a piece informed by many of the shamanistic motifs we have noted in earlier visionary works:

> Spirit of many a solemn day and many a savage scene—
>   electric spirit,
> That with muttering voice through the war now closed,
>   like a tireless phantom flitted,
> Rousing the land with breath of flame, while you beat
>   and beat the drum,
> Now as the sound of the drum, hollow and harsh to the
>   last, reverberates round me,
> . . . .
> Touch my mouth ere you depart, press my lips close,
> Leave me your pulses of rage—bequeath them to me—
>   fill me with currents convulsive,
> Let them scorch and blister out of my chants when
>   you are gone,
> Let them identify you to the future in these songs.
>
> (324–25.4–7, 15–18)

The poem expresses sorrow at the departure of a beloved spirit; but is there not also a hint of propitiation in the poet's wish to "identify" that spirit to the future, thereby insuring that it shall cease to stalk the nation in a role no longer desirable? The last four lines of the poem beg for an aggrandizement of the poet's power through the spirit's acquiescence in his purposes.

The propitiatory function is notable also in "Ashes of Sol-diers," originally of *Drum-Taps* but later moved to the "Songs of Parting" cluster. The poem praises the dead of the war as it conducts them to their "resting place" and invokes spiritual aid to purge the nation of war's lingering influence—the dan-

THE ECSTATIC WHITMAN • 148

ger of continued disharmony. In a visionary, "retrospective" trance the poet first calls upon all dead soldiers to gather round him in a spiritual procession, led not by war-drums,

> But aside from these and the marts of wealth and the crowded
> promenade,
> Admitting around me comrades close unseen by the rest
> and voiceless,
> The slain elate and alive again, the dust and debris alive,
> I chant this chant of my silent soul in the name of all
> dead soldiers.
>
> (491.19–22)

The relationship between the poet and his dead comrades strongly echoes that between the poet and his friends, living and dead, in "These I, Singing in Spring."

> Faces so pale with wondrous eyes, very dear, gather closer
> yet,
> Draw close, but speak not.
>
> Phantoms of countless lost,
> Invisible to the rest henceforth become my companions,
> Follow me ever—desert me not while I live.
>
> (491.23–27)

If "These I Singing in Spring" dramatized the discovery of symbolic resources for a new poetic group ("Calamus") in 1860, "Ashes of Soldiers," curiously parallel in many respects, seems closely linked to the inspiration of "When Lilacs Last in the Dooryard Bloom'd." The domination of "perfume" and love, the vision of the war "resuming," the interest in embalming, "bathing" the memories of the dead and making ashes "to nourish and blossom"—all seem closely related to the inspiration of Whitman's ceremony for the dead president. "Ashes of Soldiers" is, in fact, an important link in the chain that connects "Calamus," *Drum-Taps,* and "Lilacs." Praise and the promise of faithful love calm vengeful passions while the foetor of death is purified into wholesome perfume and the ashes of the dead made finally to nourish rather than haunt the living:

> Sweet are the blooming cheeks of the living—sweet are
> the musical voices sounding,
> But sweet, ah sweet, are the dead with their silent eyes.

Dearest comrades, all is over and long gone,
But love is not over—and what love, O comrades!
Perfume from battle-fields rising, up from the foetor
  arising.

Perfume therefore my chant, O love, immortal love,
Give me to bathe the memories of all dead soldiers,
Shroud them, embalm them, cover them all over with tender
  pride.

Perfume all—make all wholesome,
Make these ashes to nourish and blossom,
O love, solve all, fructify all with the last chemistry.

Give me exhaustless, make me a fountain,
That I exhale love from me wherever I go like a moist
  perennial dew,
For the ashes of all dead soldiers South or North.

(492.28–41)

"When Lilacs Last in the Dooryard Bloom'd"

As "Ashes of Soldiers" implies, Whitman interpreted the war not simply as deliverance, but as a purging experience that also made possible new life. No event so condensed these meanings as the assassination of the American Osiris, President Lincoln. "The actual murder," as Whitman described it, "transpired with the quiet and simplicity of any commonest occurrence—the bursting of a bud or pod in the growth of vegetation, for instance."[21] And in another context he claimed, "The tragic splendor of [Lincoln's] death, purging, illuminating all, throws round his form, his head, an aureole that will remain and will grow brighter through time, while History lives, and love of Country lasts" (*Memoranda*, p. 49). A tragic and sacred culmination of centuries of western history had finally condensed America into a nation and "rung down the curtain" forever on lingering feudal influences and disunion.[22] Whitman's calling in this instance was not simply to articulate or assuage a nation's grief but to complete the rite of passage and purification symbolized in the historic event. Hence, unlike an elegy, "Lilacs" mediates both Lincoln's passage from life to death and the nation's passage from a wartime to a peacetime identity; within the poet's experience, these two aspects of the national transition have personal ramifications as well, but private crisis is thoroughly wedded to the visionary functions of the artist *cum* spiritual intermediary.

In "Lilacs," as in "Song of Myself," the poet mediates between the sacred and profane worlds within an essentially triadic dramatic situation, and the poem brilliantly integrates drama, narrative, and lyric in the course of a cycle focusing upon the ritual "journey" of the singing hero. A dual narrative structure allows the journey of the dead and the change in the poet to parallel each other and finally to converge immediately before the bird's carol. Similarly, the role process includes an orientation toward the grieving community (most evident in the narrative of the coffin's journey to its "burial house" and the community's envelopment in the "long black trail"), as well as an orientation toward the spiritual world (most evident in the speaker's awakening to the thrush's song). These orientations fully converge at the lyric climax of the ecstasy, when the speaker's experience becomes a "solution" of grief both for himself and for the community at large. Moreover, the lyric of the bird-poet, which shows the least orientation to audience, comes at the point of greatest spiritual concentration—it is the transforming center of the ecstasy, made possible by the poet's symbolic death.

A number of critical symbolic exchanges occur during this crisis and are important evidence of the poem's functional, ritual core. Perhaps the most telling of these exchanges is indicated, most obviously, by the disappearance of the coffin from the poem after section fourteen. The significance of this fact has been obscured by an almost universal failure to recognize the coffin as a major symbol; critics have noted a symbolic "trinity" where there is actually a quaternity.[23] The burial of the coffin, with the delivery of the deceased into the great "mother's" arms, forms, after all, the chief public occasion of the poem; and the speaker himself, as "bird," acts as messenger for the "delivery."

Jane A. Nelson has previously compared the ecstasy of sections fourteen and fifteen of "Lilacs" to exercises in which a shaman "'escorts' the dead to their final resting place and reveals for the community the significance and nature of the experience of death."[24] The practice of escorting the dead assures spiritual, and therefore social, equilibrium; it derives from the perception of a link between earthly affairs and those of the underworld, a respect for hidden causes of disharmony that the shaman is particularly suited to manipulate. Yet it also incorporates the basic structure and function of a rite of passage, for the community and purportedly for the deceased, who must be conveyed to a new status, a new mode of "existence" in the hidden world. As the community participates vicariously in an experience that illuminates the meaning of death, it also undergoes a transition toward a new equilibrium without the person that has died. (This is, of course, all the more true when that person is the symbolic "head" of the society.) It can better accomplish the transition insofar as the person's death acquires a rationale and symbolism that strengthen the identity of the surviving community, thereby inverting the threat of disintegration posed by death—and especially by assassination.

Any rite of passage entails the momentary destruction of a system of differences that normally defines both the status or identity being left behind and that being newly assumed. The moment of transition is the liminal core of the rite, requiring contact with higher level transformational principles, a "transcendent" ground that provides both the meaning of status distinctions and the possibility of their dissolution or reorientation.[25] In suspending the boundaries between two antithetical states along a socially or historically defined (horizontal) axis, however (e.g., boy and man; person living and person dead; nation at war and nation at peace), the liminal moment also violates the distinction between the sacred and the profane, as quotidian affairs are inundated with spiritual "realities."

The higher-level "transcendent" principles or symbols that are drawn upon in the climax of the liminal rite situation "are defined . . . with reference to the specific states or statuses that form the terminal points of the ritual."[26] As "Lilacs" mediates the transition between states of war and peace ("death" and "rebirth") in national identity—paralleling a transition between states of life and death in Lincoln's identity—it does so climactically by dramatizing the courtship and even celebration of death as the "deliveress" and mother to which the nation's leader and all the soldiers of the war return for rest. (As they are "delivered" into a peaceful condition, the republic is "reborn" out of the compost they comprise.) This is a most appropriate strategy, and it does not by any means indicate a rejection of Whitman's earlier views of the "dark mother," but rather an adaptation of the ecstatic process to its occasion.

If the "dark mother" serves, however, as the transcendent

symbol presiding over the passage of the nation and its former leader from one state of being to another, "Lilacs" also brings together two normally antagonistic attitudes to death at the moment of transformation. In order for the passage to occur, sacred and profane orientations must be fused momentarily in a dangerous connection through the poet himself—who exists, for that moment of fusion, in a state of symbolic death (at the threshold between "appearance" and "reality"). Hence, the profane "thought" of death and the "sacred knowledge of death"—represented specifically as spectral companions— hold either hand of the poet as he enters the swamp in the moment preparatory to the bird's climactic aria.

The transformational process of "Lilacs" depends upon the complex interrelationships between the four major symbols that are subordinate to and embraced by the dark mother. These four symbols operate simultaneously on three different levels of significance relating to the problem of death: historical occurrence versus perennial recurrence, sacred versus profane understanding, and public versus private response. The poem's first five stanzas introduce two perennial and two historical symbols: lilac and star appear annually to precipitate the poet's observance; bird and coffin are historically "fixed" except by virtue of the ritual reenactment. Each of these symbolic pairs includes one symbol associated with the "sacred knowledge" of immortality or "death's outlet song of life" (lilac and thrush) and one symbol totally lacking in this value, connected instead with the profane "thought" of death (star and coffin). Furthermore, each of *these* pairs (sacred and profane) includes one "shy," "private" symbol (star and bird) and one "exposed," "public" symbol (lilac and coffin).[27] Finally, of the "private" symbol pair and the "public" symbol pair, each includes both a perennial and a nonperennial element. The matrix of oppositions is striking for both its economy and its comprehensiveness with relation to the problem of death which is the poem's occasion.

Lilac	Star	Thrush	Coffin
perennial	perennial	historical	historical
"sacred knowledge"	profane "thought"	"sacred knowledge"	profane "thought"
public	private	private	public

If this schema seems excessively formal, it is because "Lilacs" is by far the most complexly and carefully ordered of all Whitman's poems—the most truly ceremonial of his performances.

CHAPTER FIVE • 153

In emotional terms the two perennial symbols, which first evoke the ceremonial situation by reminding the poet of the season of Lincoln's death, directly oppose each other. The opposition resounds powerfully in the contrast between sections two and three, which introduce the symbols. Section two is dominated by the exclamations of a voice gasping in helpless grief:

> O powerful western fallen star!
> O shades of night—O moody, tearful night!
> O great star disappear'd—O the black murk that hides the star!
> O cruel hands that hold me powerless—O helpless soul of me!
> O harsh surrounding cloud that will not free my soul.
>
> (329.7–11)

The constricted vocal quality and broken lines stand in direct opposition to the succeeding section three, which introduces the lilac. Here serenely flowing lines, an extended sentence that moves calmly to a poised ending, complement images equally opposed to those associated with the star:

> In the dooryard fronting an old farm-house near the white-wash'd palings,
> Stands the lilac-bush tall-growing with heart-shaped leaves of rich green,
> With many a pointed blossom rising delicate, with the perfume strong I love,
> With every leaf a miracle—and from this bush in the dooryard,
> With delicate-color'd blossoms and heart-shaped leaves of rich green,
> A sprig with its flower I break.
>
> (329.12–17)

Whereas section two ends with an image of "cruel hands" holding the poet powerless, at the end of section three with his hands he willfully breaks off a sprig from the "tall-growing lilac bush," whose "pointed blossom" rises "delicate" with "strong perfume" by "white-wash'd palings." The imagery comprehensively opposes the "powerful . . . fallen star" hidden behind "black murk" while a "harsh surrounding cloud" entraps the poet's soul. It is significant that the star and lilac "hold" the poet before he enters the swamp, impeding his response to the thrush. Mentioned at the close of section thirteen but not at all in section fourteen, they also drop behind as the apparently equivalent "thought" and "knowledge" of death take a hand on either side of the poet and lead him toward the bird. If the lilac and star thus oppose each other, we might well expect some form of merging in the ecstatic heart of the poem. Indeed, the "rising and falling" aria of the singing bird, "as warning and warning, and yet again bursting with joy," fuses the qualities of the joyous, tall-growing lilac and the drooping, foreboding star.

In sections four and five, Whitman continues to introduce his major symbols; the connection of these movements with the previous ones is evident at the very least in the echoing syntactic inversions of key main clauses in sections three, four, and five: "a sprig with its flower I break"; "Solitary the thrush . . . Sings by himself a song"; and "Night and day journeys a coffin." Whitman's peculiarly ceremonial manipulation of sentence structure thus reinforces the coffin's participation in the symbolic level of the lilac and bird. Neither the bird nor the coffin is perennial, of course, except by virtue of the poem itself. Yet they oppose each other symbolically as sacred knowledge opposes the profane thought of death; when the poet answers the thrush in section fourteen the coffin is being buried. In other words his subjection to the symbolism of the coffin is exchanged for his "possession" by the bird. Interestingly, the symbolic oppositions here divide the oppositional relations between star and lilac. The thrush is withdrawn and solitary, "shy and hidden" in "secluded recesses" of the swamp, like the star hidden by "black murk." Yet its "song of the bleeding throat" is "Death's outlet song of life"—carrying a message of release and rebirth at odds with the tortured hopelessness conveyed by the star and closer to the symbolism of the lilac. The coffin, on the other hand, travels openly across the land, "amid cities," towns, farms and fields (where lilacs bloom) to where the corpse "shall rest in a grave," just as the star (which the poet says "will soon depart" immediately before he goes to the swamp) will set in the west. No "outlet" is mentioned here; moreover, the coffin decisively reflects the emotional values of the star (and its "harsh surrounding cloud") through the "great cloud darkening the land" that accompanies it to Springfield. The relationship between coffin and lilac is foreshadowed in grains of "yellow-spear'd wheat" "uprisen" from their "shrouds" "in the dark-brown fields" as the train passes—echoing the image of the "tall-growing" lilac "with many a pointed blossom rising delicate." Also, the poet places his *broken* sprig of lilac on the coffin as it passes him on its way to the grave; but at the end of the poem, he leaves a growing bush intact in the dooryard. Finally, whereas the coffin is *spoken to* early in the poem and is gone utterly at its end, the lilac is not spoken to until the end of the poem, when the speaker takes his "leave."

What I am striving to point out is a striking complex of oppositions between the four symbols that are introduced in sections two through five. Because of the interweaving of contiguous and opposing values between the symbols as they relate to death, the "dark mother," that transcendent symbol of an ultimate merging and janus-like "life-outlet" (*into* and *out of* death) has transformational power over them. Hence, the disappearance of the coffin and the giving of the corpse to the "strong deliveress" in section fourteen allows a decided shift in emphasis toward the symbolic values shared by the (nonperennial) thrush and the (perennial) blooming lilac, indicating the successful "passage" of poet, community, and deceased to a new equilibrium. At the close of the poem the coffin is not even mentioned; the perennial star, however, does remain to counterbalance what might be a too-easy reconciliation with death, a total abandonment of the sorrowful thoughts that are, after all, necessary to the tragic sense, intimately bound to love, and as important to communal identity as is happiness. Only the binding influence of the historical and public grief associated with the coffin has been relinquished, along with the body of the deceased.

Section six marks the beginning of a new orientation for the poet as he turns to actually address the major symbols (except the lilac). The emphasis now is not upon bringing symbols into the ken of a human audience (as in section four, for example: "In the swamp in secluded recesses, / A shy and hidden bird is warbling a song"), but upon speaking personally to those symbols themselves.

It is important to take account of the different modes of address deriving from the dramatic situation created by the poem. "Lilacs" as a whole seems written for the benefit of an intimate human audience that is able to identify silently the unnamed "comrade" who has died and to grieve for the countless victims of the war. But within the role process the poem enacts, the poet frequently addresses symbols (star, lilac, coffin, and bird), turning from the audience to face the nonhuman elements which he eventually masters, through "transcendence," by pivoting to communicate with death herself. Specifically, in sections six, seven, eight, and nine the poet turns away from the audience to address the coffin (sections six and seven), the star (section eight, where he reminds himself and the star of the murky communication foreshadowing Lincoln's death), and the thrush (section nine). In all of these apostrophes the poet expresses his subjection to grief, which is most obvious in the fact that he cannot tear himself from the hold of the star (and, later, the lilac) to answer the bird's call.

The lilac symbol he never addresses, however; there is a gap, rather, in which the poet, at a loss concerning how to prepare the "burial house," asks questions. It is as if he asks these questions of the bird, whom he addresses both immediately before and after the hiatus. The absence of the lilac is all the more noticeable because of the nature of the questions suddenly posed in sections ten and eleven (where, to complete the symbolic cycle, the lilac might have been addressed):

> O how shall I warble myself for the dead one there I loved?
> And how shall I deck my song for the large sweet soul that has
>   gone?
> And what shall my perfume be for the grave of him I love?
>
> Sea-winds blown from east and west,
> Blown from the Eastern sea and blown from the Western sea,
>   till there on the prairies meeting,
> These and with these and the breath of my chant,
> I'll perfume the grave of him I love.
>
> (322.71–77)

In section eleven the speaker goes on to ask what he shall hang on the chamber walls "To adorn the burial house of him I love." "Lilacs!" might seem the appropriate answer, but it is carefully avoided. Instead are suggested "pictures of growing spring and farms and homes," of grass growing, of leaves on trees, of hills, of cities, and of workshops. Elements with symbolic values appropriate to the lilac in fact dominate sections eleven and twelve, yet the lilac is not once mentioned as an adornment or perfume for the burial chamber. Neither is it called upon in apostrophe, as if the "seed" of the broken lilac has yet to sprout and the poet works around it with strategies of displacement. Conversely, the coffin—which has been addressed, and which is a dominating symbol before the poet's entry into the swamp—disappears from the poem when the speaker finally "tallies" the bird's song. Such exchanges, replacements, and echoes reinforce the mysterious resonance of the "burial house" in the theatre of the "farmhouse" dooryard where the poet apparently sings while lilacs bloom.

Whitman has carefully chosen the dramatic arena for his performance with reference to the interrelations between his symbols. Whereas the coffin journeys to its "burial house" never to return, the lilac with "heart-shaped leaves" returns each spring *in the dooryard of a farmhouse,* giving the poet the occasion for his ceremony. In Whitman's verse doorways most often represent thresholds between states of being—the "exquisite flexible doors" of birth, for example, or the "doors of time" ("hospital doors") he leads us through in "The Wound-Dresser." A farm in spring, besides being associated with a virtuous and "average" America, obviously evokes connotations of regeneration to reinforce the symbolic values of the perennial lilac. Such regenerative motives also inform the adornments with which the poet, prior to the entombment of the coffin, determines to prepare the burial house; they even match the qualities of the landscape through which the coffin passes on its way to Springfield (a destination Whitman declined to designate specifically, although its name must have tempted him). Just as lilacs are connected with the coffin and ultimately take its place, "returning with spring," the dooryard of the farmhouse replaces the tomb—decked, adorned, and perfumed with blossoming lilacs just as the tomb is adorned with "pictures of growing spring and farms and homes," perfumed with sea-winds meeting on the prairies of the midwest.

It is not only the idea of the burial house that informs the spell of the farmhouse dooryard, however; for the burial house is but the public space correspondent to the swamp that, in the poet's private transformation and illumination, forms the liminal ("threshold") landscape. The swamp is the interface between the sacred and the profane (on the "vertical" axis, so to speak), whereas the tomb is a place of transition on the social and historical ("horizontal") axis. The dooryard facilitates a theatrical montage of both the personal and public landscapes of action. In the original experience, the coffin entered the burial house as the poet entered the swamp. This parallelism suits the fact that the poet performs a sort of funerary rite, and the locus of descent in Whitman is often symbolized as a body of water—a natural, secluded place that allows one to perceive the connections between "reality" and "appearances."

An interesting gloss here is that in shamanic rites of the American Northwest the performer frequently mimes diving into a lake, a pond, or an ocean (which are regarded as interfaces with the underworld) even as he or she performs a ceremony in the house of death, in the presence of the corpse. Whitman does not literally enter a swamp in the (audience-oriented) "present" moment of his poem's unfolding but ritually re-enacts the entry that coincided with Lincoln's burial. Hence the role process that the poem creates allows the meaning of the farmhouse dooryard to unfold as both burial house and swamp—connecting them. In fact, all four primary symbols of the poem (lilac, star, coffin, and bird), as well as the two primary thresholds (tomb and swamp) and the audience-spiritual world axis, connect through the poet as he "warbles" his "lilac leaf" in the dooryard of the farmhouse in spring, courting and celebrating Mother Death.

In section fourteen the narrative of the coffin's journey and that of the poet's experience merge when the poet, looking out upon his land and people, is enveloped by the cloud that falls upon all, indicating his participation in a shared grief, a sorrow no longer merely personal. (Note that communication with the "murk"-enshrouded star, as opposed to the sight of the coffin and its surrounding cloud, is strictly private.) Only now does he move to the sacred wood from which the bird has been calling. In his movement to the liminal "recess" of the swamp the speaker enters an altered state of consciousness that has been induced by the combined influences of the thrush's hypnotic song and his own debilitating grief. Joined by spiritual companions—the "thought" of death and the "knowledge of death"—he is received by the bird in a setting that, as Jane A. Nelson indicates in detail, archetypally resembles entrances to the underworld.[28] At this point, engrossed in his spiritual experience and unaware of audience, the poet merges with the identity of the bird/"psychopomp" in a state of rapture and ritual death.[29] As the poet achieves equality with the possessing agent, the song becomes his own.[30]

In becoming the bird, the speaker both "dies" and overcomes his subjection to the condition that first prompted the ecstatic experience. He achieves transcendence by opening communication with the highest-level symbol (the mother) and, in the song, synthesizing the values of the four major subordinate symbols. As usual, Whitman "transcends upward," to use Kenneth Burke's terminology; he interprets the positive term of an antinomy as closest to the "essence" of the situation, although he gives the other term its full "existential" integrity.[31] When he finally does break through to "tally" the bird's song, the coffin (the other "historical," nonperennial symbol, opposite in emotional values) is implicitly being interred.

The function of the bird's carol has never been adequately understood, as most critics have focused upon the consolatory qualities of the poem, often against the background of the English elegiac tradition.[32] The poet does not simply seek solace in a new knowledge of death, although this is certainly one effect of the carol. Close attention to the language of the lyric indicates that the bird/poet actually "woos" death:

> *From me to thee glad serenades,*
> *Dances for thee I propose saluting thee, adornments and*
> *feastings for thee*

(335.151–52)

It is as if the bird, by whom the poet is "possessed," courts a god—in a tone similar to that of the address to the dead in "Ashes of Soldiers." We hear, successively, the initial invocation of (or invitation to) death, the praising of it, the chant of welcome, the implied report of death's response (*"Approach strong deliveress, / When it is so, when thou hast taken them I joyously sing the dead"*), dances of salutation and serenades, the placing (through song) of the soul and body of the deceased in the "mother's" arms, and finally the chant of joy and celebration *"Over the rising and sinking waves, over the myriad fields and the prairies wide, / Over the dense-pack'd cities all and the teeming wharves and ways"* (335.160–61). The hidden bird's song is wafted over the roofs of the nation, and as the dead "nestle close" to the mother, the poet's affliction is cured. Moreover, the reader cannot help but share—by vicarious regression—in the comfort provided here.

By including the American landscape and its inhabitants in the serenade to "lovely and soothing death" and then triumphantly "floating" the song over the continent, the bird/poet effectively merges subject and audience—as Whitman had done in most of his earlier ecstatic poems, from "Song of Myself" through "Proto-leaf." Furthermore, he establishes contact between the nation and the sacred ground of his rite; he "decks" the burial site with that nation in the same movement by which he woos death to "approach unfalteringly" and take the community's dead to her bosom. Hence the transformation in the country's wartime and mourning status (its passage from "death" to "rebirth") is achieved simultaneously with the transformation in the status of Lincoln and those others that gave "the last full measure of devotion," as the sacred and profane are fused by the liminal power of the song. The poet can then celebrate this achievement in a manner joining its private and public aspects. The public voyage of the coffin finds its transmuted echo in the song that rides over the waves, fields, prairies, and cities of the nation. All the axes of the poem converge here—in the very moment that the poet has miraculously taken on the identity of the bird.

The "tallying" of the bird's song completes the poet's service to the dead one; following the coffin's journey and the preparation of the burial place, it lodges Lincoln and his soldiers in the embrace of a caring mother. There is a correspondence here with that moment in "The Sleepers" when the speaker covers a body as a shroud and then has his sight unbound to visions of ancestral loss. Indeed, in section fifteen, which returns the poem to an orientation toward the audience, the carol of the bird gives way to the visions of Civil War losses it has induced in the poet—visions with direct implications for the community, and which implicitly enjoin the survivors of the war to put off grief. That the poet does not underestimate the suffering occasioned by the war is proven by this vision; it establishes his authentic sharing in the community's pain:

> I saw battle-corpses, myriads of them,
> And the white skeletons of young men, I saw them,
> I saw the debris and debris of all the slain soldiers of the war.
>
> (336.177–79)

The repetitive "I saw," catching the full weight of the human debris in these three carefully-timed lines, conveys the sense of burden connatural with grief. The poet cannot, on his own account, assuage the community's sorrow, but by attesting to the restfulness of the departed he draws out the causes of grief and makes possible their purgation.

> But I saw they were not as was thought,
> They themselves were fully at rest, they suffer'd not,

The living remain'd and suffer'd, the mother suffer'd,
And the wife and the child and the musing comrade suffer'd,
And the armies that remain'd suffer'd.

(336.180–84)

If the poem attempts to overcome grief, it does so not simply through consolation of the living, but by helping establish equilibrium in the sacred sphere and reporting that equilibrium to the community, at the same time accomplishing a rite of passage by which the national identity is transformed through contact with sacred "realities." This way lies an end to spiritual disharmony, the lingering destructive influences of the war.

In section sixteen the poet's "passage" indicates his emergence from his ecstasy, from night, from the spiritual companions (the "thought of death" and "the sacred knowledge of death"), from the call of the bird, and from subservience to the lilac and the star. This movement occurs in a direct reversal of the order leading to visionary climax—such inversion as we noted particularly in the gyric form of "Starting from Paumanok," a device appropriate to the pattern of descent and emergence, the induction and deactivation of the ecstasy.[33] Furthermore, by echoing the lines associated with the coffin's public journey in section five ("Passing the yellow-spear'd wheat, every grain from its shroud in the dark-brown fields uprisen, / Passing the apple-tree blows of white and pink in the orchards" [330.29–30]), the lines narrating the poet's passage out of the visionary experience ("Passing the visions, passing the night, / Passing, unloosing the hold of my comrades' hands" [336.185–86]) reiterate the union of personal and public functions which was established at the point of entrance into the swamp. And if the journey of section five passed toward the grave (and the swamp, the poet's "death"), that of section sixteen passes out of it, leaving the night, the coffin, and the dark cloud behind: both personal and public cycles of mourning are implicitly closed by the poet's action. Clearly the structure of the poem in this sense reinforces the idea that Whitman's stance toward the relationship between life and death has not altered radically since 1855. It is more likely that, as he so often claimed, his belief was only deepened by experience.

If the sense of immortality or rebirth implicit in the image of death as mother does not receive great emphasis, that is because of the poem's function rather than a change in Whitman's attitude toward death. From the point of view of a nation just emerging from civil war, the knowledge that the dead are at peace is of incalculably greater consequence than the assurance that they will be reborn, and this functional context should be taken into consideration when we interpret both the poem's symbolism and its participation in a larger social drama. Not the dead leader, but the national community as a whole is "reborn" through a symbolic sacrifice—"the bursting of a bud or pod in the growth of vegetation"—which engenders, in "Lilacs," "every grain from its shroud in the dark-brown fields uprisen," prophesying the spring blooming of lilacs and of America whenever the rite is repeated. Furthermore, we can see how the initiatory shamanistic experience has provided the skeletal pattern for this functionally different ritual exercise.

Charles Feidelson has said that "Lilacs" dramatizes "the achievement of a poetic utterance"—a claim that might be made equally for "Out of the Cradle," Whitman's representation of poetic initiation. In fact, Whitman repeatedly responded to crises in his life (usually connected with national crises from 1855 to 1865) by seeking symbolic mastery over them through ecstatic art, repeating the pattern of initiatory death and rebirth with results adapted to the situation giving rise to the performance. "The achievement of a poetic utterance" in "Lilacs" serves a primary social function and represents the attainment of control over a volatile and potentially dangerous personal as well as social condition. With this poem, Whitman put his seal on the war, announcing its end, dissipating its potential for negatively "haunting" the Republic, and imbuing it with a sacred significance only reinforcing, revivifying the identity of the Union.

I have been speaking of the poem as if it were a funerary rite, but actually the opening and closing stanzas, together with Whitman's complex manipulations of verb tense, indicate that it is a reenactment of such a rite, a form of annual observance rather than a ceremony conducted only at the time of Lincoln's burial. The ritualistic nature of the poem makes complex demands upon the representation of time. Consider, for example, the logical difficulty presented by the idea, implicit in all rites that are repeated periodically, that the contemporary performance does not simply narrate or imitate an originating event but abolishes all distance from that event in space and time so that the primary experience is radically "present" in the core of the ceremony.[34] It is not "remembered" but enacted. Whitman's genius was to overcome the difficulty such a necessity poses for a "monodramatic," quasi-narrative poetic structure, not only through the parallelism established between landscapes (swamp/burial house/farmhouse)—which effectively collapses spatial differences coordinated with separable moments—but by the manipulation of verb tense. The temporal structure of the poem is frame-like.

If we consider the bird's song as the liminal center of the poem—given in a "lyric present" that transcends difference in time, space, and human identity as the poet "becomes" the bird that warbled in an originating event that "really" happened in the past—and work in either direction from there, the frame structure becomes apparent. The song, given in present tense and actually composed of "performatives" or illocutionary acts (utterances that perform the actions they name), is preceded and followed by statements in past tense, which in turn are framed by present tense addresses to and introductions of the major symbols, which are again framed by statements defining the actual relationship (in "profane" or diachronic time) between the separable moments brought together by the poem. ("When lilacs last in the dooryard bloom'd . . . / I mourned and yet shall mourn with ever-returning spring.") Perhaps the most important effect of this manipulation of tense in concert with shifts in dramatic orientation is to heighten the effect when the singer joins his voice with that of the bird, so that we have the illusion of hearing the thrush address death and we "confuse" the moment of that address with our own present moment. We are "surprised" out of separation from the transformational event.

The use of the simple "lyric present" tense, which we find throughout the bird's song, gives an expression, according to George T. Wright, an "elevation" and "solemnity" that are "appropriate to visionary experience. . . . When poets use the tense, therefore, to describe their own actions or those of others, these actions acquire a faintly or strongly ceremonial character. This is especially true in first-person examples, where the poet, in announcing his ceremonial actions, seems at times to be playing a priestlike role."[35] The "priestlike" effect is heightened, moreover, when the statements embody illocutionary acts, as C. Carroll Hollis points out.[36] Although Hollis has warned against equating Whitman's role-playing process with the shamanistic process, his objections (as I have argued earlier) spring from ill-considered assumptions about the mechanisms of ecstatic role-playing and the status of so-called "natural discourse." It cannot be shown that the shaman's performance is more "spontaneous" and "natural" than Whitman's utterance—that *unlike* a "true" shaman, Whitman was "imitating" an ecstatic form of expression. To perform ecstatically is to wear a mask. The work of students of shamanism thus indirectly supports Jonathan Culler's answer to certain speech-act theorists' attempts to differentiate "fictional" from "natural" speech acts. As Culler points out, "There is a sense in which all speech acts are imitation speech acts. To perform a speech act is to imitate a model, to take on the role of someone performing this particular speech act."[37] Nowhere is this more evident than in ceremonial or prophetic situations.

The importance of "performative" illocutionary acts in ceremonial observances seems linked to the fact that their linguistic function corresponds to the function of ritual itself in the larger realm of social action. The ritual is a self-referential phenomenon, just as the performative speech act (particularly what John R. Searle calls the "declaration") is one. The ritual, like the declaration, establishes the reality that it signifies,[38] as in our well-known rite that climaxes in the statement, "I now pronounce you husband and wife." According to Searle, the success of the declaration normally depends upon extra-linguistic conditions, such as the respective positions of the speaker and hearer within a religious or social institution, but such conditions are unnecessary if the declaration concerns language itself, "as, for example, when one says 'I define, abbreviate, name, call or dub.'"[39] The bird's carol is in precisely this way performed—"I joyously sing the dead."

Furthermore, because the carol is an apostrophe, the peculiar qualities of the performative are enhanced. The "strangeness" of apostrophe, as Culler points out (the singer becoming that type of subject that can address the nonhuman as another "I")—its brazen artificiality that constitutes the poet as visionary outside a diachronic progression—indicates "that what is at issue is not a predictable relation between a signifier and a signified, a form and its meaning, but the uncalculable force of an event. Apostrophe is not the representation of an event; if it works, it produces a fictive, discursive event."[40] This, of course, is precisely what a performative speech act or a rite of passage does—the difference being that in the cases of the rite and the performative, given the "felicitous" conditions, a community agrees that the act is not "merely" fictive, much as they do in apostrophic prayer. We should not be surprised, then, that ritual "texts" depend heavily upon performative speech acts and apostrophe, nor that the climactic drama of "Lilacs," set in an "eternal now," makes use of precisely these techniques.

Framing the bird's song, which is the transformational center of the poem, the narrative movements at the beginning of section fourteen and in section fifteen are rendered in past tense and are addressed to the audience. It is as if the poet momentarily steps into "our" time to recount an earlier experience, in this attitude bracketing the more purely liminal, lyrical, timeless orientation. In "Lilacs" the audience-orientation, when the speaker addresses us and looks upon a public spectacle or landscape, coincides with dominance of the past tense and narrative qualities, whereas an orientation to the spiritual world and symbolic elements—when he looks upon those elements to conjure them up (as in sections two through five) or to directly address them (as in sections six through thirteen)—is marked by simple present tense, often speech acts with illocutionary force. Hence, the direct manipulation of symbols upon which the ritual process depends occurs in an "eternal present" dramatized for an historically-bound audience; the process is comparable, in fact, to a Catholic mass, in which the audience moves back and forth between participation in a "timeless" event and observance of a dramatic narrative, in the heart of which a priest in his sacred role utters apostrophes (prayers) and performs illocutionary actions (sacraments, blessings).

The only possible exception to this scenario is section eight, in which we do find past tense verbs; however, the section actually embodies an address to the star in that moment following Lincoln's death that the poem makes "present":

O western orb sailing the heaven,
Now I know what you must have meant as a month since I
    walk'd,
As I walk'd in silence the transparent shadowy night.
(331.55–57)

Clearly, the poet speaks to the star about his communication with it a month preceding the assassination. The reminiscence is part of a present act of address, not merely a narration to the reader about a past event but an act of intimate dialogue with a symbolic "companion." It nicely fits with the dramatic orientation held throughout sections six through thirteen, an orientation that will recur when the poet returns from the visionary state in section sixteen and addresses the lilac and star (the perennials), taking leave of them.

There is no question but that the bird and coffin are not literally "present" in our time; they are present only through the manipulations of the poet who spans time and space. On the other hand, the lilac and the star are perennial; they both were present at the time of the originating event and are again present from the moment the poem begins, as in the moment it ends. Neither the bird nor the coffin is mentioned in the first section of the poem, for, nonperennial and historically "fixed," they cannot be immediately recalled to presence. The lilac and star offer the required mediation by virtue of their seasonal return, which prompts ceremonial return. The positioning of these symbols in section sixteen, when the poet emerges from the visionary state and deactivates the performance, is carefully determined:

> Passing the visions, passing the night,
> Passing, unloosing the hold of my comrades' hands,
> Passing the song of the hermit bird and the tallying song of my
> soul,
> Victorious song, death's outlet song, yet varying ever-altering
> song,
> As low and wailing, yet clear the notes, rising and falling,
> flooding the night,
> Sadly sinking and fainting, as warning and warning, and yet
> again bursting with joy,
> Covering the earth and filling the spread of the heaven,
> As that powerful psalm in the night I *heard* from recesses,
> Passing, I *leave* thee lilac with heart-shaped leaves,
> I *leave* thee there in the door-yard, blooming, returning with
> spring.
>
> I *cease* from my song for thee,
> From my gaze on thee in the west, fronting the west, communing
> with thee,
> O comrade lustrous with silver face in the night.
>
> (336–37.185–97, my emphasis)

The poet's identity with the bird is relinquished precisely "in time" with the return of distinction between present and past, after the long dominance of present participles that hold our sense of diachrony in suspension. There is a subtle shift (almost obscured by the linguistic echo) between "As low and wailing" (which may refer to either the poet's or the bird's voice) and "As [passing] that powerful psalm in the night I *heard* from recesses" (my emphasis). This shift derives from the giving way of the close identification between poet and bird to the more "logical" distinction between them as well as the emergence from the "eternal now" in which the bird/poet's aria transpires; it is no longer the poet who wails, but distinctly the bird he heard. Moreover, the deactivation of the visionary state and of the performance itself mirrors the original induction of the rite situation, which began with lilac and star before moving to the introduction of the bird and coffin as objects of address in the "eternal present" of the rite. As he marks his passage from what he "heard" in the swamp, the poet "leaves" the lilac in the dooryard, "returning with spring," and "ceases from" his song for the perennial star.

The idea of a repeated performance conflicts with Whitman's earlier orientation, which eschewed calendrical repetition. ("Out of the Cradle" might seem an exception, yet it is not presented as a yearly performance.) In this respect the poem prefigures a major reorientation in Whitman's entire historical and poetic stance, a reorientation that would become pronounced in 1871 and thereafter, when he began talking about "the vast rondure of the world at last accomplish'd" ("Passage to India")—a completed sphere rather than an open spiral. Moreover, the foreshadowing of this reorientation specifically in "Lilacs" is indicative of a larger and more intriguing phenomenon. For Whitman's reorientation was impelled by the triumph of Union arms and the preservation of the national identity upon which he had staked his vocation. In Whitman's interpretation Lincoln's death was an identifying tragedy (like the tragedies of the Revolution), a pivoting point in universal history that marked the decisive end of feudalism and the opening of the age of democratic fulfillment. The war had apocalyptically answered the promise of the founding generation:

> There is a cement to the whole People, subtler, more underlying, than any thing in written Constitution, or courts or armies—namely, the cement of a first-class tragic incident thoroughly identified with that People, at its head, and for its sake. Strange, (is it not?)

that battles, martyrs, blood, even assassination, should so condense—perhaps only really, lastingly condense—a Nationality.
("Death of Lincoln," in *Memoranda*, p. 12)

Whitman's emotional release in the late 1860s can hardly be
considered apart from the "family romance" of national identity that had been so important to his psyche since youth. As he
composed "Lilacs," the poet was emerging from the central
challenge of his life, the task of his generation, which had
drawn upon the most intimate resources of his being even as it
symbolized the bond between those resources and the public
world of history. For the rest of his life, Whitman would go over
and over his war experience as a consecration, the drama
through which he had been saved. Hence the manner in which
he chose to enshrine Lincoln's burial—with what is easily the
most formal and the most formally complex of his poems.
Indeed, "Lilacs" is extraordinary in the Whitman canon for the
finished brilliance of its structure, its ceremonious perfection.
Almost totally vanished is the improvisational effect of the
poems of 1855.

Whitman's view of the importance of Lincoln's death and
burial to the "condensation" of the national identity helps
explain why the rite performed in "Lilacs" is presented as a
perennial one, an annual springtime observance.[41] To enact
the rite of passage by which Lincoln entered the shades as his
country assumed its postwar status was of central importance
to the poet's developing program. However, defined in the
opening and closing stanzas as a rite repeated year by year,
"Lilacs" embodies a form of canonization that distinctly differ-
entiates it from such poems as "Song of Myself," "The Sleepers," "Crossing Brooklyn Ferry," and "Starting from Paumanok." It shows a backing away from further immersion in
history's endless betrayals and denials. In the 1876 Preface,
Whitman would call one of the two "Pillars of Promise" sustaining his faith the idea "that all the hitherto experience of The
States, their first Century, has been but preparation, adoles-
cence—and that This Union is only now and henceforth (*i.e.,*
since the Secession war) to enter on its full Democratic career."[42] He told Horace Traubel, moreover, that since the war
he could no longer feel despair. His emotional investment in
the conflict was so great that he could not afford to question
the war's religious and historical significance. In fact, his hospital experience and Lincoln's martyrdom together provided

the hoard of faith in cosmic process that he would take with him to the grave. As the decisive historical crisis was purportedly over, the moment of sacred history answering the nation's founding successfully completed, it was left for the poet to begin a final "religious" project and then to construct his cathedral—complete with "inscriptions" and "annexes"—which we know today as the "deathbed edition" of *Leaves of Grass.*

In no poem after "Lilacs" did Whitman so successfully display his engagement with the condition of his country and thus reveal the connection between his art and broader social processes. Both Robert Bellah and J. F. Wilson have indicated how the Civil War and the death of Lincoln came to be interpreted in the "American civil religion" (or "public religion," to use Wilson's phrase) as a sanctification of the nation, introducing "a new theme of death, sacrifice, and rebirth" symbolized by the President's assassination.[43] It was a theme Whitman had already incorporated in the "ancestral" underworld episodes of his 1855 poems, one that Lincoln himself had expounded in the Gettysburg Address; and it lay at the center of Whitman's ritualistic interpretation of the war. Because of the centrality of this theme we have come to perceive "Lilacs" as the effective culmination of the *Drum-Taps* project, as well as the last great ecstatic work of Whitman's poetic career. But if we look upon the Civil War as a rite, then it signals a change of status and the adoption of a new identity that would only become reified in the moment of its consolidation. Thus the ecstatic poet must continually return to the "dark mother" for renewal of his visionary resources—or give up his job.

CHAPTER SIX

The Prophet
in Repose

*T*HE EARLY 1870s mark an important turning point in Whitman's career. "Proud Music of the Storm," often considered a companion-piece to "Passage to India," clearly indicates the poet's intention to shift his focus toward "Poems bridging the way from Life to Death," and in several of the prose pieces he wrote in the 1870s Whitman attests to his greater concentration upon purely spiritual matters, a turning away from the body and the material world.[1] Coincidentally, in the prefaces of 1872 and 1876, Whitman also betrays a suspicion that he has written himself out; indeed, critics generally agree that the power of Whitman's poetry declines in the 1870s (either with "Passage to India" or immediately after it). In *The Solitary Singer,* Gay Wilson Allen writes that Whitman's sense of having perhaps finished his task as a poet "was probably the result of his physical decline. The ideas were no longer bubbling to the surface; his emotions had cooled, and the images had lost their freshness."[2] Other scholars have noted the growing fame of the "good gray poet," satisfying personal relationships, and the resolution of oedipal conflict as reasons for a growing serenity inimical to the psychic tension that had energized the great visionary poems of 1855 to 1867.[3] Stephen A. Black sees a retreat from subconscious conflicts—"Lilacs" supposedly indicating that the poet will no longer embark upon the psychological "journeys" that increasingly threatened the poet's sanity and self-image.[4] Rarely is the nation's reunification considered a major factor either in the decline of Whitman's visionary capacity or in his shift of focus.[5] Yet the change in the status of the Union is precisely the most important factor to take into account at this critical point in Whitman's career.

Psychological interpretations of Whitman's loss of creative tension have merit, but they need not obscure the intimate connection between the poet's psyche and the historical drama to which he had pledged his creative resources. The crisis of the Union was the central and catalyzing fact in Whitman's life; his personal psychological state and his view of his calling were vitally linked to the fate of the Union. If the northern victory did not herald a golden age of democratic integrity and fulfillment, it did, most assuredly in Whitman's eyes, preserve the nation from the most immediate and ultimate threat to its very continuation. Any sense of national tensions or problems is notably absent in "Passage to India" and its companion-pieces. Simultaneously, the dramatic structure of the visionary performance itself has broken down, just as the personal confrontation with loss and chaos has all but entirely disappeared. Although good short poems would continue to bubble up until the end of the poet's life, he would never again produce the sort of grand, ecstatic performance for which he is most revered.

The tendency to minimize the importance of historical change in Whitman's aesthetic shift and decline derives from the desire to separate the "poet" from the "prophet," a reaction against the hagiography and single-minded historicism of earlier critics and biographers who hardly illuminated the aesthetic value of Whitman's accomplishments. The poet's reputation grew as critics of the 1950s and 1960s succeeded in differentiating the weaker, supposedly more "prophetic" verse from the stronger, more aesthetically satisfying "poetry."[6] Although this interpretive shift contributed significantly to developing appreciation of Whitman's work, the time has come to clarify the relationship between the quality of the verse that is both poetic and prophetic and the historical situations to which the poet/prophet responded. In Whitman's case when the "poet" and the "prophet" separated they both became infirm, and "Passage to India" begins to indicate the nature of the infirmity of each.

In the preface to his pamphlet, *As a Strong Bird on Pinions Free* (1872), Whitman considers the implications of the fact that "The Four Years' War is over"; the entire essay is founded upon the assumption that the nation, having passed its greatest test, has identified itself in material terms and must now realize its deeper historical significance.[7] The poet admits that in *Leaves of Grass* (as it stood without "Passage to India" and the other poems of his new project) he had "fulfilled . . . an imperious conviction. . . . But of this Supplementary Volume, I confess I am not so certain. . . . [I]t may be that mere habit has got dominion of me, when there is no real need of saying any thing further" (Preface 1872, pp. 739–40). He states his inten-

tion to focus, in the future, upon spirituality and upon aggre-
gate nationality—*Leaves of Grass* having been more concerned with the body and the "Democratic Individual"
(Preface 1872, pp. 743–44). These views emerge even more
explicitly in the preface to the two-volume edition of 1876, the
edition composed of *Leaves of Grass* and *Two Rivulets*. Here
Whitman compares "Passage to India" and its companions in
Two Rivulets to a farewell gathering "to close the plot and the
hero's career" as the poet himself escapes "for good, from all
that has preceded them."[8] Moreover, he mentions that the Civil
War, through *Drum-Taps*, was "pivotal" to *Leaves of Grass*—
the collection of poems written "from the age of 30 to 50 years"
(Preface 1876, pp. 750n, 748).

If Whitman regards *Drum-Taps* as pivot and catalyst of
Leaves of Grass and "Passage to India" as a farewell to that
work and an introduction to a new program, it is only logical to
regard the result of the Civil War as the crucial factor in his
decision to start a new collection. If the triumph of Union arms
marked "the closing of long-stretch'd eras and ages" and "the
opening of larger ones," "Passage to India" marks the threshold of a political and spiritual future which would have been
inconceivable without a Union victory (Preface 1876, p. 750n).
In the 1876 Preface, the poet sets up a clear parallel between
the change in his focus and the change in the status of America
as a result of the war. He asserts that in *Leaves of Grass*,

> composed in the flush of my health and strength, from the age of 30
> to 50 years [1849–69], I dwelt on Birth and Life, clothing my ideas in
> pictures, days, transactions of my time, to give them positive place,
> identity—saturating them with that vehemence of pride and audac-
> ity of freedom necessary to loosen the mind of still-to-be-form'd
> America from the accumulated folds, the superstitions, and all the
> long, tenacious and stifling anti-democratic authorities of the Asiat-
> ic and European past—my enclosing purport being to express,
> above all artificial regulation and aid, the eternal Bodily Character
> of One's-Self. (P. 748)

Thus Whitman implies a correspondence between the development of the national identity and the life of the democratic
poet-hero—a correspondence that is central to *Leaves of
Grass* as a whole. Throughout the 1876 preface, Whitman alter-
nates between talking about America and talking about *Leaves
of Grass* or *Two Rivulets*. The reason for this structural device
becomes explicit in the climax and penultimate paragraph of
the essay:

Thus my form has strictly grown from my purports and facts, and is the analogy of them. . . . . . . Within my time the United States have emerg'd from nebulous vagueness and suspense, to full orbic, (though varied) decision—have done the deeds and achiev'd the triumphs of half a score of centuries—and are henceforth to enter upon their real history—the way being now, (*i.e.* since the result of the Secession War,) clear'd of death-threatening impedimenta, and the free areas around and ahead of us assured and certain, which were not so before—(the past century being but preparations, trial-voyages and experiments of the Ship, before her starting out upon deep water.) (Pp. 753–54)

The final metaphor is critically important to our interpretation of "Passage to India" and the decline of Whitman's ecstatic poetry.

Just as the poet begins to look away from the body toward a spiritual world beyond death, he would have America turn more to its moral and spiritual purposes, now that her existence is assured. "Democratic Vistas" (1871) asserts that the Union, having emerged victoriously "from the struggle with the only foes it need ever fear (namely, those within itself, the interior ones)," must seek to develop its "religious and moral character." Whitman's essay suggests what the nation lacks and plots the future task of American literature and culture: "The problem of humanity all over the civilized world is social and religious, and is to be finally met and treated by literature. The priest departs, the divine literatus comes."[9] Of course, this millennial religious vision had informed *Leaves of Grass* from the beginning; but in the past Whitman had been vitally concerned with the very survival of the republic, with assuring her "bodily" existence as a prerequisite for the nation's grander accomplishments. Thus he came to regard *Leaves of Grass* "as the indispensable deep soil, or basis, out of which, and out of which only, could come the roots and stems more definitely indicated by these later pages" (Preface 1876, p. 748). His new ambition, as stated in 1872, is to express "the present age"— the world's movement toward a great "denouement" in which the United States would play the leading part: "And on these areas of ours, as on a stage, sooner or later, something like an *eclaircissement* of all the past civilization of Europe and Asia is probably to be evolved" (Preface 1872, p. 740). "Passage to India" dramatizes the inspiration of this historical vision.

However, the supposed absence of "death-threatening impedimenta" and Whitman's belief that "the free areas around and ahead of us [are] assured and certain, which were not so before" profoundly undermine Whitman's attempts at ecstatic performance after "When Lilacs Last in the Dooryard Bloom'd" (Preface 1876, pp. 753–54). In the past his prophecy had worked as poetry in those instances when it was precipitated by threats to American identity. "Death-threatening impedimenta" had created the battlefield for spiritual struggle from the beginning of Whitman's career as a poet, since conflict was integral to the kind of absorption upon which the ecstatic process depended. In "Passage to India," poetic omnipotence responds to neither intimate pain nor personal risk.[10] Hence, the poem creates a far less intense and less personalized dramatic situation than we have noted in earlier ecstatic poems. In those poems a moral and religious problem evoked through the political and/or personal realms of material life needs to be solved. The problem may be expressed in riddles or personal difficulties to be surmounted by way of suffering and transformation—often symbolic death and rebirth. The spiraling intensity of the poetic performance achieves focus in a transformation that answers the problems giving rise to the performance. But "Passage to India" dramatizes no personal crises, and the energy of the poem is diffuse, leading several critics to say that the poet's art has become "flaccid."[11]

Certainly the internationalist subject matter does not inherently lack the drama, the problems moral and material, that could precipitate ecstatic performance. Curiously, the technological development that Whitman sees tying the nations together has also been the greatest source of conflict between nations in modern times; but this paradox Whitman fails to envision. Thinking the lands shall inevitably be tied together—and in fairly orderly fashion—he immediately invokes the corresponding development on the spiritual plane. All "strangling problems" are of the past. Rather than giving rise to conflict, the developing technology only makes possible a new concentration upon spiritual matters.[12]

Similarly, far from seeing the inherent conflict between technological development and the union of man and nature—the union that lies at the center of his religious conception—Whitman sees such development inevitably leading to that union. Where one might find the challenge of a real paradox to be surmounted in visionary fusion, one finds instead a noticeable gap in the ecstatic process. Whitman has not kept up with his times—he has continued to meditate upon the sort of religious problems that had concerned him in the 1840s and 1850s; the trappings of modern times he finds superficially inspiring, but he does not feel the need to grapple with their full significance. My point here is not that Whitman interpreted technology "wrongly," but that technology does not work as an authentic force of inspiration in "Passage to India." The inspiring elements in Whitman's successful ecstatic poems are both beneficial and demonic—lovers and executioners. Technology, in "Passage to India" and several of Whitman's other late poems, lacks "executionary" qualities. Whitman is no longer at the heart of an historical process, an ongoing challenge to his vision of the world and thus to his faith in his own being. As Richard Chase has said, "Productive tensions have been relaxed, conflicts dissipated, particulars generalized, inequities equalized. . . . The deft and flexible wit disappears along with the contraries and disparities which once produced it."[13]

This is different from saying that the weakness of the poem derives from a "patchwork" quality caused by Whitman's process of developing the poem out of different fragments. Joel R. Kehler has persuasively shown that the typological function of the formerly independent poems, "Fables" and "Thou Vast Rondure" (now incorporated in sections two and five, respectively), justifies their positions in "Passage to India." True to the millennial spirit, Whitman's most important late additions to his poem heightened the sense of a typological relationship between mythology and history.[14] They did not overcome the fundamental weakness of the poem.

Religious typology controls the development of "Passage to India" and inheres in the drama of "fusing" man and nature to achieve a paradisal state of being. Whitman had long considered such fusion the prime task of the prophet and the ultimate resource of the poet—a miraculous cure for the afflictions of human consciousness. His speculations on this subject date from the early 1850s and the birth of the ecstatic capability by which he first sounded "below the Sanscrit and the Vedas," supposedly locating the origin of all religion and of all poems in a form of creativity equal to nature itself, participating in cosmogenic power. The paradisal state of ecstasy naturally figures the historical millennium; in "Passage to India," Whitman fuses his religious primitivism and his ideology of progress. The concept of "rondure" and the unity of mankind—the core, in Whitman's view, of past ideas of heaven—appear to be on the verge of fruition. This development leads the poet to consider the ultimate metaphor of rondure and democracy—death itself, the realm toward which he sails in the poem's closing lines. If we consider the difference between the idea of *rondure* and the concept of recurring cycles of birth and death, we shall realize that in this poem Whitman conjures the end of history; concomitantly, he reifies the ecstatic process and thus traduces it. Perhaps this result is ideologically necessary: as all religions arise out of the confrontation with death, the heart of all religions is egalitarian, and democracy is the "superior law" superseding and "gradually supplanting and overwhelming" the inferior laws of the universe—to Whitman, this process had been confirmed by the result of the Civil War. The millennial correspondence between democracy and death is inescapable. But out of the historical, universal triumph of democracy, what rebirth could be imagined?

"Democratic Vistas" provides the key to Whitman's purpose in writing "Passage to India." In the essay he explains that democracy includes but surpasses the law of "physical force" with a superior law of the spirit. The "law of successions" leads inevitably to democracy, just as religion leads to the vision of heaven and life leads to death:

> [Democracy] alone can bind, and ever seeks to bind, all nations, all men, of however various and distant lands, into a brotherhood, a family. It is the old, yet ever-modern dream of earth, out of her eldest and her youngest, her fond philosophers and poets. Not that half only, individualism, which isolates. There is another half, which is adhesiveness or love, that fuses, ties and aggregates, making the races comrades, and fraternizing all. Both are to be vitalized by religion. . . . For I say at the core of democracy, finally, is the religious element. All the religions, old and new, are there.[15]

In "Passage to India," Whitman sails toward the "myth of heaven" first mentioned in "The Sleepers" and descended from archaic visions—the democracy and unity of mankind that coincide with the fusion of man and nature (this fusion being ultimately death itself, which religious ecstasy symbolically enacts). "Proud Music of the Storm" points toward a similar religious matrix of archaic origin:

> As of the far-back days the poets tell, the Paradiso,
> The straying thence, the separation long, but now the
>   wandering done,

The journey done, the journeyman come home,
And man and art with Nature fused again.[16]

Man, art, and Nature become, in the longer poem, the "Trinitas divine"—man, the poet ("true son of God"), and Nature. The three elements are fused by virtue of the poet's miraculous capacities.

The only model for such a state of affairs is what existed before history—paradise. "Passage to India" develops in alternating considerations of the present and the past (and of historical and mythical versions of human experience), so that when the "younger brother" melts in the arms of the "elder brother," God, the poem reaches its climax and then looks beyond to the deep water. One wonders, however, how history can continue once the millennium has arrived. Progress leads to the end of any possibility of progress if heaven can in fact be realized. And since "Passage to India" from the beginning denies the possibility of any ultimate despair or separation, the "myth of heaven" loses its ballast of hell. In this poem the experience of defeat—of "dejection, poverty, death"—transpires entirely in the past.

The first section of the poem sets up the relation of past to present as that of ground to growth, projector to projectile. Section two accordingly turns to the past and instructs the soul, in its passage, to "Eclaircise the myths Asiatic, the primitive fables." A typological relationship thus surfaces, indicating that the present will realize the promise of heavenly visions:

Lo, soul, seest thou not God's purpose from the first?
The earth to be spann'd, connected by network,
The races, neighbors, to marry and be given in marriage,
The oceans to be cross'd, the distant brought near,
The lands to be welded together.[17]

The apparent inconsistency between a glorification of the "fables of eld" and Whitman's "worship new" appears in several of Whitman's best poems and derives from the paradoxical relationship between his primitivism and his progressivism.[18] The visionary spiral ends in a return to creative origins out of which primal fable, legend, and poetry arose. New in form, if not in essence, the religion of democracy ultimately supersedes all previous, less "general" ones, since political democracy embodies in the historical realm what previously has been known only as a spiritual condition:

> What Christ appear'd for in the moral-spiritual field for human-
> kind, namely, that in respect to the absolute soul, there is in the
> possession of such by each single individual, something so tran-
> scendent, so incapable of gradations, (like life), that, to that extent,
> it places all beings on a common level . . . —is tallied in like
> manner, in this other field, by democracy's rule that men, the na-
> tion, as a common aggregate of living identities, affording in each a
> separate and complete subject for freedom . . . must, to the politi-
> cal extent of the suffrage or vote, if no further, be placed, in each
> and in the whole, on one broad, primary, universal, common
> platform.[19]

It is important to remember that Whitman's faith in democracy
rests upon his concept of the soul, a concept coeval with the
awareness of death. In fact, democracy supplants earlier forms
of sociality chiefly because it trains "immortal souls."[20] Hence
all of history has tended toward political democracy as a prelude to spiritual fruition, and the visions of ecstatics have pre-
figured this fruition since the moment history began.

Section three introduces a progression found in several of
Whitman's longer poems—the catalogue of a vision-journey
across the continent, leading to an invocation of ancestral
struggles in section four:

> Struggles of many a captain, tales of many a sailor dead,
> Over my mood stealing and spreading they come,
> Like clouds and cloudlets in the unreach'd sky.
> ("PI," 414.69–71)

As the idea of "rondure," symbolized as a "rivulet," runs
"down the slopes" of history, rising occasionally to the surface, we sense the poet's visionary state deepening, the past
relived until it ushers in the "rondure of the world." The end of
section four provides an historical vision of the millennium
that suddenly harks back, in the opening line of section five, to
the mythic moment of Creation, "type"—or model—of the
millennium.[21]

The poet has deliberately juxtaposed a future historical
moment and a past mythic moment of creation, giving to his
vision the effect of "rondure" in time:

> O vast Rondure, swimming in space,
> Cover'd all over with visible power and beauty,
> Alternate light and day and the teeming spiritual darkness,

Unspeakable high processions of sun and moon and countless
    stars above,
Below, the manifold grass and waters, animals, mountains,
    trees,
With inscrutable purpose, some hidden prophetic intention,
Now first it seems my thought begins to span thee.
                                            ("PI," 414.81–87)

After recalling the rondure at the moment of cosmogenesis, section five advances to the separation of man from nature consequent upon the beginning of human consciousness; but as the earth is spanned the poet arrives to join mankind to nature again. The typology allows progression as well as repetition, and the millennium, of course, bears resemblance to a heavenly state of which religious thinkers have always dreamed.

If section five lapsed from the historical to the mythic orientation, beginning with the myth of creation, section six returns to the historical. The poet again looks back to the "cradle of man," but in this case that cradle is the Caucasus and the river Euphrates, not the garden of Eden. The progression of historical events then passes through Asia, the Middle East, and Europe to America—reaching a climax in the portrait of Columbus. Indeed, when the poet returns to the idea of "primal thought" and "realms of budding bibles" in section seven, it becomes clear that he has intended an alternation of historical and mythic dimensions—the historical represented in sections three, four, and six; the mythic in sections two, five, and seven. Metaphors of germination (associated with ecstasy), which we have noted in previous poems, appear in the transition between sections six and seven to bind the historical and mythic visions. Columbus's achievement, lying like a "seed unreck'd for centuries in the ground," sprouts at the end of section six. Section seven extends the metaphor in another field:

Passage indeed O soul to primal thought,
Not lands and seas alone, thy own clear freshness,
The young maturity of brood and bloom,
To realms of budding bibles.
                                            ("PI," 418.165–68)

Sections four, five, six, and seven all end with visions of sacred creation—visions of the paradise achieved in either the historical or the mythical dimension. One of the essential qualities of millennial speculation is the sense that mythical and historical dimensions, the sacred and the profane, shall be fused; heaven, in some sense, must descend to earth as paradise returns. Such is the message of section seven in "Passage to India":

> O soul, repressless, I with thee and thou with me,
> Thy circumnavigation of the world begin,
> Of man, the voyage of his mind's return,
> To reason's early paradise,
> Back, back to wisdom's birth, to innocent intuitions,
> Again with fair creation.
>
> ("PI," 418.169–74)

The apparent contradiction between the idea of a new religion made possible by modern science and the "mind's return" to "wisdom's birth, to innocent intuitions" is not new to *Leaves of Grass;* it had informed Whitman's way of thinking since his youth.

Moreover, in a classic pattern, the return to paradise (at the end of section seven) coincides with a moment of ecstasy—much as, in "The Sleepers," for example, ancestral "underworld" scenes lead to a paradisal state and the triumph of ecstasy. From a position of inequality with ontological conditions (time, space, and death), the poet moves to equality with those conditions, even to control over them. If, previously in the poem, the poet showed a "return to fair creation," by the end of section eight he displays his own cosmogenic powers, marking a radical change in his status. Whitman's typology is completed when the hero finds God, his "Elder Brother," and "melts in fondness in his arms" ("PI," 420.223). The soul returns to its source, and Whitman's doubling ends. In fact, this poem implies no circling back to the profane state of being, no emergence from the state of ecstasy. But "Passage to India" does not concern merely the poet's voyage toward the spiritual world after death; it projects a universal process through which the religion of democracy embraces all lands. As the new religion includes and supersedes all others, its fruition must be interpreted eschatologically, the hero's evolution serving as a model of cultural and world-wide development.

If Whitman could conceive of no ultimate crises for democracy after the Civil War, and if he considered democracy to be the promise of the ages—the state of society toward which all of history has tended—then how could the future hold anything but an escape from history? The assurance with which "Passage to India" is written, the conviction that all the crises of history are past, virtually dictates that this final visionary poem must end in the open seas and not in a return to land or an emergence from "mother night." Whitman has abandoned the cyclic structure of his previous performances. Moreover, "Passage to India" includes no healing episodes, a fact with possible biographical implications.

Exploring the psychological significance of finding the "elder brother" in "Passage to India," E. H. Miller has shown that the return of the prodigal son resolves a "psychic conflict" that had plagued Whitman from youth.[22] Yet if we remember the "family romance" of the poet's early years—his idolization and "adoption" of the founding "fathers"—his deepening anxiety about American identity, and his sense of deprivation and betrayal prior to the Civil War, we develop a more refined sense of the source of Whitman's reconciliation than Miller, who rejects the nationalistic and "prophetic" side of the poet, can provide: "There were no more variations to be played upon his themes, for the tensions expressed in the themes were now quiescent. Without tensions there is no need to seek sublimation in art. Before he wrote 'Passage to India,' Whitman had achieved some kind of resolution of his conflicts—when this took place we cannot know exactly, nor need to speculate— and the poems show the result: personal serenity, unfortunately, seems to produce a flaccid art."[23] Through the Civil War, America had justified Whitman's faith in her and in the cosmos; in "Passage to India," the poet justifies our faith in a democratic god and in cosmic evolution. He need never again leave the embrace of the "elder brother" or question his relationship with that brother. By way of analogy, consider the picture Whitman bought in Washington after the war and kept until his death, the one his friends found "queer" but which he was oddly attached to—that in which Washington embraces Lincoln and crowns him with a wreath as the martyr enters heaven.[24] There can be little doubt that the Union victory had profound psychological effects upon the poet whose "fathers" were of the Revolution and whose call to poetry had been precipitated by events leading to the Civil War.

"Passage to India" is not the work of a poet under the sort of inspiration that went into Whitman's poems of 1855–67.

There is never, in "Passage to India," an ultimate confrontation with despair. Thus the triumph of sections eight and nine lacks the power of comparable moments in "Song of Myself" or "The Sleepers" of 1855. (Interestingly, it was after 1876 that Whitman deleted the "darkest" sections of "The Sleepers.") Moreover, "Passage to India" differs from earlier poems by viewing transcendence as a progressive state of being rather than part of a rhythmic, alternating process of descent and emergence, death and rebirth, or ebb and flow. The change illustrates more than a shift in thematic concerns; it indicates a degeneration of the ecstatic process itself, the loss of self-dissolution and radical self-questioning. Millennial speculation has detached itself from the "agonistic arena."

One senses that Whitman's visionary process is hardening into a system and thus losing its dynamic essence. A case in point, "The Mystic Trumpeter," appeared in the pamphlet *As a Strong Bird on Pinions Free* in 1872 and in *Two Rivulets* of 1876 as one of the pieces exemplifying the new program Whitman had begun in 1871. Lacking the luminous personal intensity of earlier visionary performances, it imitates too systematically the poem of ecstatic prophecy. Moreover, like "Passage to India," "The Mystic Trumpeter" ends within an ecstatic state (not emerging from one), ringing "most vast, but hollow" in the forced emphases of exclamation points. Like "Passage to India," it ends with a millennial vision—an escape from the pulse of life, the ebb and flow of pains and joys that in the past had accounted for so much of the exquisite pathos of Whitman's finest lyrics.

The hypnotic force of inspiration in this poem takes the form of the spirit of an ancient trumpeter, an ecstatic ghost whom the poet courts to gain "possession" of bardic song:

> Come nearer bodiless one, haply in thee resounds
> Some dead composer, haply thy pensive life
> Was fill'd with aspirations high, unform'd ideals,
> Waves, oceans musical, chaotically surging,
> That now ecstatic ghost, close to me bending, thy
>   cornet echoing, pealing,
> Gives out to no one's ears but mine, but freely gives
>   to mine,
> That I may thee translate.[25]

Note the echoes of "Out of the Cradle" and "Lilacs"; in section three the poet enters his trance as the "fretting world, the

streets, the noisy hours of day withdraw" ("MT," 468.15)—
vision always comes in some form of spiritual seclusion.

In the "holy calm" of trance, the poet reenters "Paradise"
while the trumpeter's song "launches" his spirit into controlled flight. Visions of the medieval past fill section four—
perhaps because, in Whitman's view of history, the essential
stages of cultural evolution are feudalism and democracy. Section five takes up the theme of love, which mocks time and
space and encloses all other themes. The poet feels spiritual
lovers pressing upon him in a manner we have grown ac-
customed to in earlier poems: "O how the immortal phantoms
crowd around me! / I see the vast alembic ever working, I see
and know the flames that heat the world" ("MT," 469.35–36).
Turning from love to its opposite, in section six the trumpet
"conjure[s] war's alarums" and we witness grim scenes of
bloodshed comparable to those of "Song of Myself" or "The
Sleepers." The poet now draws toward the climax of his ecstasy; completely possessed in section seven, he actually becomes the trumpet as darkness overtakes him and he knows
all the causes of despair:

> I see the enslaved, the overthrown, the hurt, the opprest of
>   the whole earth,
> I feel the measureless shame and humiliation of my race, it
>   becomes all mine,
> Mine too the revenges of humanity, the wrongs of ages, baffled
>   feuds and hatreds,
> Utter defeat upon me weighs—all lost—the foe victorious,
> (Yet 'mid the ruins Pride colossal stands unshaken to the
>   last,
> Endurance, resolution to the last.)
>
>   ("MT," 470–71.54–59)

Though no doubt bearing some relation to Whitman's knowledge of the Civil War, this stage of the poem corresponds with
section thirty-seven of "Song of Myself," in which the poet ends
his descent into suffering before discovering himself "on the
verge of a usual mistake" and emerging "replenish'd with supreme power." Indeed, from the pit of suffering and defeat the
poet-hero rises, in section eight of "The Mystic Trumpeter," to
faith, hope, and prophecy:

> Marches of victory—man disenthral'd—the conqueror at last,
> Hymns to the universal God from universal man—all joy!
> A reborn race appears—a perfect world, all joy!
>
>   ("MT," 471.67–69)

The millennial vision does not differ essentially from that noted in poems ranging from "The Sleepers" to "Passage to India," but the joy is not as spontaneous as the poet would have us believe; one is certain that the performer knew where he was heading before he set out. Whitman has been studying himself, imitating the process of his earlier work rather than engaging himself in the uncertainties of the ecstatic process.

"The Mystic Trumpeter" develops more schematically than any of Whitman's earlier ecstatic poems. One mark of this more systematic, less genuinely energetic quality is that each section treats a clearly delimited theme; moreover, we find no impulsive, unbidden shifting of dramatic orientation. Such shifts are characteristic of the more authentic possession sequences of "Song of Myself," for example, in which sudden shifts in theatrical orientation (from internal or spiritual to external and public dimensions) create a texture of spontaneity and radical psychic engagement—an illusion of lawlessness. Thus the assault upon the consciousness of the performer, which makes for much of the drama and intensity of a possession sequence, appears tamed and domesticated in "The Mystic Trumpeter"—notwithstanding the fact that the general pattern of the experience that is narrated resembles the classic shamanistic process.

Another mark of the failure of inspiration in this poem lies in the nature of the transitions between sections. In "Song of Myself" (which, in fact, was not initially divided into sections), such transitions are "organic," arising from the pulsing and spiraling current of the entranced performer's consciousness. The later successful visionary poems retained this organic and unpredictable quality. But each section of "The Mystic Trumpeter" that dramatizes experience within the possessed state begins with a nearly identical call to the possessing force: in section three, "Blow trumpeter free and clear"; in section four, "Blow again trumpeter!"; in section five, "Blow again trumpeter!"; in section six, "Blow again trumpeter"; and in section seven, with a predictable intensification of the trance, "O trumpeter, methinks I am myself the instrument thou playest." Finally, in section eight the poet calls, "Now trumpeter for thy close, / Vouchsafe a higher strain than any yet" ("MT," 471.60–61). Such transitions, coming at the opening of each section, betray the lack of inspiration, the studied design and geometry Whitman has lapsed into as he has lost the sources of tension and creativity.

External factors support the thesis that Whitman allowed his visionary capacity to harden into a system following the war. Besides the central weakness of "Passage to India" and the clean schematization of "The Mystic Trumpeter," we find in "Democratic Vistas" (1871) Whitman's first attempt to give a name, "Personalism," to his religious orientation, along with a greater tendency than before to explain discursively a form of democratic faith that had previously been conveyed through ecstatic performance. At the same time, the infamous group of admirers and would-be illuminés grew under the influence of Whitman's personal "magnetism." For a few of these followers, merely meeting Whitman or reading *Leaves of Grass* ignited a transformative experience amounting to religious conversion.[26] The pattern follows closely what A. F. C. Wallace has pointed to in charismatic movements—the point at which the solitary prophet gains a discipleship and the insights revealed in his visions are molded into a creed. The disciples surrounding Whitman helped pass on a mythologized view of him, taking down his every word and reifying his religious orientation, even founding a "Walt Whitman Fellowship" society with several branches—few but far-flung. Often regarded as a negative influence upon the poet's later work, the apostles really became important to him only after the Union victory had justified his faith and thus deprived him of the ground of ecstasy.

Scholars have often blamed the "Whitmaniacs" for seducing the poet into believing that he was what he had been claiming to be all along, as if his acceptance of the role of religious prophet and national bard helped ruin his art. But most Whitman criticism of the past thirty years has misunderstood what a "prophet" is, what conditions foster his awakening, and how he performs when he is truly inspired. In the most precise sense, Whitman was less of a prophet in 1871 than he had been in 1855, and as a result his poetry changed even as he turned increasingly to prose.

It was time for Whitman to abandon ecstatic performance and to concentrate upon the simple intimations of death, upon the threshold between worlds we find movingly rendered in such pieces as "Whispers of Heavenly Death" (1868). Fragments of shamanistic experience remain even in these less ambitious poems—phantoms, eidolons, trance-inducing cadences, and the essential rhythms of despair and hope that, when genuinely experienced, inspire fine lyrics. "Whispers of

Heavenly Death," for example, written at about the time Whitman began working on portions of "Passage to India," makes fewer claims than the latter poem, but is more authentic and moving; it indicates the most productive direction Whitman would take in his final years.

"Prayer of Columbus" is the last of the poet's works to approach authentic visionary quality. In it we find not a ritualistic performance but a prayer. No earthly audience is implied, no public function served or acquired. Having essentially completed his tasks, the hero looks back upon his life through the mask of Columbus and, in the process of private worship, receives the gift of vision and reassurance for no one but himself. One applies the term "lyric" to this poem with less qualification than to any of the other successful visionary pieces, for it is more exclusively personal; and it seems highly appropriate that at this late point in the Whitman canon we should find a poem about the European discoverer of America. Whitman has come full circle. He knows that his ecstatic work is done, and what he writes well from now on will mainly address the unknown or simply marvel in the mysteries he once plumbed—mysteries he trusts to enter again through portals of death beyond performance.

Notes

Introduction

1. Two articles have specifically analyzed shamanistic structures, symbols, and techniques in "When Lilacs Last in the Dooryard Bloom'd" and "The Sleepers." Jane A. Nelson, "Ecstasy and Transformation in Whitman's 'Lilacs,'" *Walt Whitman Review* 18(1972):113–23; and George Hutchinson, "Parallels to Shamanism in 'The Sleepers,'" *Walt Whitman Review* 26 (1980):43–52, revised and incorporated into chapter 3 of this book. Other, less rigorous references to Whitman as a "shaman" are in Albert Gelpi, *The Tenth Muse* (Cambridge, Mass.: Harvard University Press, 1975), 185, 208; Ivan Marki, *The Trial of the Poet* (New York: Columbia University Press, 1976), 238, and "The Last Eleven Poems of the 1855 *Leaves of Grass,*" *American Literature* 54 (1982):229–39; Quentin Anderson, *The Imperial Self* (New York: Alfred A. Knopf, 1971), 125–65; and Justin Kaplan, *Walt Whitman* (New York: Simon & Schuster, 1980), 190–91.

2. Roger Asselineau, *The Evolution of Walt Whitman* (Cambridge, Mass.: Harvard University Press, 1960), 2:107.

3. Henry Seidel Canby, *Walt Whitman, An American* (Boston: Houghton Mifflin, 1943), 323. Whitman quoted in F. O. Matthiessen, *American Renaissance* (New York: Oxford University Press, 1941), 539.

4. Frederik Schyberg, *Walt Whitman,* trans. Evie Allison Allen (New York: Columbia University Press, 1951), 251.

5. Mircea Eliade, *Shamanism: Archaic Techniques of Ecstasy,* trans. Willard R. Trask (New York: Bollingen Foundation, 1964), 504.

6. Whether shamanism is a phenomenon to be found in many areas of the world and once characteristic of Indo-European cultures, or whether the term should be restricted to particular cultural configurations (of Asia and/or North America and/or South America and/or Africa) is still a hotly debated issue. Ake Hultkrantz surveys some of the problems while providing a serviceable definition of shamanism in "Ecological and Phenomenological Aspects of Shamanism," in *Shamanism in Siberia,* ed. V. Dioszegi and M. Hoppál (Budapest: Akadémiai Kiadó, 1978), 27–58.

7. Anna-Leena Siikala, *The Rite Technique of the Siberian Shaman,* Folklore Fellows, FF Communications, No. 220 (Helsinki: Suomalainen, 1978), 20; Ake Hultkrantz, "A Definition of Shamanism," *Temenos* 9 (1973):30.

8. Johan Reinhard, "Shamanism and Spirit Possession: The Definition Problem" in John T. Hitchcock and Rex L. Jones, eds., *Spirit Possession in the Nepal Himalayas* (Warminster, England: Aris & Phillips, 1976), 16 (Reinhard's emphasis). See also Hultkrantz, "Ecological and Phenomenological Aspects of Shamanism."

9. Eliade, *Shamanism,* 5.

10. I. M. Lewis, *Ecstatic Religion* (Middlesex, England: Penguin, 1971), 64.

11. *The Uncollected Poetry and Prose of Walt Whitman,* ed. Emory Holloway (1921; rpt. Gloucester, Mass.: Peter Smith, 1972), 2:69. In revised form this passage was later included in section forty of "Song of Myself."

12. Hultkrantz, "A Definition of Shamanism," 33.

13. Siikala, 5.

14. Siikala, 17.

15. Schyberg, 252.

16. Hyatt H. Waggoner, *American Poets From the Puritans to the Present* (Boston: Houghton Mifflin, 1969), 175; James E. Miller, Jr., *A Critical Guide to* Leaves of Grass (Chicago: University of Chicago Press, 1957), 34.

17. Asselineau, 2:5–6.

18. T. R. Rajasekharaiah, *The Roots of Whitman's Grass* (Rutherford, N. J.: Fairleigh Dickinson University Press, 1970), 243–48. See also O. K. Nambiar, *Walt Whitman and Yoga* (Bangalore, India: Jeevan, 1966), 102–25. Nambiar shows that sexual symbolism (indicating the cross-influence of sensual and mental experience during mystical arousal) is common in Tantrism as well as in some Christian mystical experiences (e.g., that of St. John of the Cross); but in these traditions sexual arousal is allowed to play a part only as a means to its ultimate subjection during the subsequent transcendence to mystical "purity." There is a hierarchy of values embedded in the mystical experience, consonant with the religious creed, that subordinates "animality" to "spirituality." Whitman, according to this view, nearly let the "animal" in him have too free a reign because of his lack of guidance from a mystical tradition. Eliade, incidentally, points out shamanic elements in Tantrism and the general "transformation that a shamanic schema can undergo when it is incorporated into a complex philosophical system, such as tantrism" (*Shamanism,* 437). See also Kaplan, 192–93.

19. Eugene G. d'Aquili and Charles D. Laughlin, Jr., "The Neurobiology of Myth and Ritual," in *The Spectrum of Ritual: A Biogenetic Structural Analysis,* ed. d'Aquili and Laughlin (New York: Columbia University Press, 1979), 158. See also Julian M. Davidson, "The Psychobiology of Sexual Experience," in *The Psychobiology of Consciousness,* ed. Julian M. and Richard J. Davidson (New York: Plenum, 1980), 295; and Whitman's remark in Horace Traubel's *With Walt Whitman in Camden,* ed. Gertrude Traubel (Carbondale: Southern Illinois University Press, 1964), 5:376: " 'I think Swedenborg was right when he said there was a close connection—a very close connection—between the state we call religious ecstacy [sic] and the desire to copulate. I find Swedenborg confirmed in all my experience. It is a peculiar discovery.' "

20. Julian M. Davidson, 318.

21. Waggoner, 165–66.

22. I. M. Lewis, 58, notes that the ecstatic union, frequently interpreted as mystical sexual intercourse with a possessing spirit, is also considered a sort of half-death. For a discussion of possible neurophysiological connections between altered states of consciousness and the experience of dying, see Arnold J. Mandell, "Toward a Psychobiology of Transcendence: God in the Brain," in Julian M. and Richard J. Davidson, 405–6. Of course, such speculations in no way call in question the value or profundity of transcendent or death experiences from a religious or philosophical point of view. My intent is not reductionist, but rather to suggest the ways in which biological structures might be involved in the total "ecology" of ecstaticism.

23. *Uncollected Poetry and Prose*, 2:85.

24. Richard Chase, *Walt Whitman Reconsidered* (New York: William Sloane Associates, 1955), 49.

25. For comparisons of Whitman and Sufism, see Massud Farzan, "Whitman and Sufism: Towards 'A Persian Lesson,'" *American Literature* 47 (1976):572–82; Ghulam M. Fayez, "Images of the Divine in Rumi and Whitman," *Comparative Literature Studies* 17 (1980):33–43; and Ghulam M. Fayez, "Motion Imagery in Rumi and Whitman," *Walt Whitman Review* 25 (1979):39–51.

26. This view is implicit in much Whitman criticism today. It was perhaps first offered by Edward Carpenter in dealing with Whitman's sexuality, then more deeply explored by Jean Catel (*Walt Whitman: la naissance du poète* [Paris: Reider, 1929]); Asselineau connects the poet's psychological conflicts with both his sexuality and the state of the nation. In contrast Stephen A. Black claims that the poetry did not solve Whitman's psychological problems, that he never did achieve equilibrium, but this theory rests upon some very shaky readings of Whitman's major poems. See *Whitman's Journeys into Chaos* (Princeton: Princeton University Press, 1975).

27. Andreas Lommel, *Shamanism: The Beginnings of Art*, trans. Michael Bullock (New York: McGraw-Hill, 1967), 76.

28. The key word here, but not the concept, is borrowed from Alfred H. Marks's article, "Whitman's Triadic Imagery," *American Literature* 23 (1951):99–126.

29. Mircea Eliade, *Myths, Dreams, and Mysteries*, trans. Philip Mairet (New York: Harper & Row, 1960), 103.

30. Interestingly, Thomas S. Kuhn has made virtually the same point with regard to crises and revolutions in scientific communities. See *The Structure of Scientific Revolutions* (Chicago: University of Chicago Press, 1970).

31. Victor Turner, *Dramas, Fields, and Metaphors* (Ithaca, N.Y.: Cornell University Press, 1974), 70.

32. Turner, 252–53.

33. Turner, 68, 269.

34. Turner, 293.

35. Joseph Campbell, *The Masks of God: Primitive Mythology* (New York: Viking, 1959), 240–41. See also Hultkrantz, "Ecological and Phenomenological Aspects of Shamanism," 52–53.

36. See especially, by Anthony F. C. Wallace, "Mazeway Resynthesis: A Bio-Cultural Theory of Religious Inspiration," *Transactions of the New York Academy of Sciences*, ser. 2, 18 (1956):626–38; and "Revitalization Movements," *American Anthropologist* 58 (1956):264–81. McLoughlin's application of Wallace's model appears in *Revivals, Awakenings, and Reform* (Chicago: University of Chicago Press, 1978). To my knowledge, no one has yet extended this model to literature.

37. Lewis, 203–5.

38. See especially Siikala, and Sheila S. Walker, *Ceremonial Spirit Possession in Africa and Afro-America* (Leiden: Brill, 1972).

39. Hayden White, *Tropics of Discourse* (Baltimore: Johns Hopkins University Press, 1978), 10.

40. Turner, 249.

41. See, for instance, Item 62 in Part 2 of the "Notes and Fragments" edited by Richard Maurice Bucke, in *The Complete Writings of Walt Whitman,* ed. Richard Maurice Bucke, Thomas B. Harned, and Horace Traubel (New York: G. P. Putnam's Sons, 1902), 9:104–5. It is clear from his early notebooks anticipating *Leaves of Grass* that Whitman modeled his poetic persona with this idea in mind. Later, the "hot little prophets" would try to make of the poet himself a mythic-religious figure and author of a new cosmic religion. Concerning the most devoted of the "Whitmaniacs," see Artem Lozynsky, *Richard Maurice Bucke, Medical Mystic* (Detroit: Wayne State University Press, 1977).

Chapter One

1. On Americans' movement toward nationalism, see especially George Dangerfield, *The Awakening of American Nationalism, 1815–1828* (New York: Harper & Row, 1965). William R. Brock discusses the connection of religious and moral forces to the growing sense of a national character in *Parties and Political Conscience* (Millwood, N. Y.: KTO, 1979), 139–41.

2. See Robert N. Bellah, *The Broken Covenant* (New York: Seabury, 1975), 49, on the contribution of evangelism to American "civil religion" and national feeling.

3. George B. Forgie, *Patricide in the House Divided* (New York: W. W. Norton, 1979), 29, 101. Biographers—especially Justin Kaplan—have frequently noted Whitman's feelings for the Union and early worship of the founders, but neither the psychological force and complexity of this attach-

ment nor its relationship to the "social drama" of his generation have been sufficiently illuminated. Forgie provides excellent background and commentary for students of the American Renaissance.

4. John F. Wilson, *Public Religion in American Culture* (Philadelphia: Temple University Press, 1979), 34.

5. The critique of Forgie from which I have quoted is a review of *Patricide in the House Divided* by Edwin G. Burrows, in *Journal of American History* 66 (1979):653–54. Forgie discusses the replacement of fathers by "founding fathers," p. 28.

6. Horace Traubel, *With Walt Whitman in Camden* (Boston: Small, Maynard, 1906), 1:78.

7. Traubel (New York: Mitchell Kennerley, 1914), 3:139. "Specimen Days," in *Prose Works 1892*, ed. Floyd Stovall (New York: New York University Press, 1963), 1:14. See also William White, "A Tribute to William Hartshorne: Unrecorded Whitman," *American Literature* 42 (1971):554–58.

8. Whitman, *The Early Poems and the Fiction,* ed. Thomas L. Brasher (New York: New York University Press, 1963), 99. See also Forgie, 35–49.

9. Mason Locke Weems, *The Life of Washington,* ed. Marcus Cunliffe (1809; rpt. Cambridge, Mass.: Belknap, 1962), 120. Further references to this work will be noted parenthetically in the text.

10. See especially Whitman's *Eagle* editorial of 4 December 1846, on Washington's farewell to the army. In *The Gathering of the Forces by Walt Whitman,* ed. Cleveland Rodgers and John Black (New York: G. P. Putnam's Sons, 1920), 1:76–80.

11. "The Sleepers," in *Leaves of Grass:* Comprehensive Reader's Edition, ed. Harold W. Blodgett and Sculley Bradley (New York: New York University Press, 1965), 429, lines 92, 94.

12. See John Marshall, *The Life of George Washington* (Philadelphia: C. P. Wayne, 1804), 2:446.

13. Stephen A. Black, *Whitman's Journeys Into Chaos* (Princeton: Princeton University Press, 1975), 16–25.

14. "The Sleepers," 429, ll. 98–99. Concerning possible sources of this scene see Henry B. Rule, "Walt Whitman's 'Sad and Noble Scene,'" *Walt Whitman Review* 27 (1981):165–70.

15. *With Walt Whitman in Camden,* ed. Gertrude Traubel (Carbondale: Southern Illinois University Press, 1964), 5:93.

16. Edwin Haviland Miller, *Walt Whitman's Poetry* (New York: New York University Press, 1968), 50.

17. Traubel, 5:362; see vol. 1 (Boston: Small, Maynard, 1906), 62.

18. Traubel, 1:62.

19. Traubel, 3:134.

20. Forgie, 51n.

21. Joseph Jay Rubin, *The Historic Whitman* (University Park: Pennsylvania State University Press, 1973), 15. See also Justin Kaplan, *Walt Whitman: A Life* (New York: Simon & Schuster, 1980), 65–66; and Traubel, 5:29–30.

22. See Forgie, 168–74, on the movement to restore Mount Vernon, which spearheaded a general determination to preserve historic landmarks.

23. Walt Whitman, "Tear Down and Build Over Again," *American Review*, November 1845; rpt. in *The Uncollected Poetry and Prose of Walt Whitman*, ed. Emory Holloway (1921; rpt. Gloucester, Mass.: Peter Smith, 1972), 1:95.

24. *Uncollected Poetry and Prose*, 1:96.

25. Editorials in the Brooklyn *Daily Eagle* of 9 July 1846 and 3 December 1847, rpt. in *The Gathering of the Forces*, 2:46–52.

26. See also Kaplan, 66–67.

27. Walt Whitman, *I Sit and Look Out: Editorials from the Brooklyn Daily Times by Walt Whitman*, ed. Emory Holloway and Vernolian Schwarz (New York: Columbia University Press, 1932), 72.

28. Walt Whitman, "The Centenarian's Story," in *Leaves of Grass*, 299, ll. 97–99.

29. See especially Douglas T. Miller, *Jacksonian Aristocracy* (New York: Oxford University Press, 1967), 188–89.

30. Dangerfield, 299.

31. See Floyd Stovall, *The Foreground of* Leaves of Grass (Charlottesville: University Press of Virginia, 1974), 42; and Carl N. Degler, "The Locofocos: Urban 'Agrarians,'" *Journal of Economic History* 16 (1956):322–33.

32. See Denton E. Morrison, "Some Notes Toward Theory on Relative Deprivation, Social Movements, and Social Change," *American Behavioral Scientist* 14 (1971):688.

33. Walt Whitman, "The Columbian's Song," in *The Early Poems and the Fiction*, 13.

34. See his Brooklyn *Daily Eagle* article of 5 November 1846, "Morbid Appetite for Money," in *The Gathering of the Forces*, 2:130–36.

35. Walt Whitman, "A Backward Glance O'er Travel'd Roads," in *Leaves of Grass*, 571.

36. Dangerfield, 291.

37. Degler, 333.

38. "A Song for Occupations," in *Leaves of Grass*, 213, ll. 41–43, 55–58.

39. Norman Ware, *The Industrial Worker, 1840–1860* (1924; rpt. Chicago: Quadrangle, 1964), 19.

40. Ware, 25; see also John Higham, *From Boundlessness to Consolidation* (Ann Arbor: William L. Clements Library, 1969), 17–18.

41. Hartman, "Romanticism and 'Anti-Self-Consciousness,'" in *Romanticism and Consciousness*, ed. Harold Bloom (New York: W. W. Norton, 1970), 52n.

42. Of the biographers, Roger Asselineau in particular emphasizes the importance of the "political crisis" Whitman experienced in the late 1840s; see *The Evolution of Walt Whitman* (Cambridge, Mass.: Harvard University Press, 1960), 1:37–40. See also Jerome Loving, *Emerson, Whitman, and the American Muse* (Chapel Hill: University of North Carolina Press, 1982), 67–82.

43. Rpt. in *The Early Poems and the Fiction*, 39–40. The poem appeared as "Europe" in *Leaves of Grass*, with some changes.

44. See especially Brock, 140–51.

45. Walt Whitman, "American Workingmen, versus Slavery," Brooklyn *Daily Eagle*, 1 September 1847; rpt. *The Gathering of the Forces* 1:209–10 (Whitman's emphasis).

46. "American Workingmen, versus Slavery," in *The Gathering of the Forces*, 1:212. It is instructive to recall a passage from Whitman's more optimistic period: "'It is well that the benefactors of a state be . . . kept alive in memory and in song, when their bodies are mouldering. Then will it be impossible for a people to become enslaved; for though the strong arm of their old defender come not as formerly to the battle, his spirit is there, through the power of remembrance, and wields a better sway even than if it were of fleshly substance'" ("The Last of the Sacred Army" [1842], 99).

47. Walt Whitman, "New States: Shall They Be Slave or Free?" Brooklyn *Daily Eagle*, 22 April 1847; rpt. *The Gathering of the Forces*, 1:201.

48. Walt Whitman, "The House of Friends," New York *Tribune*, 14 June 1850; rpt. *The Early Poems and the Fiction*, 36–37. See Gay Wilson Allen's discussion of the poem's relation to Whitman's sense of personal betrayal in *The Solitary Singer*, rev. ed. (New York: New York University Press, 1967), 104.

49. Walt Whitman, "Collect," in *Prose Works 1892*, 2:431.

50. "The House of Friends," 37 (my ellipsis).

51. Roger Asselineau's insight, in *The Evolution of Walt Whitman*, 1:38.

52. Asselineau, 1:39.

53. Anthony F. C. Wallace, *Religion: An Anthropological View* (New York: Random House, 1966), 213.

54. George Rosen, "Social Change and Psychopathology in the Emotional Climate of Millennial Movements," *American Behavioral Scientist* 16 (1972):164.

55. "Preface 1855," in *Leaves of Grass*, 713.

56. John Jay Chapman, "Walt Whitman," rpt. in *A Century of Whitman Criticism*, ed. E. H. Miller (Bloomington: Indiana University Press, 1969), 103–4.

57. See William G. McLoughlin, *Revivals, Awakenings, and Reform* (Chicago: University of Chicago Press, 1978).

58. Donald G. Matthews, "The Second Great Awakening as an Organizing Process, 1780–1830," 1969; rpt. *Religion in American History: Interpretive Essays*, ed. John M. Mulder and John F. Wilson (Englewood Cliffs: Prentice-Hall, 1978), 203.

59. Wallace, *Religion*, 211.

60. Charles C. Cole, Jr., *Social Ideas of Northern Evangelists, 1826–1860* (New York: Columbia University Press, 1954), 77.

61. Loving, 6–11.

62. This is now common knowledge among historians of the early humanitarian reform movement. See, for example, Dangerfield, 290; Ware, 18–42; and John L. Thomas, "Romantic Reform in America, 1815–1865," *American Quarterly* 17 (1965):656–81.

63. Although it hardly deals with religious movements of the period, Edward K. Spann's *The New Metropolis* (New York: Columbia University Press, 1981) comprehensively discusses the socioeconomic transformations and the failure of the political order in New York City between 1840 and 1857, as well as the rising anxiety that these conditions created.

64. I. M. Lewis, *Ecstatic Religion* (Middlesex: Penguin, 1971), 203.

65. Lewis, 39.

66. Lewis, 39.

67. Lewis, 44. Lewis insists that orthodox Christianity has "generally sought to belittle mystical interpretations of trance where these were claimed by those who experienced them to represent Divine revelation. Thus, though it is difficult to ignore the countless visions of Christian mystics, where the church has approved or honored these ascetic figures it has often done so on other grounds. The sanction of heresy has proved a powerful deterrent in curtailing and discrediting wayward personal mystical experiences" (p. 39).

68. Whitney Cross, in *The Burned-Over District* (Ithaca: Cornell University Press, 1950), points out the difficulties Finney had in restraining some of

his itinerants, whose meetings became increasingly sensational and whose ideas shaded into heresy. One missionary's description of his power over an audience betrays a strong correspondence to ideas of mesmerists and early spiritualists; he told an alarmed colleague of Finney's that he was "*'recipient and channel of a sensible divine emanation, which he caused to pass from him by a perceptible influence,* as electricity passes from one body to another'" (p. 175).

69. *A Shopkeeper's Millennium* (New York: Hill and Wang, 1978), 102.

70. Cross, 341–42; Robert Laurence Moore, *In Search of White Crows: Spiritualism, Parapsychology, and American Culture* (New York: Oxford University Press, 1977), 9–12.

71. Cross, 341.

72. Harold Aspiz, *Walt Whitman and the Body Beautiful* (Urbana: University of Illinois Press, 1980), 160. See also Cross, 342; and Robert C. Fuller, *Mesmerism and the American Cure of Souls* (Philadelphia: University of Pennsylvania Press, 1982), 16–104, whose treatment of mesmerism and spiritualism, and their connections with the Christian revivals, parallels mine in many respects, including his use of the insights of A. F. C. Wallace and Victor Turner. Aspiz (163–72), Stovall (*The Foreground of* Leaves of Grass, 154–55, 247–48), and Howard Kerr (*Mediums and Spirit-Rappers and Roaring Radicals* [Urbana: University of Illinois Press, 1972], 199, 20–21) have considered the possible influence of Swedenborg and American spiritualists upon Whitman.

73. Aspiz, 167. A recent student believes the upset to traditional religious views caused by scientific advance, combined with changing social conditions, fostered the rise of modern spiritualism: "Modern Spiritualism can therefore be seen as a 'new religion,' emerging from the essentially magical world view of Shamanism and witchcraft. A religion influenced by the teachings and practices of previous higher religions, but whose basic elements derive from an older and more traditional religion, which continued to underlie the veneer of Christianity, and emerged when the superficial layer of Christian influence was removed by the changing social conditions of mass migration and urbanism." Geoffrey K. Nelson, *Spiritualism and Society* (New York: Schocken Books, 1969), 269.

74. Alice Felt Tyler, *Freedom's Ferment* (1944; rpt. New York: Harper & Row, 1962), 81.

75. John Humphrey Noyes, *History of American Socialisms* (Philadelphia: Lippincott, 1870), 596, 611, 604–5.

76. Anna-Leena Siikala, *The Rite Technique of the Siberian Shaman,* Folklore Fellows, FF communications, no. 220 (Helsinki: Suomalainen, 1978), 61; R. M. White, "A Preface to the Theory of Hypnotism," *Journal of Abnormal and Social Psychology* 36 (1941):503.

77. Herbert W. Schneider and George Lawton, *A Prophet and A Pilgrim* (New York: Columbia University Press, 1942), 52.

78. Schneider and Lawton, 46–47. In a note collected by Bucke, Whitman said Shelley "must have been quite such another as T. L. Harris." *Notes and Fragments*, ed. Richard Maurice Bucke, in *The Complete Writings of Walt Whitman*, ed. Richard Maurice Bucke et al. (New York: G. P. Putnam's Sons, 1902), 9:84.

79. Schneider and Lawton, 46–47.

80. Schneider and Lawton, 51.

81. Schneider and Lawton, 52.

82. See Nelson, 78:

The middle of the nineteenth century in America was a period of acute stress for the majority of individuals in that country, for they were involved in a series of rapid changes unparalleled in history. This resulted in the rise of many movements whose latent function was the relief of tension; such movements included political organizations such as the "Know Nothing" Party, the Locofocos and the Anti-masons, such reform movements as the Temperance movement and the Abolition movement, as well as religious revivals and the rise of many new and often extravagant sects and cults.
    Spiritualism was one of these cults, and during the eighteen fifties was probably the most successful of all the movements which arose from the chaos of social change.

Nelson applies social deprivation theory to this movement, as well (266–69).

83. *Complete Writings*, 9:127 (Item 99 of the "Notes and Fragments").

84. Timothy L. Smith, *Revivalism and Social Reform* (New York: Abingdon, 1957), 62.

85. Smith, 145; see also John L. Thomas.

86. Smith, 145.

87. Victor Turner, *Dramas, Fields, and Metaphors* (Ithaca: Cornell University Press, 1974), 47.

88. Turner, 46–47.

89. See Perry Miller, "From the Covenant to the Revival," in Mulder and Wilson, eds., *Religion in American History*, 158 (rpt. from *The Shaping of American Religion*, ed. James Ward Smith and A. Leland Jamison [Princeton University Press, 1961]).

90. Bellah, 44–45.

91. Quoted in Thomas B. Harned, "Walt Whitman and Oratory," in *Complete Writings*, 8:245.

92. When the movement for spiritual regeneration had obviously failed to preserve the Union, the Civil War took its place, according to John F.

Wilson, as "a battle for possession of the covenant. . . . In this framework, the national covenant is the moral claim that the community continues elect under divine authorization. So the Civil War sanctified the nation through the terrible blood sacrifice of lives" (*Public Religion in American Culture*, 38). Whitman's war memoranda and *Specimen Days*, not to mention *Drum-Taps*, exemplify this point of view. Moreover, his view of Lincoln's symbolic role as martyr, with echoes of the Christian archetype, was widespread in the North, according to Robert Bellah; through the President's death, which concentrated the deaths of thousands more in a single event, "The theme of sacrifice was indelibly written into the civil religion" ("Civil Religion in America," 1967; rpt. in *American Civil Religion*, ed. Russell E. Richey and Donald G. Jones [New York: Harper & Row, 1974], 32). The relevance of this insight to "When Lilacs Last in the Dooryard Bloom'd" is obvious; see also Thomas Parkinson, "'When Lilacs Last in the Dooryard Bloom'd' and the American Civil Religion," *Southern Review* 19 (1983):1–16.

Chapter Two

1. Floyd Stovall, *The Foreground of* Leaves of Grass (Charlottesville: University Press of Virginia, 1974); Joseph Jay Rubin, *The Historic Whitman* (University Park: Pennsylvania State University Press, 1973); Harold Aspiz, *Walt Whitman and the Body Beautiful* (Urbana: University of Illinois Press, 1980). See also Paul Zweig, *Walt Whitman: The Making of a Poet* (New York: Basic Books, 1984).

2. Albert Gelpi, *The Tenth Muse: The Psyche of the American Poet* (Cambridge, Mass.: Harvard University Press, 1975), 165. See also Anna-Leena Siikala, *The Rite Technique of the Siberian Shaman*, Folklore Fellows, FF Communications, no. 220 (Helsinki: Suomalainen, 1978), 48; and Hans Mol, *Identity and the Sacred* (Oxford: Basil Blackwell, 1976), 47.

3. Sigmund Freud, *Totem and Taboo*, trans. James Strachey (New York: W. W. Norton, 1950), 75–99.

4. See, for example, Hayden White, *Tropics of Discourse* (Baltimore: Johns Hopkins University Press, 1978), 10. For related views of Whitman's poetry, see especially Gustav Bychowski, "Walt Whitman, A Study in Sublimation," *Psychoanalysis and the Social Sciences*, 3 (1951):223–61; Edwin Haviland Miller, *Walt Whitman's Poetry* (New York: New York University Press, 1968), 22; and Stephen A. Black, *Whitman's Journeys into Chaos* (Princeton: Princeton University Press, 1975), 14.

5. Barbara Lefcowitz, "Omnipotence of Thought and the Poetic Imagination: Blake, Coleridge, and Rilke," *Psychoanalytic Review* 59 (1972):431. See Bychowski, 212: "It seems quite clear that by his poetic creation, Whitman did not only regain faith in himself, but also found gratification for his narcissism. Moreover, this fulfillment was of such a nature as to help him transcend the limitations of his own ego and, in so doing, escape what might have been a psychotic overcathexis."

6. Miller, in *Walt Whitman's Poetry*, locates the power of Whitman's work precisely in the ability to tap the "subterranean currents that we have tried to forget when we put away childish things" (p. 22). Cf. Black, 46, who

claims the poems are successful insofar as they help the reader to confront unconscious conflicts, but finds the resolution of those conflicts in ecstasy evasive and unsuccessful; in fact, Whitman's probing of the unconscious "exacerbated neurotic anxieties" until Whitman could no longer risk his "journeys into chaos" (p. 45). It should be evident that my reading of the ecstatic poems is fundamentally opposed to Black's, although I concur in his recognition of unconscious conflicts and the impulse to "infantile omnipotence."

7. S. M. Shirokogoroff, *Psychomental Complex of the Tungus* (London: Routledge and Kegan Paul, 1935), 368: "[I]n case of psychic troubles, due to unmastered spirits, the shaman actually masters himself, regulates his own psychomental complex, after which he is no more affected by the condition which was the initial cause of his becoming a shaman."

8. Klopfer and Boyer, quoted in Robert F. Kraus, "A Psychoanalytic Interpretation of Shamanism," *Psychoanalytic Review* 59 (1972):29.

9. Klopfer and Boyer, quoted in Kraus, 29.

10. Black, 25.

11. For an overview of scholarship relating to the psychology of shamanism, see Youngsook Kim Harvey, *Six Korean Women: The Socialization of Shamans* (New York: West, 1979), 241–50.

12. Mircea Eliade, *Shamanism*, trans. Willard R. Trask (New York: Bollingen Foundation, 1964), 29.

13. Black, 36; Horace Traubel, "Notes From Conversation With George W. Whitman, 1893: Mostly in His Own Words," in *In Re Walt Whitman* (Philadelphia: D. McKay, 1893), 38.

14. *Notes and Fragments,* ed. Richard Maurice Bucke, in *The Complete Writings of Walt Whitman,* ed. Richard Maurice Bucke, Thomas B. Harned, and Horace Traubel (New York: G. P. Putnam's Sons, 1902), 9:135. Further references to this work will be noted parenthetically in the text with the abbreviation "*CW,*" followed by volume and page numbers.

15. Gay Wilson Allen, *The Solitary Singer,* rev. ed. (New York: New York University Press, 1967), 147.

16. Eliade, 13–19, 23–32. See also Eliade's *Myths, Dreams, and Mysteries,* trans. Philip Mairet (New York: Harper & Row, 1960), 75–81.

17. Emory Holloway obtained this testimony from Mrs. Orvetta Hall Brenton, daughter-in-law of Mr. and Mrs. James J. Brenton, with whom Whitman lived in 1839–40; *The Uncollected Poetry and Prose of Walt Whitman,* ed. Emory Holloway (1921; rpt. Gloucester, Mass.: Peter Smith, 1972), 1:xxxiv in a note.

18. Walt Whitman, "Lingave's Temptation," in *The Early Poems and the Fiction,* ed. Thomas L. Brasher (New York: New York University Press, 1963), 333. Further references to "Lingave's Temptation" will be noted parenthetically in the text.

19. George Whitman told Horace Traubel in 1893 that Walt took up his new notion of dressing as a laborer sometime after returning from New Orleans in 1848. See Traubel, "Notes From Conversation with George W. Whitman," 34.

20. Walt Whitman, "The Shadow and the Light of a Young Man's Soul," in *The Early Poems and the Fiction*, 327. Further references to this work will be noted parenthetically in the text.

21. Shirokogoroff, 368. Justin Kaplan's view of Whitman's transformation, similar to mine in broad outline, also compares that change to shamanistic "conversion" (though Kaplan is imprecise in his references to shamanism), and emphasizes its self-healing character. See *Walt Whitman: A Life* (New York: Simon & Schuster, 1980), 187–93.

22. Claude Levi-Strauss, *Structural Anthropology*, trans. C. Jacobson and B. C. Schoepf (New York: Basic Books, 1963), 181.

23. Siikala, 28.

24. See especially Floyd Stovall; Robert D. Richardson, Jr., *Myth and Literature in the American Renaissance* (Bloomington: Indiana University Press, 1978), 138–64; David Goodale, "Some of Walt Whitman's Borrowings," *American Literature* 10 (1938):202–13; Robert D. Faner, *Walt Whitman and Opera* (Carbondale: Southern Illinois University Press, 1951); William L. Finkel, "Walt Whitman's Manuscript Notes on Oratory," *American Literature* 22 (1950):29–53; and C. Carroll Hollis, *Language and Style in* Leaves of Grass (Baton Rouge: Louisiana State University Press, 1983), 1–27.

25. *CW*, 10:17n.

26. Stovall, like Gay Wilson Allen, mentions the *Ruins* chiefly as an example of early deistic influence upon Whitman. So does Richardson (pp. 18, 143). Goodale records some of Whitman's notes on the *Ruins* and indicates instances of direct borrowing for *Leaves of Grass* in addition to perceiving "the impregnation of Whitman's mind with the fundamental concepts of Volney" (p. 211), but he goes no further than this hint in showing how Volney most profoundly affected Whitman's development. Betsy Erkkila's more illuminating discussion of its influence—in *Walt Whitman Among the French* (Princeton: Princeton University Press, 1980), 14–19—deals briefly with some of the aspects I will emphasize.

27. Horace Traubel, *With Walt Whitman in Camden* (New York: D. Appleton, 1908), 2:445. Volney's *Ruins* was one of the few books Walter Whitman, Sr., owned.

28. Allen, 122.

29. Constantin François Chasseboeuf Volney, *A New Translation of Volney's Ruins; or, Meditations on the Revolution of Empires* (Dublin: Hood & Cuthell, Walker & Ogelvy, 1811), 130–67. Further references to this work will be noted parenthetically in the text.

30. Diane Kepner, "From Spears to Leaves: Walt Whitman's Theory of Nature in 'Song of Myself,'" *American Literature* 51 (1979):189.

31. Allen, 162.

32. Allen, 163.

33. The most recent and complete examination of Whitman's interest in, and possible indebtedness to, the quasi-scientific "animal magnetism," phrenological, and health fads of his era is Harold Aspiz's *Walt Whitman and the Body Beautiful.* See also Myrth Jimmie Killingsworth, "Another Source for Whitman's Use of 'Electric,'" *Walt Whitman Review* 23 (1977):129–32; Edmund Reiss, "Whitman's Debt to Animal Magnetism," *PMLA* 78 (1963):80–88; and Justin Kaplan, 146–53. Maria M. Tatar has discussed the influence of mesmerism and electrical theory upon romantics in her book *Spellbound: Studies on Mesmerism and Literature* (Princeton: Princeton University Press, 1978), 45–81.

34. *Uncollected Poetry and Prose,* 2:66.

35. *Uncollected Poetry and Prose,* 1:41. Interestingly, Whitman's quest here follows an archaic pattern similar to that of Volney's narrator.

36. *Uncollected Poetry and Prose,* 1:42.

37. *Uncollected Poetry and Prose,* 1:256.

38. *Uncollected Poetry and Prose,* 1:256.

39. See Arnold J. Mandell, "Toward a Psychobiology of Transcendence: God in the Brain," in *The Psychobiology of Consciousness,* ed. Julian M. and Richard J. Davidson (New York: Plenum, 1980), 404–5.

40. Justus George Lawler, *Celestial Pantomime* (New Haven: Yale University Press, 1979).

41. *CW,* 9:112–13, 120, and 97–98. See also Stovall, 127–28. In this critical stance, of course, Whitman was influenced by Carlyle and Emerson as well as by a host of nonliterary sources.

42. See Faner, 30–31.

43. To recall just one example, "Death of Carlyle" in *Specimen Days* indicates Whitman's continued interest in the idea of the spirit as he had developed that idea out of the concepts of Volney: "And now that he has gone hence, can it be that Thomas Carlyle, soon to chemically dissolve in ashes and by winds, remains an identity still? In ways perhaps eluding all the statements, lore, and speculations of ten thousand years—eluding all possible statements to mortal sense—does he yet exist, a definite, vital being, a spirit, an individual—perhaps now wafted in space among those stellar systems, which, suggestive and limitless as they are, merely edge more limitless, far more suggestive systems? I have no doubt of it" (*Prose Works 1892,* ed. Floyd Stovall [New York: New York University Press, 1963], 1:253). It is startling that Whitman's general concept of spiritual survival changed so little over time.

44. Stovall, 178.

45. Quoted in Stovall, 178, from "Personal," *Harper's Weekly,* 23 April 1887. Whitman told Traubel in 1890 that he was enraptured by " 'Walter Scott first, for many early years—the initial predilection—O! the joy and wonder! and what it has done for me!' " See *With Walt Whitman in Camden,* ed. Gertrude Traubel and William White (Carbondale: Southern Illinois University Press, 1982), 6:242. In his later years, he continued to find *Minstrelsy of the Scottish Border* a "feast" "never exhausted."

46. Cf. Goodale, 211n.

47. Walter Scott, *Letters on Demonology and Witchcraft Addressed to J. G. Lockhart, Esq.,* 2d ed. (London: John Murray, 1831), 47.

48. Scott, 88.

49. Nora K. Chadwick, *Poetry and Prophecy* (Cambridge: Cambridge University Press, 1942), 10. See also Eliade, 379–84. Carlyle, in *On Heroes and Hero-Worship and the Heroic in History* (London: Chapman, 1840), discusses Odin at length in "The Hero As Divinity," regarding Odin as an historical person, an enlightened man who had been deified in legend and had become a central figure in Norse culture. But Carlyle does not discuss Odin's methods of inspiration. Whitman reviewed Carlyle's book for the *Eagle* in 1846.

50. *Daybooks and Notebooks,* ed. William White (New York: New York University Press, 1978), 3:674.

51. Chadwick, 5–10.

52. Hugh Blair, "Critical Dissertation on the Poems of Ossian," in James Macpherson, *The Poems of Ossian* (1830; rpt. New York: Thomas Y. Crowell, n.d.), 122–28. See also Stovall, 116–19; and *Daybooks and Notebooks,* 3:683: "Socrates had his demon—the word, ~~in its ancient~~ till toward modern times, having ~~only~~ as much the signification of spirit, or one of the genii, or heavenly visitor, as of an evil spirit" (Whitman's cross-outs).

53. Carlyle, "The Nibelungen Lied," in *Critical and Miscellaneous Essays* (1839; rpt. Boston: Dana Estes & Co., 1869), 2:242. Stovall (p. 180) has no doubt that Whitman read Carlyle's essay on the epic in an 1848 edition of *Critical and Miscellaneous Essays;* he identifies some of Whitman's notes, apparently of the late 1840s or early 1850s, which were from this work (p. 109). Most of the notes on the poem may be found in *CW,* 9:83, 117, 187. See also Stovall, 200–201, and his article, "Notes on Whitman's Reading," *American Literature* 26 (1954):344, 347–49, 357–58.

54. William A. Little, in "Walt Whitman and the *Nibelungenlied*" (*PMLA* 80 [1965]:562–70), states that Whitman's knowledge of the epic probably came from secondary sources but may have come from a translation by Joseph Gostwick published in 1854; evidence proves only that Whitman had read it by 1857. Whitman's critical and interpretive response to the epic largely follows Carlyle's, but Stovall argues convincingly that Whitman did read and take notes from Gostwick's 1854 edition of *German Literature.* He also apparently paraphrased forty-one lines of Gostwick's translation of passages from the *Niebelungenlied;* see *Foreground,* 196.

55. Stovall, *Foreground,* 109–10 and 200–201.

56. Carlyle, *Sartor Resartus* (New York: F. M. Lupton, n.d.), 227–28. Whitman reviewed this work in late 1846.

57. Carlyle, "Characteristics," in *Critical and Miscellaneous Essays,* 2:353–54.

58. Whitman, *Prose Works 1892,* 1:257, 256.

59. *Prose Works 1892,* 1:254–55.

60. Ibid., 261. For other discussions of Carlyle's early influence on Whitman, see especially Stovall, *Foreground,* 104–10; Fred Manning Smith, "Whitman's Debt to Carlyle's *Sartor Resartus," Modern Language Quarterly* 3 (1942):51–65; Fred Manning Smith, "Whitman's Poet-Prophet and Carlyle's Hero," *PMLA* 55 (1940):1,146–64; W. S. Kennedy, "An Annotated Edition of 'Sartor Resartus,' " *Conservator* 8 (1897):28–29; and Kaplan, 171–73.

61. *With Walt Whitman in Camden,* 2:300.

62. *CW,* 9:104–5. This is a theory that shows up repeatedly in Carlyle's works, particularly in *Heroes and Hero-Worship.* More recently, Weston La-Barre has suggested that the first "gods" were shamans—a hypothesis that has surfaced periodically in the study of ancient religion and mythology; see *The Ghost Dance: Origins of Religion* (Garden City, N. Y.: Doubleday, 1970), 161.

63. Quotation from Richard Maurice Bucke, *Walt Whitman* (Philadelphia: David McKay, 1883), 52.

64. *CW,* 9:228: "Subjective—out of the person himself. Objective—of other persons, things, events, places, characters. As the *Iliad* is profoundly objective, *Leaves of Grass* are profoundly subjective."

65. Hollis, "Rhetoric, Elocution, and Voice in *Leaves of Grass:* A Study in Affiliation," *Walt Whitman Quarterly Review* 2 (1984):3.

66. F. O. Matthiessen, *American Renaissance* (London: Oxford University Press, 1941), 556; Whitman's note is in *Walt Whitman's Workshop,* ed. Clifton Joseph Furness (Cambridge, Mass.: Harvard University Press, 1928), 37. Further references to this work are noted parenthetically in the text with the abbreviation *WWW.*

67. Quoted by Thomas B. Harned, "Walt Whitman and Oratory," in *CW,* 8:249.

68. On the dating of Whitman's notes on oratory, see Finkel. See also Hollis, *Language and Style,* 9–14, 207.

69. Quoted by Harned, *CW,* 8:253–54.

70. See I. M. Lewis, *Ecstatic Religion* (Middlesex, England: Penguin, 1971), 128. Consider the relevance of this insight to the popularity of mes-

meric and spiritualistic healing both in Europe just prior to the French Revolution and in Whitman's America: among others, the spiritualist Andrew Jackson Davis got his start as a mesmeric healer (as noted in chapter 1). Mesmer himself caused a sensation in prerevolutionary France with his spectacular, charismatic curing sessions.

71. See Aspiz, 42, on the connection of hydropathy and homeopathy with Transcendentalism and Swedenborgianism.

72. *Uncollected Poetry and Prose,* 2:65.

73. *Uncollected Poetry and Prose,* 2:90, 85.

74. Carlyle, "Characteristics," 361. Cf. Whitman's editorials of 1858 on "Reformers" and "The Radicals in Council," reprinted from the Brooklyn *Daily Times* in *I Sit and Look Out,* ed. Emory Holloway and Vernolian Schwarz (New York: Columbia University Press, 1932), 44–46. "If there be balm in Gilead for the correction of abuses and the healing of moral and physical evil, it can be found in no such little doses as you make specialties and hobbies withal. . . . [Y]ou approach this mighty mystery [of evil], and hold forth in your puny hands your potent 'specific' for its cure" (pp. 44–45).

75. Carlyle, "Characteristics," 365, 358.

76. *Uncollected Poetry and Prose,* 2:75. On Whitman's view of Goethe, see also Stovall, *Foreground,* 132–37; *CW,* 9:112, 113, 114.

77. *Leaves of Grass:* Comprehensive Reader's Edition, ed. Harold W. Blodgett and Sculley Bradley (New York: New York University Press, 1965), 718.

78. *Leaves of Grass,* 724, 725.

79. R. M. White, quoted in Theodore R. Sarbin, "Contributions to Role-Taking Theory: I. Hypnotic Behavior," *Psychological Review* 57 (1950):262. See also Siikala, 49–51. Further references to Siikala will be noted parenthetically in the text.

80. E. H. Miller, 53.

81. Hollis, *Language and Style,* 79–81; and "Rhetoric," 14.

82. Charles T. Kollerer indeed claims that Whitman's manipulation of language and rhythm not only records a mystical experience, but is intended to engage the reader in a comparable experience. See "The Valved Voice: A Stylistic Analysis of Whitman's 1855 *Leaves of Grass,*" *DAI* 35 (1974):3687A (Ph.D. diss., University of California at Berkeley).

83. This outline of the pattern of the shamanic experience is based upon Siikala's analysis of what might be called "classic" Siberian seances. See especially pp. 330–41.

84. The symbol of the spiral is widely associated with the shaman. Bodies of water are often supposed to be the doors to the underworld; in fact,

among the Yukagir of Siberia the shaman's drum—the most intimate sign of his passage between sacred and profane states as well as his most important trance-inducing tool—is referred to with the word that also means "lake" (Siikala, 99).

85. Douglas Sharon (*Wizard of the Four Winds* [New York: The Free Press, 1978], p. 150) points out that the themes underlying the Peruvian shaman's system are "equilibrium and metamorphosis," which "mediate the tension between opposites symbolized by both power objects [like Whitman's grass] and curing rituals . . . . The shaman is seen as the centered, or integrated, man who focuses his conscious and unconscious faculties . . . in a balanced fashion upon other psyches and his total environment." He dances between "natural and supernatural universes" and can thus enter and leave them at will. "In this process of equilibrium the tension of opposing forces is transcended or channeled and the shaman becomes one with the cosmos. This implies a symbolic death and rebirth which makes ecstatic magical flight, vision, and conquest of the barriers of space and time a reality."

Chapter Three

1. Some might argue that the Preface accomplished the creation of subject and audience, but the Preface was a last-minute thought, whereas "Song of Myself" was the gradually-developed announcement of the poet's presence and purpose. Later he questioned whether the Preface was even worth preserving. This is not, of course, to impugn it as a valuable piece in its own right. Cf. Ivan Marki, *The Trial of the Poet: An Interpretation of the First Edition of* Leaves of Grass (New York: Columbia University Press, 1976).

2. Emory Holloway, *Whitman: An Interpretation in Narrative* (New York: Alfred A. Knopf, 1926), 123; Gay Wilson Allen, *Walt Whitman Handbook* (New York: Packard, 1946), 122.

3. Cf. Edwin Haviland Miller, *Walt Whitman's Poetry* (New York: New York University Press, 1968), 72–84.

4. See Mircea Eliade, *Shamanism*, trans. Willard R. Trask (New York: Bollingen Foundation, 1964), 32. Further references to this work will be noted parenthetically in the text.

5. Walt Whitman, "The Sleepers," in *Walt Whitman's* Leaves of Grass: *The First (1855) Edition*, ed. Malcolm Cowley (New York: Viking, 1959), 105, section 1, line 4. Further references to this work will be noted parenthetically in the text by section and line numbers, following Cowley's numbering (i.e., 1.4). I have chosen Cowley's edition for simplicity's sake, as following the integral text of the 1855 edition is easier than following the new variorum edition. But I have identified passages by section rather than page numbers so that those without easy access to Cowley's edition can follow the discussion without difficulty. Although the original version of the poem did not give section numbers, they are useful for locating passages.

6. Ivan Marki touched on my subject without exploring it when he commented on this passage, noting that the use of the hands is related to a

sort of magical intent: "The protagonist escapes his anguish by inducing, like a shaman of sorts, his own redemptive and illuminating sleep as if it were a ritual trance" (*The Trial of the Poet*, 238). More recently, Marki has confirmed my own reading (as it was originally published) in "The Last Eleven Poems in the 1855 *Leaves of Grass*," *American Literature* 54 (1982):238.

7. Sister Eva Mary, O. S. F., "Shades of Darkness in 'The Sleepers,' " *Walt Whitman Review* 15 (1969):187–90.

8. James E. Miller, Jr., *A Critical Guide to* Leaves of Grass (Chicago: University of Chicago Press, 1957), 133.

9. Quoted in F. O. Matthiessen, *American Renaissance* (London: Oxford University Press, 1941), 539–40.

10. See especially Ake Hultkrantz, "A Definition of Shamanism," *Temenos* 9 (1973):32; and Anna-Leena Siikala, *The Rite Technique of the Siberian Shaman*, Folklore Fellows, FF Communications, no. 220 (Helsinki: Suomalainen, 1978), 26. Siikala, in particular, notes as a commonly-recognized feature of shamanism the "erotic dependence of the shaman on the world of spirits." Hultkrantz, pointing out the frequency of sex-change in the shamanic complex, specifies three forms of sexual versatility: true homosexuality, change of sex only during the trance, and transvestism.

11. Richard Maurice Bucke, ed., *Notes and Fragments* (1899; rpt. Folcroft, Pa.: Folcroft Library Editions, 1972), Item 135, p. 19. The fragment also appears among the lines rejected from *Leaves of Grass* and edited by Oscar Lovell Triggs, in *The Complete Writings of Walt Whitman*, ed. Richard Maurice Bucke, Thomas B. Harned, and Horace Traubel (New York: G. P. Putnam's Sons, 1902), 3:265, Item 33.

12. Eliade, 479. A Peruvian *curandero* has described the beginning of the visionary state as a moment in which " 'the spirit has unfolded in order to go and commune with the spirits of exterior worlds, of other planes, of other dimensions; and matter remains in a state of symbolic death. . . . There is an unfolding and it is symbolically an attitude of death.' " Quoted in Douglas Sharon, *Wizard of the Four Winds* (New York: The Free Press, 1978), 110.

13. "A Reading of 'The Sleepers,' " *Walt Whitman Review* 18 (1972):25.

14. Bucke, *Notes and Fragments*, 19. In the collection of rejected passages edited by Triggs, only the earlier version (Item 38 in Bucke's collection) appears. See *The Complete Writings of Walt Whitman*, 3:263, item 29.

15. See Sharon, 103.

16. Whitman's elision makes for a critical difference in comparing "The Sleepers" and "Song of Myself." Howard Waskow, interpreting the later version of "The Sleepers," says that in "Song of Myself," unlike the shorter poem, the poet "accepts the 'pains of hell' and looks beyond them"—whereas in "The Sleepers" he turns away from death. However, in the original versions of both poems there is no such differentiation. See *Whitman: Explorations in Form* (Chicago: University of Chicago Press, 1966), 186.

17. S. M. Shirokogoroff, *Psychomental Complex of the Tungus* (London: Routledge and Kegan Paul, 1935), 368.

18. Cf. Richard Maurice Bucke, *Walt Whitman* (Philadelphia: David McKay, 1883), 171–72; Frederik Schyberg, *Walt Whitman*, trans. Evie Allison Allen (New York: Columbia University Press, 1951), 99–100; Richard Chase, *Walt Whitman Reconsidered* (New York: William Sloane Associates, 1955), 54–57; Edwin Haviland Miller, 72–84; Stephen A. Black, *Whitman's Journeys Into Chaos* (Princeton: Princeton University Press, 1975), 46; and Robert E. Abrams, "The Function of Dreams and Dream Logic in Whitman's Poetry," *Texas Studies in Language and Literature* 17 (1975):599–616.

19. Mircea Eliade, *Myths, Dreams, and Mysteries*, trans. Philip Mairet (New York: Harper & Row, 1975), 18.

20. See especially Thomas J. Rountree, "Whitman's Indirect Expression and its Application to 'Song of Myself,' " *PMLA* 73 (1958):549–55; Charles T. Kollerer, "The Valved Voice: A Stylistic Analysis of Whitman's 1855 *Leaves of Grass*," *DAI* 35 (1974):3687A (Ph.D. diss., University of California at Berkeley); and C. Carroll Hollis, *Language and Style in Leaves of Grass* (Baton Rouge: Louisiana State University Press, 1983), 65–123. Hollis objects to calling Whitman a prophet or shaman specifically because the poet experimented diligently with language in order to "sound like" an ecstatic performer. The assumption behind such an objection is that the performances of "true" shamans are naive and spontaneous, free of "artfulness." If we abandon this assumption—as studies of shamanic role-taking indicate we must—we will find Hollis's linguistic analysis to serve our interpretation admirably. Mitchell Robert Breitwieser's examination of the uses of "I" in *Leaves of Grass* also supports my interpretation, although he does not speak of religious, ecstatic, or ritualistic elements as such. See his "Who Speaks in Whitman's Poems?" in *The American Renaissance: New Dimensions*, ed. Harry R. Garvin and Peter C. Carafiol (Lewisburg: Bucknell University Press, 1983), 121–43.

21. Cf. Edwin Haviland Miller, 19.

22. Helge Normann Nilsen, "The mystic message. Whitman's 'Song of Myself,' " *Edda* 56 (1969):401.

23. See, for instance, Roy Harvey Pearce, *The Continuity of American Poetry* (Princeton: Princeton University Press, 1961), 72; Chadwick Hansen, "Walt Whitman's 'Song of Myself': Democratic Epic," in *The American Renaissance*, ed. George Hendrick (Frankfurt: Diesterweg, 1961), 77–88; Peter Wolfe, " 'Song of Myself'—The Indirect Figure in the Word-Mosaic," *American Transcendental Quarterly* 12 (1971):20–25; and James E. Miller, Jr., *The American Quest for a Supreme Fiction: Whitman's Legacy in the Personal Epic* (Chicago: University of Chicago Press, 1979), 31–43.

24. Pearce, 73.

25. James E. Miller, Jr., *The American Quest for a Supreme Fiction*, 36.

26. James E. Miller, Jr., *A Critical Guide*, 6; Waskow, 139; Chaviva Hosek, "The Rhetoric of Whitman's 1855 'Song of Myself,' " *Centennial Re-*

view 20 (1976):264. Cf. Gay Wilson Allen, *The Solitary Singer,* rev. ed. (New York: New York University Press, 1967), 164. The fact that Whitman came to poetry from an interest in oratory would tend to support the "monodrama" designation, and "Song of Myself" has its generic ancestry in Whitman's wish to "counterpart," " 'in the first person, present time, the divine ecstasy of the ancient Pythia, oracles, priests, possessed persons, demoniacs &c.' " Quoted by Thomas B. Harned, "Walt Whitman and Oratory," in *The Complete Writings of Walt Whitman,* 8:249.

27. Mutlu Blasing, *The Art of Life* (Austin: University of Texas Press, 1977), 40–41. Eliade has speculated that shamanism contributed "a large number of epic 'subjects' or motifs, as well as many characters, images, and clichés of epic literature," which were borrowed from narratives of ecstatic adventures in the superhuman worlds (*Shamanism,* 510). This is certainly true of many ancient Asian epics and Native American narratives, but may be true of many Western epics, as well, and such myths as that of Orpheus. Cf. Andreas Lommel, *Shamanism: The Beginnings of Art,* trans. Michael Bullock (New York: McGraw-Hill, 1967), 138. Lommel believes that the shaman's soul-journey is the "mimed repetition of a myth" that is based upon "the travels and adventures of a shamanistic tribal hero of ancient times." The question of which comes first—the myth or the rite—is still a sticky one in anthropological circles when the origin of these two *forms* is considered; but it is clear that many *particular* myths and epics are based upon ecstatic adventures. Indeed, as indicated in the preceding chapter, Carlyle had probably led Whitman to believe that such was the case.

28. Related views are expressed by E. H. Miller, who perceives a movement in the poem "from aloneness to entry into society" (p. 92), and J. Albert Robbins, who finds the narrative structure based upon the poet's gradual awakening to his messianic responsibilities ("The Narrative Form of 'Song of Myself,' " *American Transcendental Quarterly* 12 [1971]:17–20). Both of these scholars, however, focus upon the poet's self-realization without considering the intended social function of the poem.

29. Views similar to mine concerning the importance of audience-creation appear in Hosek, 263; and Marki, 226.

30. See, for example Pearce, 74–77; Cowley's "Introduction" to the 1855 *Leaves of Grass;* and James E. Miller, Jr., *A Critical Guide,* 8.

31. This idea is the foundation of Marki's view of "the curious triplicate process" of the poem (pp. 47–52).

32. Eugene G. d'Aquili and Charles D. Laughlin, Jr., "The Neurobiology of Myth and Ritual," in *The Spectrum of Ritual,* ed. Eugene G. d'Aquili, Charles D. Laughlin, Jr., and John McManus (New York: Columbia University Press, 1979), 177. The neural basis of the ritual trance-induction process, which I will not elaborate on here, is outlined by d'Aquili and Laughlin, and also, in greater detail, by Barbara W. Lex ("The Neurobiology of Ritual Trance") in *The Spectrum of Ritual,* chapter 4. The important point is that the ecstatic state allows simultaneous stimulation of two different spheres of consciousness—one causal and "analytic" (presenting paradoxes and antinomies), the other "holistic" and "gestaltic"; thus logical paradoxes appear

simultaneously "as antinomies and as unified wholes" (d'Aquili and Laughlin, 175–76).

33. Interpretations of Whitman's catalogue technique support this view of its function. See Roger Asselineau, *The Evolution of Walt Whitman* (Cambridge, Mass.: Harvard University Press, 1962), 2:102; Rountree, 552; Lawrence Buell, *Literary Transcendentalism* (Ithaca: Cornell University Press, 1973), 166–86; and John B. Mason, "Walt Whitman's Catalogues: Rhetorical Means for Two Journeys in 'Song of Myself,' " *American Literature* 45 (1973):34. It is worth pointing out that the catalogue is commonly used in many types of ritual and prayer.

34. See Laughlin and d'Aquili, "The Neurobiology of Myth and Ritual," 177: "Ritual is often performed to solve a problem that is presented via myth to the verbal analytic consciousness" (a view held by Levi-Strauss as well). Another scientific discussion of this phenomenon is that of Arnold J. Mandell, "Toward a Psychobiology of Transcendence: God in the Brain," in *The Psychobiology of Consciousness*, ed. Julian M. and Richard J. Davidson (New York: Plenum Press, 1980), pp. 404–5; driving rhythms and repetitive stimuli lead to a progressive change in brain functions, including disintegration of the normal cognitive system. Then a break-down of inhibitions upon the reticular arousal system "brings the feelings of high energy . . . along with the loss of comparator function [causing the sense of one's fluidity— union with God, loss of ego boundaries]. Dualistic debates, conflicts, and ruminations between alternatives suddenly disappear with a feeling and perception of unity, as the internal organization . . . becomes the dominant subjective world."

35. See Waskow, 16–17 and 28: "The touchstone of fusion, the blending of two extremes, is applied to almost every area about which Whitman records an opinion." William White seems to impugn "mystical" explanations for this fusion while emphasizing the sexual quality of Whitman's conception: "An examination of the process of Whitman's bringing together what seem to be polar opposites and his synthesizing (mating) of them to form a new wholeness at a higher level can aid the reader in comprehending what often passes for mysticism in *Leaves of Grass*." White, "The Dynamics of Whitman's Poetry," *Sewanee Review* 80 (1972):349. However, as many critics have come to realize, this "mating" differs from the dialectical pattern of thesis-antithesis-synthesis.

36. See Victor Turner (*The Forest of Symbols* [Ithaca: Cornell University Press, 1967], 30), who points out that a "dominant" ritual symbol "encapsulates the major properties of the total ritual process." A good example of this, which is very similar to Whitman's use of the leaf of grass, is found in the symbolism of the San Pedro plant (a night-blooming cereus) in Peruvian *curanderos'* seances; the object of the rite is to make the people and symbolic elements "bloom" at midnight, obviously a moment of symbolic transition (in Whitman's poem, the daybreak of sections 24–28). After that the power "generated" by the shaman's performance is directed toward therapy. "Thus, in essence, what a *curandero* does during a seance is to replicate symbolically the growth cycle of the San Pedro, which provides the prototype for traditional *curanderismo*" (Sharon, 47).

37. "Song of Myself," in Cowley's edition of the 1855 *Leaves of Grass,* section 2, lines 25–29; further references to this work will be noted parenthetically in the text in the same manner I have used in discussing "The Sleepers."

38. Walter Scott, *Letters on Demonology and Witchcraft,* 2d ed. (London: John Murray, 1831), 45–46.

39. Harold Aspiz, *Walt Whitman and the Body Beautiful* (Urbana: University of Illinois Press, 1980), 169. Critics have often compared Whitman's invocation of the soul to epic invocations of the Muse—a valid comparison, but I would suggest, with Eliade, that the epic invocations descend from religious practices of "possession" or shamanistic inspiration, and Whitman's aim was to get behind the epic form to the "subjective" ritual performance.

40. E. H. Miller has protested that the experience of section five "is not to be explained away or conventionalized by vague descriptions in terms of an even vaguer mysticism" (p. 20), but we must be careful about whose "conventions" we adopt, and what limitations accompany them. The psychological process embodied in the episode in no way compromises the importance of the religious aspect of the passage. Psychological analysis of religious experience, as William James cautioned, does not "explain away" its religious value.

41. Victor Turner, *The Forest of Symbols,* 28. Further references to this work will be noted parenthetically in the text.

42. E. H. Miller, 91–92. Interestingly, the dominant symbol among the Ndembu whom Victor Turner studied—the "milk tree"—has very similar associations.

43. Joseph M. DeFalco, "The Narrative Shift in Whitman's 'Song of Myself,'" *Walt Whitman Review* 9 (1963):82–84.

44. DeFalco, 84.

45. Cf. Robin Magowan, "The Horse of the Gods: Possession in 'Song of Myself,'" *Walt Whitman Review* 15 (1969):67–76. Magowan compares the ecstatic process of sections twenty-five through twenty-seven to the possession sequence in a Haitian *hounfor* ceremony.

46. Eliade, *Shamanism,* 99: "Friendship with animals, knowledge of their language, transformation into an animal are so many signs that the shaman has re-established the 'paradisal' situation lost at the dawn of time."

47. Eliade, *Myths, Dreams, and Mysteries,* 63.

48. Cf. Waskow, 179–80; Nilsen, 408; Richard R. Adicks, "The Sea-Fight Episode in 'Song of Myself,'" *Walt Whitman Review* 13 (1967):20; E. H. Miller, 106; and Robbins, 18.

49. Cf. F. DeWolfe Miller, "The Partitive Studies of 'Song of Myself,'" *American Transcendental Quarterly* 12 (1971):11–17. This scholar compares Whitman to the Christian revivalist preacher.

50. Cf. Waskow, 182; James E. Miller, Jr., *Critical Guide,* 26.

51. Although I feel that he overemphasizes the comic aspects of "Song of Myself," I have benefited from Richard Chase's highlighting of Whitman's humor. See *Walt Whitman Reconsidered,* especially 74–75.

52. See Victor Turner's discussion of pilgrimage, liminality, and *communitas,* particularly in *Image and Pilgrimage in Christian Culture* (New York: Columbia University Press, 1978).

53. Cf. James E. Miller, Jr., *Critical Guide,* 34: "As Whitman's dramatization of the entry into the mystical state [through erotic ecstasy] is inverted, so also is the hint at the meaning of self and existence grasped from the quickly receding mystical consciousness. At some stage in the traditional mystical experience, 'the human instinct for personal happiness must be killed.' Whitman has used the mystical experience as a framework within which to deny some of its basic traditions."

54. See Turner on the dominant ritual symbol, *The Forest of Symbols,* 30.

Chapter Four

1. An early hint of this development is the subtitle of Whitman's unpublished pamphlet of 1856, *The Eighteenth Presidency! Voice of Walt Whitman to each Young Man in the Nation, North, South, East, and West.* See the critical text edited by Edward F. Grier (Lawrence: University of Kansas Press, 1956).

2. Of the biographers, Roger Asselineau has most emphasized Whitman's political frustration as contributor to a "crisis" between 1856 and 1860; but even Asselineau believes that the political aspect of the crisis had become secondary by 1858–59, when the main source of despair was Whitman's supposed discovery of his homosexuality and possibly the loss of a lover. Support for this widely-accepted assumption is remarkably sparse. See *The Evolution of Walt Whitman* (Cambridge, Mass.: Harvard University Press, 1960), 1:98–126. See also Gay Wilson Allen, *Walt Whitman Handbook* (Chicago: Packard, 1946), 146.

3. As evidence of Whitman's optimism in early 1858, see the editorial of 2 April 1858, "Lecompton in the House" (in *I Sit and Look Out,* ed. Emory Holloway and Vernolian Schwarz [New York: Columbia University Press, 1932], 94–95): "As Senator Seward remarked in a recent speech, the turning point of the contest between Freedom and Slavery has been passed, and henceforth the black tide is on the ebb." Whitman believed the "healthy" masses were beginning to wake up and split from the dishonorable politicians on the conservative wing of the Democratic party; see "Sneaking Politicians," an editorial of 23 April 1858, in *I Sit and Look Out,* 95–96. But in an editorial of 7 March 1859 (shortly before Whitman was apparently kicked off the staff of the Brooklyn *Daily Times*) he is very pessimistic, believing the "ultra Southerners" would prevent Douglas's nomination, thus causing the defeat of the Democratic party, "hoping thereby to precipitate a disruption of the Union." This is precisely what happened in the following year. See *I Sit and Look Out,* 99.

NOTES · 211

4. Roy Harvey Pearce, "Introduction," in Walt Whitman, *Leaves of Grass*, Facsimile Edition of the 1860 Text (Ithaca: Cornell University Press, 1961), x–xviii. For a long time, some of the best Whitman scholars have insisted upon the differentiation of poet from prophet; see also Gay Wilson Allen, *The Two Poets of* Leaves of Grass (Westwood, N. J.: The Kindle Press, 1969); and Malcolm Cowley, "Introduction," in *Walt Whitman's* Leaves of Grass: *The First (1855) Edition*, ed. Malcolm Cowley (New York: Viking, 1959), xxvii.

5. "So long!" in *Leaves of Grass*, Facsimile Edition of the 1860 Text, 451–52, stanza 3.

6. Robin P. Hoople, "'Chants Democratic and Native American': A Neglected Sequence in the Growth of *Leaves of Grass*," *American Literature* 42 (1970):181–82.

7. Thomas, "Whitman's Achievements in the Personal Style in *Calamus*," *Walt Whitman Quarterly Review* 1 (1983):38. See also Whitman's "All About a Mocking-bird" (1859), in *A Child's Reminiscence by Walt Whitman*, ed. Thomas Ollive Mabbott and Rollo G. Silver (Seattle: University of Washington Bookstore, 1930), 19–20: "'Leaves of Grass' has not yet been really published at all," said the poet in his self-advertisement and defense of "A Word Out of the Sea" for the *Saturday Press*. "Walt Whitman, for his own purposes, slowly trying his hand at the edifice, the structure he has undertaken, has lazily loafed on, letting each part have time to set,—evidently building not so much with reference to any part itself, considered alone, but more with reference to the ensemble."

8. "Democratic Vistas," in *Prose Works 1892*, ed. Floyd Stovall (New York: New York University Press, 1964), 2:414. James E. Miller, Jr., has also emphasized this point and, like myself, finds "at the center of the 'Calamus' emotion . . . a profound religious feeling." *A Critical Guide to* Leaves of Grass (Chicago: University of Chicago Press, 1957), 66.

9. "Calamus" number five, in *Leaves of Grass*, Facsimile Edition of the 1860 Text, p. 349, stanza 5.

10. "Calamus" number four, in *Leaves of Grass*, Facsimile Edition of the 1860 Text, p. 347, lines 4–13. Further citations of the poem will refer to this edition and will be noted parenthetically in the text by page and line numbers.

11. "Song of Myself," in *Walt Whitman's* Leaves of Grass: *The First (1855) Edition*, 56, lines 694–701.

12. See Fredson Bowers, "Introduction," in *Whitman's Manuscripts, Leaves of Grass (1860)*, ed. Fredson Bowers (Chicago: University of Chicago Press, 1955), lxx.

13. Thomas, 41.

14. Paul Ricoeur, *The Symbolism of Evil*, trans. Emerson Buchanan (Boston: Harper & Row, 1967), 5–8. Cf. Asselineau, 1:127: "The gravity of the political situation was not his only torment, there were many other reasons

for distress. The dangers menacing democracy were after all only one aspect among many of an infinitely greater problem, the problem of evil. . . . [I]t was this omnipresence of evil in creation and in himself which obsessed him." See also R. Galen Hanson, "Anxiety as Human Predicament: Whitman's 'Calamus' no. 9," *Walt Whitman Review* 21 (1975):73–75. Hanson emphasizes existential anxiety in the poem later entitled "Hours Continuing Long," which, he shows, has a profound religious thrust.

15. "Leaves of Grass" number one, in *Leaves of Grass*, Facsimile Edition of the 1860 Text, p. 195, stanza 1. Further references to this poem will be cited parenthetically in the text by page and stanza numbers.

16. "Calamus" number seven, in *Leaves of Grass*, Facsimile Edition of the 1860 Text, 352–53, lines 1–6. Further references to this poem will be cited parenthetically in the text by page and line numbers.

17. For other views of how Whitman sublimated homoerotic yearnings in his poetry of "adhesiveness" and democratic brotherhood, see especially Gustav Bychowski, "Walt Whitman, A Study in Sublimation," *Psychoanalysis and the Social Sciences* 3 (1951):252–53, 258–61; James E. Miller, Jr., *A Critical Guide*, 70; Edwin Haviland Miller, *Walt Whitman's Poetry* (Boston: Houghton Mifflin, 1968), 152; and Asselineau, 2:121–25.

18. In *Leaves of Grass:* Comprehensive Reader's Edition, ed. Harold W. Blodgett and Sculley Bradley (New York: New York University Press, 1965), 661, lines 18–19. Cf. Kenneth Burke, *Attitudes Toward History*, 3d ed. (Berkeley: University of California Press, 1984), 218: "People try to combat alienation by *immediacy,* such as the senses alone provide."

19. *Leaves of Grass*, Facsimile Edition of the 1860 Text, 376.

20. *Leaves of Grass*, Facsimile Edition of the 1860 Text, 276, stanza 31.

21. Asselineau, 2:13.

22. See the 1876 Preface, in *Leaves of Grass:* Comprehensive Reader's Edition, 751n.:

> I also sent out Leaves of Grass to arouse and set flowing in men's and women's hearts, young and old, (my present and future readers,) endless streams of living, pulsating love and friendship, directly from them to myself, now and ever. To this terrible, irrepressible yearning, (surely more or less down underneath in most human souls,)—this never-satisfied appetite for sympathy, and this boundless offering of sympathy—this universal democratic comradeship—this old, eternal, yet ever-new interchange of adhesiveness, so fitly emblematic of America—I have given in that book, undisguisedly, declaredly, the openest expression.

23. See especially Bowers, li–lxiii.

24. Charles Feidelson, overstating the case, called "Starting From Paumanok" " 'Song of Myself' in minature" (*Symbolism and American Liter-*

ature [Chicago: University of Chicago Press, 1953], 19). However, discussions of the development of the poem until now have paid little attention to the growth of the ecstatic structure. The most detailed reading of correspondences between lines of the poem and the clusters and poems of the 1860 edition is in Elizabeth Wells, "The Structure of Whitman's 1860 *Leaves of Grass*," *Walt Whitman Review* 15 (1969):131–61.

25. Bowers, lii.

26. Cf. Bowers, lxi; on the early organization of "Premonition" (precursor to "Proto-leaf"), see Bowers, lx.

27. "Proto-leaf," in *Leaves of Grass,* Facsimile Edition of the 1860 Text, 7, stanza 9. Further references to the poem will be noted parenthetically in the text by page and stanza number.

28. See "All About a Mocking-bird," 19–20.

29. The most recent and sustained confusion of the shamanistic coitus and the earthly sexual experience is that of Robert K. Martin, in his discussion of Whitman's ecstatic poems (*The Homosexual Tradition in American Poetry* [Austin: University of Texas Press, 1979], 8–33). Of course, that the shamanic tryst is frequently homosexual in Whitman's poems is undeniable and significant.

30. Clifford Geertz, *The Interpretation of Cultures* (New York: Basic Books, 1973), 90. Geertz's emphasis.

31. Geertz, 108.

32. Geertz, 114, 118.

33. Geertz, 116, 122.

34. "All About a Mocking-bird," 19.

35. *The Solitary Singer,* rev. ed. (New York: New York University Press, 1967), 233. The "real incident" was probably one concerning a mocking bird at Egg Harbor, Long Island, which became a local legend. See Florence MacDermid Chace, "A Note on Whitman's Mockingbird," *Modern Language Notes* 61 (1946):93–94; Robert D. Faner, *Walt Whitman and Opera* (Carbondale: Southern Illinois University Press, 1951), 67; and Courtland Y. White, "A Whitman Ornithology," *Cassinia* 35 (1945):16. Notice that Whitman did *not* say the poem was founded on a *personal experience.*

36. *Solitary Singer,* 233–35. The most important "biographical" readings of the poem are in Frederik Schyberg, *Walt Whitman,* trans. Evie Allison Allen (New York: Columbia University Press, 1951), 147–48; Floyd Stovall, "Main Drifts in Whitman's Poetry," *American Literature* 4 (1932):8–10; Stephen Whicher, "Whitman's Awakening to Death: Toward a Biographical Reading of 'Out of the Cradle Endlessly Rocking,'" *Studies in Romanticism* (1961), 1:9–28; and C. Griffith, "Sex and Death: The Significance of Whitman's *Calamus* Themes," *Philological Quarterly* 39 (1960):18–38.

37. Faner, 104.

38. Faner, 67, 87. See also Justin Kaplan, *Walt Whitman: A Life* (New York: Simon & Schuster, 1980), 178.

39. Faner, 8, 198. Faner does not specify whether or not Alboni and Bettini actually performed *together* in this opera—only that Bettini played Fernando and that one of Alboni's favorite parts was that of the king's mistress (and Fernando's lover), which she played often.

40. See the quotation from "Goodbye My Fancy," in Faner, 3: "'I should like well if Madame Alboni and the old composer Verdi (and Bettini the tenor, if he is living), could know how much noble pleasure and happiness they gave me then, and how deeply I always remember them and thank them to this day.'"

41. "Letters From Paumanok [No. 3]," New York *Evening Post*, 14 August 1851, rpt. in *The Uncollected Poetry and Prose of Walt Whitman*, ed. Emory Holloway (1921; rpt. Gloucester, Mass.: Peter Smith, 1972), 1:258–59; my emphasis.

42. Whicher makes the strongest case for a different point of view, deemphasizing the importance of Whitman's first awakening for interpretation of "Out of the Cradle."

43. Whitman, "The Dead Tenor," in *Leaves of Grass:* Comprehensive Reader's Edition, 523, lines 3–10.

44. See, for instance, Item 108 in the "Notes and Fragments" edited by Richard Maurice Bucke, in *The Complete Writings of Walt Whitman*, ed. Richard Maurice Bucke, Thomas B. Harned, and Horace Traubel (New York: G. P. Putnam's Sons, 1902), 9:130–32.

45. Cf. Whicher, 27. "Where 'Song of Myself' had dramatized the omnipotence of bardic vision, 'Out of the Cradle' dramatizes the discovery that the power of the bard is only to sing his own limits." This is a very common view; see also Stovall, 9; Griffith; and Richard Chase, *Walt Whitman Reconsidered*, 112. My own view is much closer to that of James E. Miller, Jr., *A Critical Guide*, 104–5.

46. See Robert J. Bertholf, "Poetic Epistemology of Whitman's 'Out of the Cradle,'" *Walt Whitman Review* 10 (1964):73–77; and Richard Chase, 122.

47. I. M. Lewis, *Ecstatic Religion* (Middlesex, England: Penguin, 1971), 189.

48. Andreas Lommel, *Shamanism: The Beginnings of Art*, trans. Michael Bullock (New York: McGraw-Hill, 1967), 11.

49. "A Word Out of the Sea," in *Leaves of Grass*, Facsimile Edition of the 1860 Text, 274, stanza 21. Further references to this poem will be noted parenthetically in the text by page and stanza numbers.

50. See Pearce, xliii, on how the points of view of the bird and the boy are "hypnotically merged" beginning at this point in the poem.

51. Lewis, 64. Compare Bertholf's statement concerning the "brotherhood" of boy and bird: "Such an association is possible only when the boy can hear and feel meaning in the bird's song, only when he knows the core, the essence, of the bird. Brotherhood with the bird is the first step in the process of the boy-exile becoming the man-poet" (p. 75).

52. Cf. Leo Spitzer, "*Explication de Texte* Applied to Walt Whitman's Poem 'Out of the Cradle Endlessly Rocking,'" *ELH: Journal of English Literary History* 16 (1949):229–49.

53. Spitzer, 247–48.

54. Spitzer, 248.

55. Spitzer, 249.

56. Chase, 123.

57. Discussing the relation of the initiation crisis to the experience of chaos, I. M. Lewis explains that "the initial experience withdraws the victim from the secure world of society and of ordered existence, and exposes him directly to those forces which, though they may be held to uphold the social order, also ultimately threaten it" (p. 188).

58. The discussions of "*So long!*" are so rare and brief that they are hardly worth mentioning. Those who have written about the poem have generally felt that it expresses a "tragic" consciousness, in accord with their view that the 1860 edition is flooded with darkness because of the poet's inner problems or a lost love. See Allen, *Walt Whitman Handbook*, 161, 185–86; Asselineau, 2:64–65; and John Snyder, *The Dear Love of Man* (The Hague: Mouton, 1975), 160–63.

59. "*So long!*" in *Leaves of Grass*, Facsimile Edition of the 1860 Text, 455, stanza 18. Further references to the poem will be noted parenthetically in the text with page and stanza numbers.

60. 1876 Preface, 745n.

61. Cf. Allen, *Walt Whitman Handbook*, 161, 185–86; Asselineau, 2:64–65; and Snyder, 160–63.

Chapter Five

1. Roy P. Basler, ed., *Walt Whitman's Memoranda During the War and Death of Abraham Lincoln* (Bloomington: Indiana University Press, 1962), 65n. Future references to this work will be noted parenthetically in the text as "*Memoranda.*"

2. "Death of Abraham Lincoln," in *Memoranda,* 12.

3. "Preface 1876," in *Leaves of Grass:* Comprehensive Reader's Edition, ed. Harold W. Blodgett and Sculley Bradley (New York: New York University Press, 1965), 750n.

4. See also Edwin Haviland Miller, *Walt Whitman's Poetry* (New York: New York University Press, 1968), 16.

5. Quoted by Gay Wilson Allen in *The Solitary Singer,* rev. ed. (New York: New York University Press, 1967), 272, from a Whitman notebook entry of 16 April 1861.

6. Roger Asselineau, *The Evolution of Walt Whitman* (Cambridge, Mass.: Harvard University Press, 1960), 1:146–47. See also Albert Gelpi, *The Tenth Muse* (Cambridge, Mass.: Harvard University Press, 1975), 185: "Whitman's care for the victims of both sides of the Civil War in military hospitals became only a practical application of the mystical and visionary role of American medicine man." Gelpi repeatedly refers to Whitman as a "shaman" in a rather loose way.

7. Letter to Nicholas Wyckoff or Daniel L. Northrup, 14 May 1863, in Walt Whitman, *The Correspondence,* ed. Edwin Haviland Miller (New York: New York University Press, 1961), 1:102.

8. Letter to Margaret S. Curtis, 4 October 1863, in *The Correspondence,* 1:155.

9. Letter to Hugo Fritsch, 8 October 1863, in *The Correspondence,* 1:159.

10. Letter to Thomas Jefferson Whitman, 13 February 1863, in *The Correspondence,* 1:75. Whitman would repeat the hospital metaphor in a letter to Emerson and in the *Memoranda,* 5: ". . . the marrow of the tragedy concentrated in those Hospitals—(it seem'd sometimes as if the whole interest of the land, North and South, was one vast central Hospital, and all the rest of the affair but flanges)—those forming the Untold and Unwritten History of the War." See also *With Walt Whitman in Camden,* ed. Gertrude Traubel and William White (Carbondale: Southern Illinois University Press, 1982), 6:353: regarding antebellum America, Whitman says abolitionism was " 'a pimple, a boil—yes, a carbuncle, that's it—out of the nation's bad blood: out of a corpus spoiled, maltreated, bruised, poisoned. . . . [I]t had to come out—and out it came: a great flood, leading upwards!' "

11. "The Wound-dresser," in *Leaves of Grass:* Comprehensive Reader's Edition, 310, lines 23–24. Further references to the poems will use this edition, noted parenthetically in the text by page and line numbers. I have used the Reader's Edition text in this chapter because of its easy availability and because the poems discussed were not significantly altered following their original publication in *Drum-Taps and Sequel.*

12. M. Wynn Thomas, "Whitman and the American Democratic Identity Before and During the Civil War," *Journal of American Studies* 15 (1981):73–93.

13. See especially James E. Miller, Jr., *A Critical Guide to* Leaves of Grass (Chicago: University of Chicago Press, 1957), 220–25.

14. *The Correspondence,* 1:69.

15. Whitman's very method of composition during the war supports this interpretation. He later described to Horace Traubel how he had composed *Drum-Taps* poems "on the spot" in little notebooks, sometimes weeping as he wrote. He would record scenes "in snatches" while he mixed with the crowds and the soldiers, then put the material together when he returned home—" 'by writing at the instant the very heart-beat of life is caught.' " The notebooks were among his most "sacred" possessions. See *With Walt Whitman in Camden* (New York: Mitchell Kennerley, 1915), 2:137, 25–26.

16. Letter to Nathaniel Bloom and John F. S. Gray, 19–20 March 1863, in *The Correspondence,* 1:81–82.

17. *The Correspondence,* 1:82.

18. Cf. Richard Chase, *Walt Whitman Reconsidered* (New York: William Sloane Associates, 1955), 136.

19. Cf. Chase, 137.

20. *Specimen Days,* in *Prose Works 1892,* ed. Floyd Stovall (New York: New York University Press, 1963), 1:99.

21. *Memoranda,* 47. Whitman's testimony here goes directly counter to Mutlu Blasing's recent assertion (in "Whitman's 'Lilacs' and the Grammars of Time," *PMLA* 97 [1982]:31–39) that, awakening to the "terrorism of history" as a result of Lincoln's death, the poet relinquished "the fiction of natural continuity, the grandest of fictions" (p. 38).

22. See "Death of Lincoln," in *Memoranda,* 11; and "Preface 1876," 750n.

23. To my knowledge only Howard Waskow has previously judged the coffin to be part of a symbolic "quarternity" including the lilac, the star, and the bird. See *Whitman: Explorations in Form* (Chicago: University of Chicago Press, 1966), 222–42. Probably the reason for the common oversight is the absence of the coffin at the end of the poem (when the speaker mentions star, lilac, and bird) and the reference to a "trinity" in the opening section. Note, however, that the "trinity" is composed of the lilac, the star, and "thought of him I love"—the two perennial symbols and the poet's reflection upon the dead "comrade," which is awakened in spring by the return of the star and lilac. Only through considerable symbolic reduction can we find in the bird an allegorical representation of the "thought of him I love"; careful reading of the carol hardly supports such an interpretation. Neither bird nor coffin appears in the first section because they are historically "past" and can be invoked only after the return of the perennial symbols evokes the poet's "thought." Some scholars have anaiyzed the "dark cloud" as a fourth symbol. See E. H. Miller, 187.

24. Jane A. Nelson, "Ecstasy and Transformation in Whitman's 'Lilacs,' " *Walt Whitman Review* 18 (1972):113.

25. Terence S. Turner, "Transformation, Hierarchy and Transcendence: A Reformulation of Van Gennep's Model of the Structure of Rites de

Passage," in Sally F. Moore and Barbara G. Myerhoff, ed., *Secular Ritual* (Amsterdam: Van Gorcum, 1977), 53–70.

26. Terence Turner, 68.

27. Whitman was not the only mourner to note the profusion of lilacs in the capitol at the time of Lincoln's death; lilacs were, in fact, conspicuous among the flowers surrounding the bier as it lay in state, and later heaped upon the coffin as it was conveyed to Springfield. See Thomas Parkinson, "'When Lilacs Last in the Door-yard Bloom'd' and the American Civil Religion," *Southern Review* 19 (1983):1–16.

28. Nelson, 114.

29. See Nelson, 115–17; Mircea Eliade, *Shamanism*, trans. Willard R. Trask (New York: Bollingen Foundation, 1964), 98. See also E. H. Miller's speculations concerning the "composite bird-poet" archetype and the association of the bird with the flight of the soul, 189–90. Birds are common tutelary spirits in shamanism, and shamans of Siberia and the American Northwest often imitate bird calls during their ecstatic performances.

30. Harsharan Singh Ahluwalia ("The Private Self and the Public Self in Whitman's 'Lilacs,'" *Walt Whitman Review* 23 [1977]:173) has pointed out that before the carol begins the poet claims his voice "tallied the song of the bird," whereas the first line following the carol states that the thrush sings "to the tally of [the poet's] soul." The achievement of equality with (possibly even control over) the possessing agent marks a transcendence to "self-possession" and mastery of the symbolic elements which have, prior to the carol, held the poet in subjection.

31. Burke, *Attitudes Toward History,* 3d ed. (Berkeley: University of California Press, 1984), 336–38.

32. Objections to the designation of "Lilacs" as pastoral elegy have been as common as defenses of it, but the elegiac tradition has remained a point of reference for many scholars. See especially Richard P. Adams, "Whitman's 'Lilacs' and the Traditional Pastoral Elegy," *PMLA* 72 (1957):479–87; Charles Clay Doyle, "Poetry and Pastoral: A Dimension of Whitman's 'Lilacs,'" *Walt Whitman Review* 15 (1969):242–45; and E. J. Hinz, "Whitman's 'Lilacs': The Power of Elegy," *Bucknell Review* 20, no. 2 (1972):35–54. Opposing stands are taken by David Daiches, "Walt Whitman: Impressionist Prophet," in Leaves of Grass One Hundred Years After, ed. Milton Hindus (Stanford: Stanford University Press, 1955), 118; Chase, 141–42; Charles Feidelson, Jr., *Symbolism and American Literature* (Chicago: University of Chicago Press, 1953), 21–22; W. P. Elledge, "Whitman's 'Lilacs' As Romantic Narrative," *Walt Whitman Review* 12 (1966):59; Ellen S. Goodman, "'Lilacs' and the Pastoral Elegy Reconsidered," *Books at Brown* 24 (1971):119–33; and Thomas Parkinson, 1–16.

33. For the parallel phenomenon in a shamanic "lyric," see P. Simoncsics's transcription and analysis, "The Structure of a Nenets Magic Chant," in V. Dioszegi and M. Hoppal, ed., *Shamanism in Siberia* (Budapest: Akademiai Kiado, 1978), 397–402.

34. Cf. John Lynen, who in *The Design of the Present* (New Haven: Yale University Press, 1969), 310–33, analyzes the poem as an "act of remembering," an exploration of a present moment in which the past is revived.

35. Quoted in C. Carroll Hollis, *Language and Style in* Leaves of Grass (Baton Rouge: Louisiana State University Press, 1983), 86–87. Wright's article is "The Lyric Present: Simple Present Verbs in English Poems," *PMLA* 89 (1974):563–79. He does make brief reference to "Lilacs" in illustrating his theory of the "lyric present."

36. Hollis, 87. For an extended discussion of speech acts and illocutionary force in Whitman's poetry, focusing upon "Song of Myself," see chapter 3, 65–123, in Hollis's book. Although I am indebted to Hollis for pointing out the importance of speech acts in *Leaves of Grass*, and to John R. Searle (whom Hollis cites extensively) for his taxonomy of speech acts, with Emile Benveniste I stop short of accepting the "general theory" of illocutionary acts, pioneered in J. L. Austin's later works and extended toward a philosophical theory of "intentionality" by Searle. See Benveniste, *Problems in General Linguistics*, trans. Mary Elizabeth Meek (Coral Gables, Florida: University of Miami Press, 1971), 230–38.

37. "Problems in the Theory of Fiction," *Diacritics* 14 (1984):10.

38. See Karen Lystra, "Clifford Geertz and the Concept of Culture," *Prospects* 8 (1983):31–47. In relation to a Balinese rite Geertz studied, Lystra says, "The cockfight . . . creates the reality that it also represents" (p. 36).

39. *Expression and Meaning* (Cambridge: Cambridge University Press, 1979), 18.

40. *The Pursuit of Signs* (Ithaca: Cornell University Press, 1981), 152–53.

41. Whitman did, in fact, perform a sort of ritual observance on 14 or 15 April each year in his old age, by reading his lecture on the "Death of Lincoln." He told Traubel, " 'I ought never let that day pass without a word hailing it' "; " 'It is a sentiment with me, to keep this day sacred for Lincoln' "; " 'I must not speak that speech but on Lincoln's own day. It has a sacred import—a sacred origin: it is a fire on the altar.' " *With Walt Whitman in Camden*, 6:328, 331, 339.

42. "Preface 1876," 748.

43. Robert N. Bellah, "Civil Religion in America," in *American Civil Religion*, ed. Russell E. Richey and Donald G. Jones (New York: Harper & Row, 1974), 32. See also John F. Wilson, *Public Religion in American Culture* (Philadelphia: Temple University Press, 1979), 38. Thomas Parkinson treats, in part, the same issue.

Chapter Six

1. Gay Wilson Allen regards the *Passage to India* annex to the 1871 edition as "the best of all indications that Whitman was planning a major

change in strategy." *The New Walt Whitman Handbook* (New York: New York University Press, 1975), 134.

2. Allen, *The Solitary Singer,* rev. ed. (New York: New York University Press, 1967), 443.

3. See, for example, Edwin Haviland Miller, *Walt Whitman's Poetry* (New York: New York University Press, 1968), 18, 219–21.

4. Stephen A. Black, *Whitman's Journeys Into Chaos* (Princeton: Princeton University Press, 1975), 182.

5. Richard Chase gives more consideration than others have to the effect of the end of the war upon Whitman's decline as a poet. See *Walt Whitman Reconsidered* (New York: William Sloane Associates, 1955), 149.

6. For the most concerted effort of this sort, see Gay Wilson Allen, *The Two Poets of* Leaves of Grass (Westwood, N. J.: The Kindle Press, 1969).

7. "Preface 1872—As a Strong Bird on Pinions Free," in *Leaves of Grass:* Comprehensive Reader's Edition, ed. Harold W. Blodgett and Sculley Bradley (New York: New York University Press, 1965), 743. Future references to this work will be noted parenthetically in the text as "Preface 1872."

8. "Preface 1876—Leaves of Grass and Two Rivulets," in *Leaves of Grass:* Comprehensive Reader's Edition, 745n. Future references to this work will be noted parenthetically in text as "Preface 1876."

9. "Democratic Vistas," in *Prose Works 1892*, ed. Floyd Stovall (New York: New York University Press, 1964), 2:365.

10. For a similar view, see E. Fred Carlisle, *The Uncertain Self: Whitman's Drama of Identity* (East Lansing: Michigan State University Press, 1973), 173.

11. Arthur Golden, "Passage to Less than India: Structure and Meaning in Whitman's 'Passage to India,' "*PMLA* 88 (1973):1102n.3; E. H. Miller, 210–21; Carlisle, 40; Hyatt H. Waggoner, *American Poets From the Puritans to the Present* (Boston: Houghton Mifflin, 1969), 179–80; Roy Harvey Pearce, *The Continuity of American Poetry* (Princeton: Princeton University Press, 1961; rev. 1965), 173; Chase, 147–49; Jerome Loving, *Emerson, Whitman, and the American Muse* (Chapel Hill: University of North Carolina Press, 1982), 186–88.

12. E. H. Miller sees in the poem "evidences of unacknowledged loss of faith in democratic man and of (middle-aged) retreat from the complexities of an industrial civilization" (p. 215). It would be more correct to say not that Whitman was "retreating" from an earlier faith and from new complexities, but that the world-view he had formed prior to the war could not accommodate the new conditions of American society. Whitman failed to keep abreast of his times after the war, as he occasionally admitted to Horace Traubel; he continued to apply an antebellum point of view to postwar realities.

13. Chase, 147–48.

14. See Joel R. Kehler, "A Typological Reading of 'Passage to India,'" *Emerson Society Quarterly* 23 (1977):123–29. Though his reading is close to mine in many respects, Kehler overemphasizes the importance to Whitman of the Christian form of typology. What has been called "typology" in the Christian tradition is an archaic form of thought, allied to the very nature of religious ecstasy and to the problem of reconciling "synchronic" with "diachronic" frames of reference. Insofar as ecstasy represents a conjunction of the sacred and the profane, it naturally entails the typological attitude once it is transposed into an historically-oriented awareness. In many religious traditions, this conjunction appears in the interpretation of the millennium according to which history ends with reestablishment of a paradisal condition. Whitman had imaginatively reconstructed this condition in several of his ecstatic poems preceding "Passage to India."

15. "Democratic Vistas," 381.

16. "Proud Music of the Storm," in *Leaves of Grass:* Comprehensive Reader's Edition, 405, lines 48–51.

17. "Passage to India," in *Leaves of Grass:* Comprehensive Reader's Edition, 412, lines 31–35. Future references to this work will be noted parenthetically in the text as "PI," followed by page and line numbers.

18. Cf. Golden, 1096–97; and Stanley K. Coffman, Jr., "Form and Meaning in Whitman's 'Passage to India,'" *PMLA* 70 (1955):348–49. Kehler refutes Golden and Coffman in his "typological reading."

19. "Democratic Vistas," 380.

20. "Democratic Vistas," 380.

21. My reading holds with Kehler's here (125).

22. E. H. Miller, 219.

23. Miller, 221. Cf. *With Walt Whitman in Camden,* ed. Gertrude Traubel and William White (Carbondale: Southern Illinois University Press, 1982), 6:313–14. Whitman tells Traubel that despite the serious flaws in postwar American society, "'I have no despair—I am free to say that. Since the war, I have no longer had the least fear but an eventual issue of freedom was secure. Since the war I have sat down contentedly, convinced that we were to be righted at last. Oh! there is no doubt of it!'"

24. *With Walt Whitman in Camden* (New York: Mitchell Kennerley, 1914), 3:134. See also George B. Forgie's study of Lincoln's and Whitman's generation, *Patricide in the House Divided* (New York: W. W. Norton, 1979). Forgie's analysis of Lincoln's "oedipal" motivations applies inescapably to Whitman.

25. "The Mystic Trumpeter," in *Leaves of Grass:* Comprehensive Reader's Edition, 468, lines 6–12. Future references to this poem will be noted parenthetically in the text as "MT," followed by page and line numbers.

26. See especially Artem Lozynsky, *Richard Maurice Bucke* (Detroit:

Wayne State University Press, 1977). The volumes of *With Walt Whitman in Camden* (six to date) are also filled with evidence of men and women who were "converted" by *Leaves of Grass* and either visited Whitman or wrote "gushing" letters of discipleship under the influence of what he called "Leaves of Grass on the brain." Some of these converts he considered literally insane, to the consternation of Horace Traubel, who claimed they only took the poet at his word.

Index

Abolitionism, 196 n.82, 216 n.10
Adhesiveness, 98, 106–7, 115, 120, 132, 176, 212 n.22. *See also* "Calamus"; Comradeship
Alboni, Marietta, 124, 214 n.39, 214 n.40
Allen, Gay Wilson, 16, 59, 124, 219–20 n.1; on Whitman's decline, 170; on Whitman's religious views, 35, 37; on Whitman's role-transformation in the 1850s, 30, 33
American Indians. *See* Native Americans
American Renaissance, 1, 25, 54
American Revolution: importance of, to Whitman, 1–8, 10, 12, 13–14, 25, 104, 142, 167–68, 181; in *Drum-Taps,* 140–42; in edition of 1860, 95, 104; in "The Sleepers," 63, 64, 140–41; in "Song of Myself," 86–87, 140, 142. *See also* Civil religion; Founding Fathers
"American Workingmen, versus Slavery" (editorial), 12–13
"An Army Corps on the March," 145–46
Animal magnetism, 38. *See also* Electricity; Mesmerism
Animals, poet's relationship with: in "Song of Myself," 78, 83, 85–86; in "When Lilacs Last in the Dooryard Bloom'd," 150, 158–60, 166–67; in "A Word Out of the Sea" ("Out of the Cradle"), 124, 126–28
Animals, shaman's relationship with: 83, 85, 127–28, 209 n.46
Antistructure, xx–xxv, 24, 92. *See also* Liminality
Apostrophe, as discursive act: 164–65
"Artilleryman's Vision, The," 138

As a Strong Bird on Pinions Free, 171
"Ashes of Soldiers," 147–49, 159
"As I Ebb'd with the Ocean of Life" ("Bardic Symbols," "Leaves of Grass" no. 1), 102, 103–6, 107
Aspiz, Harold, 26, 49, 74
Asselineau, Roger, xiv, 15, 109, 137, 211–12 n.14
Audience, poet's relationship with, xviii, 10–11, 15, 40, 48–49, 53–54, 55–56; in "Calamus," 99, 102, 105, 107, 108–10; in edition of 1860, 95; in "Proto-leaf" ("Starting from Paumanok"), 112–14, 118–22; in "The Sleepers," 60; in "So Long!", 131–34; in "Song of Myself," 56, 58, 69–73, 77–80, 83, 84, 88–89, 91–94; in "When Lilacs Last in the Dooryard Bloom'd," 155–56, 158, 159–63, 165–66; in "A Word Out of the Sea" ("Out of the Cradle Endlessly Rocking"), 125, 129–30
Audience, shaman's relationship with, xviii, 33, 55–56, 109
Audience, subject's fusion with, 68, 119–20, 159–60

"Backward Glance O'er Travel'd Roads, A," 10
Bali, ritual in, 122, 219 n.38
"Bardic Symbols." *See* "As I Ebb'd with the Ocean of Life"
Bellah, Robert N., 25, 169, 197 n.92
Benito Cereno (Melville), 64
Biological structures: involvement in ecstaticism, 189 n.22. *See also* Neurophysiology; Psychobiology
Black, Stephen A., 5, 28, 170
Bonhomme Richard, 86, 142
Brooklyn, Battle of, 4–5, 140

xx–xxvi, 24; and scene of ritual action, xxi–xxii, 157–58; and setting in Whitman's poems, 91, 100–102, 112, 144–45, 157–58, 182–83

Lincoln, Abraham, 1, 6, 105, 141; death and burial of, 146, 149, 153, 156, 158, 160, 165, 167–69, 197 n.92, 218 n.27; "Gettysburg Address," 169; Whitman's tributes to, 219 n.41

"Lingave's Temptation," 31–32, 33, 51

Literature, origins of, 45, 47, 74, 177

"Live-Oak with Moss," 98. *See also* "Calamus"

Locofocos, 9, 10, 196 n.82

Lucifer (Satan), 63–64, 65, 130

"Magical flight," xix, 62. *See also* Soul-journey

"Magnetism," Whitman's, 29, 48, 138, 185

"March in the Ranks Hard-Prest, and the Road Unknown, A," 144–45

"Mazeway" disintegration and re-synthesis, xxii–xxviii, 18, 49

Memoranda During the War, 136, 138, 140, 141, 142, 144, 146, 147, 149, 216 n.10

Mesmerism, 20–21, 37, 195 n.68, 200 n.33, 202–3 n.70. *See also* Hypnotism; Spiritualism; Swedenborg, Emanuel

"Messenger Leaves" (1860 cluster), 96

Millennium: American views of, 22–23, 24–25, 66; in Whitman's works, 85, 95, 119, 131, 173, 175–80, 182, 184

Miller, Edwin Haviland, 5, 27, 53, 75, 181, 209 n.40, 220 n.12

Miller, James E., Jr., xiv, 68–71, 93, 210 n.53, 211 n.8

Minstrelsy of the Scottish Border (Scott), 43, 210 n.45

Monodrama, xviii, 58, 69, 163, 207 n.26

Mysticism: and approaches to "Song of Myself," 67, 68, 69,

210 n.53; eastern forms of, xiv, 67, 93, 188 n.18; relationship to shamanism, x–xii, xiv–xvi, xvii–xviii, 70–71; role of the senses in, xiv; and sexual experience, xiv–xv, 188 n.18; western forms of, xiv, 67, 93, 188 n.18, 194 n.67; Whitman's, x–xii, 109, 208 n.35, 209 n.40. *See also* Ecstaticism; Ecstatic performance; Shamanism

"Mystic Trumpeter, The," 182–85

Mythology: American, xx, 2, 6, 25, 65–66; Carlyle's view of, 44–45; classical, 44, 128; in "Passage to India," 175–80; relationship to ritual, 207 n.27, 208 n.34

Native Americans (American Indians), 104; Naskapi, xiii; in Shaker ceremony, 21–22; shamanism among, xiii, xiv, 44, 158, 207 n.27, 218 n.29; in Whitman's poetry, 63, 64, 78, 119; Whitman's view of, 47

Neurobiology of myth and ritual, 208 n.34. *See also* Ecstasy: neurophysiology of

New York City: failure of political order in, 18; revivalism in, 23

Nibelungen Lied, The, 44–45, 201 n.54

Norse culture, 44, 201 n.49

Ode, "Out of the Cradle" as, 128

Odin (Othin), 44, 45, 201 n.49

"Of the Terrible Doubt of Appearances." *See* "Calamus" number one

Opera, 42, 83–84, 124–26, 214 n.39, 214 n.40

Oratory, 42, 47–49, 207 n.26

Orpheus, 35, 41, 207 n.27

Ossian, 47

Ossian, Poems of, 44

"Out of the Cradle Endlessly Rocking." *See* "A Word Out of the Sea"

Paine, Thomas, 3, 35

Paradise, 39, 221 n.14; visions of, in